## LEGAL INNOVATION

*Legal Innovation* explores the impact of technology on the legal profession and societal change. Reflecting contributions from an international group of experts, the volume provides a comprehensive overview of the challenges and opportunities facing the legal profession today. With a particular focus on artificial intelligence, the book covers a wide range of topics, from dispute resolution and corporate governance to financial services and regulatory oversight. The conversational style of the chapters makes the content accessible while still maintaining academic rigour. This book is an essential read for policymakers, academics, lawyers, entrepreneurs, regulators and students who are interested in legal innovation and its impact on the legal profession as well as anyone interested in the intersection of law and technology. This title is also available as Open Access on Cambridge Core.

Felix Steffek is Professor of Law at the University of Cambridge, Senior Member of Newnham College and Global Distinguished Professor of Law at the University of Notre Dame. He serves as Director of the Centre for Corporate and Commercial Law and holds a J. M. Keynes Fellowship in Financial Economics.

Mihoko Sumida holds a Research Professorship at Hitotsubashi University. Her work focuses on private law theory and the position of citizens in a changing society. Together with Shunsuke Kudo she has published the book *Social Life with Robots* (2018), which unpacks the legal challenges posed by technology.

# Legal Innovation

## CONVERSATIONS ABOUT TECHNOLOGY, THE LEGAL PROFESSION AND SOCIETAL CHANGE

Edited by

**FELIX STEFFEK**

University of Cambridge

**MIHOKO SUMIDA**

Hitotsubashi University

CAMBRIDGE
UNIVERSITY PRESS

CAMBRIDGE
UNIVERSITY PRESS

Shaftesbury Road, Cambridge CB2 8EA, United Kingdom

One Liberty Plaza, 20th Floor, New York, NY 10006, USA

477 Williamstown Road, Port Melbourne, VIC 3207, Australia

314–321, 3rd Floor, Plot 3, Splendor Forum, Jasola District Centre, New Delhi – 110025, India

103 Penang Road, #05-06/07, Visioncrest Commercial, Singapore 238467

Cambridge University Press is part of Cambridge University Press & Assessment, a department of the University of Cambridge.

We share the University's mission to contribute to society through the pursuit of education, learning and research at the highest international levels of excellence.

www.cambridge.org
Information on this title: www.cambridge.org/9781009427357

DOI: 10.1017/9781009427371



First published 2025

*A catalogue record for this publication is available from the British Library.*

*Library of Congress Cataloging-in-Publication Data*
NAMES: Steffek, Felix, editor. | Sumida, Mihoko, editor.
TITLE: Legal innovation : conversations about technology, the legal profession, and societal change / edited by Felix Steffek, University of Cambridge; Mihoko Sumida, Hitotsubashi University.
DESCRIPTION: Cambridge, United Kingdom ; New York, NY : Cambridge University Press, 2024. | Includes index.
IDENTIFIERS: LCCN 2024022102 (print) | LCCN 2024022103 (ebook) | ISBN 9781009427357 (hardback) | ISBN 9781009427395 (paperback) | ISBN 9781009427371 (epub)
SUBJECTS: LCSH: Technology and law. | Technology and law–Japan. | Artificial intelligence–Law and legislation | Practice of law–Technological innovation. | Practice of law–Social aspects.
CLASSIFICATION: LCC K487.T4 L441 2024 (print) | LCC K487.T4 (ebook) | DDC 340.028–dc23/eng/20240527
LC record available at https://lccn.loc.gov/2024022102
LC ebook record available at https://lccn.loc.gov/2024022103

ISBN 978-1-009-42735-7 Hardback

# Contents

*List of Figures* — *page* vii
*List of Contributors* — ix
*Foreword* — xiii
Kazuhiko Yamamoto
*Preface* — xvii

**Conversation 1 Why Innovate? Technological, Economic and Societal Change from a Japanese Perspective** — 1
Hiroto Koda, Mihoko Sumida and Felix Steffek

**Conversation 2 Dispute Resolution Transformed by Technology** — 32
Felix Steffek, Masato Fujita, Keisuke Takeshita, Hiroaki Yamada, Kazuhiko Yamamoto and Mihoko Sumida

**Conversation 3 The Entrepreneur's Perspective on Innovation** — 64
Ludwig Bull, Wojtek Buczynski, Holli Sargeant, Yuya Ishihara, Ryutaro Ohara, Felix Steffek and Mihoko Sumida

**Conversation 4 What Can We Learn from the Okawa Elementary School Tsunami Litigation?** — 88
Masahiro Saito, Kazuhiro Yoshioka, Mikiharu Noma, Felix Steffek and Mihoko Sumida

**Conversation 5 Corporate Governance in the Age of Artificial Intelligence** — 119
Takuya Izumi, Souichirou Kozuka, Kiyotaka Sasaki, Felix Steffek and Mihoko Sumida

Conversation 6 **Innovation in Financial Services and Supervision** 146
Norichika Ikeda, Akira Nozaki, Kiyotaka Sasaki, Felix Steffek and Mihoko Sumida

Conversation 7 **Artificial Intelligence and Legal Services** 171
Mari Sako, Masakazu Iwakura, Felix Steffek and Mihoko Sumida

Conversation 8 **Will Digitalisation Help the Five Billion People without Meaningful Access to Justice?** 199
Maaike de Langen, Takashi Kikkawa, Philip Scholz, Tatyana Teplova, Ignacio Tirado, Anna Veneziano, Felix Steffek and Mihoko Sumida

**Epilogue: What Is Legal Innovation?** 235
Felix Steffek and Mihoko Sumida

*Index* 241

# Figures


1.1 Digital society and capital markets *page* 3
1.2 Major issues in Japan 5
1.3 Declining birth rate and ageing population in Japan 6
1.4 Population pyramid: rapid ageing in Japan 6
1.5 Wage difference 8
1.6 Japanese corporations today: market cap comparison 9
1.7 Big change in industry structure after collapse of 'bubble economy' 10
1.8 Price-to-book value ratio comparison: Japanese banks 11
1.9 Venture capital environment: comparison with China and the United States 12
1.10 Start-up company fundraising 13
1.11 Building a venture ecosystem to support innovation 14
1.12 Venture capital investment and entrepreneurship 15
1.13 Innovation cycle of industry–academia collaboration 18
2.1 Lawyers vs Case Crunch technology 34
2.2 Artificial intelligence at work 39
2.3 AI prediction precision and dispute resolution 40
2.4 The robot lawyers are here – and they're winning 42
2.5 AI use cases for courts and parties 43
2.6 Bias 46
3.1 Network of relationships and interests 73
3.2 Regulatory themes 76
5.1 Two types of corporate seals 127
5.2 Ideal approaches to AI governance 134
7.1 Three effects of AI on lawyers' work 174
7.2 AI-enabled legal service delivery pipeline 175
7.3 Opportunities to work in MDTs, by organisation 177
7.4 Usage of AI-assisted legal technology, by organisation 177

7.5 Usage of AI-assisted legal technology in MDTs, by organisation 178
7.6 Four business models in legal services 181
7.7 Founders' social networks 184
7.8 Speed of scaling up 184
7.9 Lawyers in law firms prefer lawyers with programming skills over technicians 187
7.10 Possible legal career paths 188
8.1 Digitalisation of civil court procedures in Japan 207
8.2 Digitalisation of the justice sector in Japan 209
8.3 Access to justice as an enabler for creating prosperity and sustainable development 212
8.4 Justiciable problems are highly prevalent 212
8.5 The most vulnerable to legal problems – Australia Law Legal Needs Survey 213
8.6 Legal problems affect certain disadvantaged groups more severely 214
8.7 Share of justiciable problems for which action has been initiated in justice institutions 214
8.8 Good country practices 216
8.9 Justice for growth and inclusion: towards people- and business-centred justice systems 217
8.10 Taskforce on Justice: Pathfinders for Peaceful, Fair and Inclusive Society 220
8.11 Reports by Pathfinders on Justice in the pandemic 221
8.12 Introduction to UNIDROIT 225
8.13 UNIDROIT instruments 226

# Contributors

**Wojtek Buczynski** is a PhD student at the University of Cambridge and a financial technology, regulation and governance consultant.

**Ludwig Bull** is CEO and Founder of CourtCorrect Ltd.

**Maaike de Langen** is Programme Director for Justice for All with the Pathfinders for Peaceful, Just and Inclusive Societies at the NYU Centre on International Cooperation.

**Masato Fujita** is Counsellor at the Civil Affairs Bureau of the Japanese Ministry of Justice.

**Norichika Ikeda** was Project Professor at the Graduate School of Public Policy of the University of Tokyo.

**Yuya Ishihara** is AI Consultant at Xspear Consulting.

**Masakazu Iwakura** is Visiting Professor at Hitotsubashi University and Senior Partner at TMI Associates.

**Takuya Izumi** is Information Policy Planning and Coordination Officer in the Information Economy Division at the Commerce and Information Policy Bureau of the Japanese Ministry of Economy, Trade and Industry.

**Takashi Kikkawa** is Head of the Secretariat of the Minister's Department in the Japanese Ministry of Justice.

**Hiroto Koda** is Visiting Professor at the Graduate School of Business Administration of Hitotsubashi University, Professor at the Graduate School of Management of Kyoto University, Professor in the Business Management Course of SBI Graduate School and President of the Innovation Intelligence Research Institute.

**Souichirou Kozuka** is Professor of Law at the Faculty of Law of Gakushuin University.

**Mikiharu Noma** is Professor at the Graduate School of Business Administration of Hitotsubashi University.

**Akira Nozaki** is Director of the Fintech Office in the Strategy Development Division of the Japanese Financial Services Agency.

**Ryutaro Ohara** is Attorney at Law at Nakamura, Tsunoda & Matsumoto.

**Masahiro Saito** is Attorney at Law at Yotsuuya-no-Mori.

**Mari Sako** is Professor of Management Studies at the Saïd Business School of the University of Oxford.

**Holli Sargeant** is a PhD student at the Faculty of Law of the University of Cambridge.

**Kiyotaka Sasaki** is Visiting Professor at the Graduate School of Business Administration of Hitotsubashi University and former Director General at the Policy Bureau of the Japanese Financial Services Agency.

**Philip Scholz** is Head of the Division 'Legal Tech and Access to Justice' at the German Federal Ministry of Justice.

**Felix Steffek** is Professor of Law at the Faculty of Law of the University of Cambridge, Senior Member of Newnham College and Global Distinguished Professor of Law at the University of Notre Dame Law School.

**Mihoko Sumida** is Professor of Law at the Graduate School of Law of Hitotsubashi University.

**Keisuke Takeshita** is Professor of Law at the Graduate School of Law of Hitotsubashi University.

**Tatyana Teplova** is Head of Division for Policy Coherence on SDGs and Senior Counsellor for Gender, Justice and Inclusiveness at the OECD.

**Ignacio Tirado** is Secretary General of UNIDROIT, the International Institute for the Unification of Private Law, and Professor at the Faculty of Law of the Autonomous University of Madrid.

**Anna Veneziano** is Deputy Secretary General of UNIDROIT, the International Institute for the Unification of Private Law, and Professor of Comparative Law at the Faculty of Law of the University of Teramo.

**Hiroaki Yamada** is Assistant Professor at the School of Computing of the Tokyo Institute of Technology.

**Kazuhiko Yamamoto** is Professor of Law at the Graduate School of Law of Hitotsubashi University.

**Kazuhiro Yoshioka** is Attorney at Law at Kazuhiro Yoshioka Law Firm.

# Foreword

*Kazuhiko Yamamoto*

This book is a compilation of the lectures and discussions on legal innovation held at Hitotsubashi University in the year 2021. All contributions were updated in 2022 (with some additions in 2023) and further texts were added. The lectures were not limited to the Faculty of Law but were open to students of other faculties. They were conducted online due to the COVID-19 pandemic. The lectures were part of a joint research project titled 'Legal Systems and Artificial Intelligence' between Hitotsubashi University in Tokyo and the University of Cambridge. Given the nature of this collaboration, the project also involved many lecturers from other countries, particularly the United Kingdom. The results of this project are reflected in this lecture series.

In the words of Professor Mihoko Sumida, who is one of the outstanding organisers of this lecture series as well as the aforementioned joint research project and who demonstrates exceptional conceptual abilities, 'We want to tell the students, who will be the next generation, exactly how the world of "law" is changing, and we want to give them the opportunity to think about and explore the concept of "legal innovation" together, at a stage when the concept has not yet been properly established.' It is strongly intended to prevent students and readers from turning into 'great white sharks that have been washed up on the beach'. Even organisms that have been optimised for survival in a certain environment become helpless when the existing environment is completely changed. Accordingly, even though it is important to study law based on the current environment in depth, what is more important is to equip students with the ability to cope with any change in the environment. This awareness of the problem must have made Professor Sumida work hard to realise this lecture series.

With this in mind, the methodology of the lectures and the book was to expose students and readers directly to a variety of issues. Although many of these issues are based on new technologies (digitalisation, artificial intelligence, etc.), as Conversation 4 ('What Can We Learn from the Okawa Elementary School

Tsunami Litigation?') clearly shows, legal innovation is not necessarily limited to technology in the narrow sense. Rather, legal innovation also includes the creation of new legal interpretations. In a sense, the book rejects the systematisation of legal innovation and confronts readers with the practice of various 'live' innovations, expecting them to develop their imagination and creativity. The question-and-answer sessions with the students reflected in the chapters, in which we see their bewilderment but also their joy at being confronted with new 'knowledge', are testimony to the success of this lecture series.

The contents of this book are, as mentioned earlier, extremely diverse. They include dispute resolution (Conversation 2), corporate governance (Conversation 5), law enforcement and financial regulation (Conversation 6), and the transformation of law firms (Conversation 7). The chapters provide a kind of 'battlefield diary' of the debaters who are at the forefront of their respective fields and who are trying to achieve innovation in the face of major environmental changes, particularly digitalisation. The readers will feel a sense of worry that they are becoming 'great white sharks' but also a sense of excitement at being on the frontline of innovation. The specific findings from Japan and the United Kingdom are useful, but what is more important is the methodology used by each of the commentators to confront the issues. Naturally, the methodologies vary from one commentator to another (e.g. in Conversation 5, Professor Sumida expresses some discomfort with the idea of 'functional equivalence' presented by Professor Kozuka). This, however, is not surprising, and the lack of a common methodology is in itself a characteristic of innovation. The reader has no choice but to develop their own methodology, with this book by their side.

Needless to say, the lectures on which this book is based are aimed at students, but the book itself is an essential read not only for students but also for anyone involved in 'law' in the broadest sense. Lawyers, judges, corporate lawyers, government officials and alternative dispute resolution (ADR) and other legal advisors stand to benefit from this book. They should first read the chapters on topics relevant to them and then expand their interests to include other areas that the book discusses. Additionally, we would like to encourage people in the sciences, such as data scientists, to pick up a copy of this book. We hope that many of them will enter the new professions discussed in Conversation 3 or become legal engineers who will support new law firms, as elaborated in Conversation 7.

Lastly, the part of the book that made the greatest impression on me was where, in Conversation 5, Mr Takuya Izumi of the Ministry of Economy, Trade and Industry (who also has a science background), quotes Heisenberg as reported by Professor Iwao Nakatani of Hitotsubashi University as follows:

> [O]nly those revolutions in science will prove fruitful and beneficial whose instigators try to change as little as possible and limit themselves to the solution of a particular and clearly defined problem. Any attempt to make a clean sweep of everything or to change things quite arbitrarily leads to utter confusion.

As rightly captured by this quote, innovation is always based on the accumulated wisdom of our predecessors. Hence, traditional legal education in universities is extremely useful. At the same time, it is also important to pay attention to the finer points of practice, without which innovation is not possible. In this sense, the theme of Conversation 8, 'Will Digitalisation Help the Five Billion People without Meaningful Access to Justice?', is pertinent. This book will give all readers the opportunity to make such a contribution. This is why I recommend it to all those interested in the law and its innovation.

# Preface

This book is an experiment. It addresses the complex topic of legal innovation with a specific focus on technology, the legal profession and societal change. Particular consideration is given to artificial intelligence. The style of this book is, however, different from the typical form of academic publications. The chapters come in the form of conversations. Leading experts from ministries, international organisations, academia, legal practice, start-ups and regulators present their thoughts and comments and engage in discussions with a group of students. The topics dealt with remain challenging, but we hope that the style of presentation makes the book an accessible and entertaining read.

Why are we interested in legal innovation? Recent technological advances are transforming the way we use and experience law and the justice system. Artificial intelligence is used to predict the outcome of court proceedings and legal chatbots explain the law. However, it is not only technology impacting the law; law can also facilitate innovation and even effect it. We wanted to discuss this transformation with those making the law, advising clients and analysing current changes. Hence, we invited experts, mainly based in Japan and the United Kingdom, to offer their perspectives on legal innovation.

What topics does this book cover? The chapters investigate the motivation and conditions for legal innovation, the impact of technology on dispute resolution, corporate governance, financial services and regulatory oversight. The conversations also address the success factors and barriers for entrepreneurs and legal practitioners innovating the law. A final round table brings together policymakers for a discussion about the impact of technology on access to justice. Legal innovation is considered from a range of perspectives including not only legal considerations but also economic, environmental, social and justice viewpoints.

Why are we presenting this book in the form of conversations? All experts presented their views in a setting that involved comments and questions. The sessions took place in 2021, in the midst of the COVID-19 pandemic, via videoconferencing. Key presentations were followed by comments from other experts. Then, students of Hitotsubashi University, Tokyo, were invited to ask critical questions. When we looked at the transcripts of the eight sessions, we thought that there is a special value in the conversational form. It reveals how experts are searching for answers in a fast-moving field and the discussions bring out interesting contrasts and nuances.

How did the session transcripts become this book? We changed as little as necessary. Hence, the chapters are documents of conversations that took place at a certain time, in the first half of 2021. While the speakers reviewed the chapters, no rewriting took place. However, we have cleaned the language for a better reader experience. Selected figures and slides from the presentations are included, and a few footnotes referring to useful information have been added. The texts reflect the dynamic between speakers and students, and we hope that the conversational style reflects well the joint effort to explore legal innovation while giving room for different perspectives. As editors, we have added a concluding conversation to each chapter and a list of questions for further thought.

Finally, we would like to thank all speakers and students contributing to the conversations. They all shared their thoughts in an open atmosphere driven by curiosity. We had the best speakers we could hope for. We are also grateful to the outstanding translators of NHK Global Media Services, who made communication possible and provided us with the transcripts that became the starting point for this endeavour. This book is part of the UK Economic and Social Research Council (ESRC) and Japan Science and Technology Agency (JST) funded project on 'Legal Systems and Artificial Intelligence'. We also received generous financial support from the Graduate School of Law of Hitotsubashi University and Newnham College of the University of Cambridge. We would like to thank the team at Koubundou with whom we have published a prior version of this book in Japanese in 2022. Last, but not least, we are grateful to Matt Gallaway and Jadyn Fauconier-Herry of Cambridge University Press, who guided us expertly towards publication. Nikhil Purohit and Quentin Schäfer have provided excellent editorial assistance.

# Conversation 1

## Why Innovate?

### *Technological, Economic and Societal Change from a Japanese Perspective*

ABSTRACT

In this conversation, Professor Hiroto Koda investigates the innovation needs of Japanese society. They include embracing digital transformation, addressing the contraction of the population, in particular outside of the Tokyo metropolitan area, and finding solutions for environmental challenges. Against this background, this chapter focuses on five issues: (i) the economic effects of the COVID-19 pandemic, accelerating regional degeneration and the delay in digital transformation, (ii) the development of new business models, (iii) the solution of social issues that arise, (iv) collaboration between industry, government, academia and financial institutions and (v) the strengthening of human resources.

| | |
|---|---|
| *Speaker* | Hiroto Koda |
| *Moderator* | Mihoko Sumida |
| *Concluding Conversation* | Felix Steffek and Mihoko Sumida |
| *Questions for Further Thought* | Mihoko Sumida |

INTRODUCTION

**Sumida:** Why does Japan need innovation now? Today, we have Professor Hiroto Koda who steers financial institutions in the midst of capital market reforms and also engages in FinTech and other innovation support. He is going to clarify Japan's place by comparing its position with the rest of the world as well as by discussing the urgent social issues Japan faces. He will then specifically explain the approach to solving social issues. Following Professor Koda's talk, I will speak about why 'legal' innovation is considered necessary and share some perspectives on the relevant issues.

## WHY IS THERE A NEED FOR 'LEGAL INNOVATION' NOW?

**Sumida:** I would first like to talk about the purpose of 'legal innovation'. The term 'legal innovation' might not be familiar to you, but it was coined by Professor Felix Steffek at the University of Cambridge. In 2018, Professor Steffek asked what changes will be brought about by fast-evolving technologies permeating the legal world, and he suggested that those changes could be seen through the lens of 'innovation'.

Luckily, we had an opportunity to launch a collaborative research project titled 'Legal Systems and Artificial Intelligence' with the University of Cambridge and our colleagues at Hitotsubashi University in 2020. I would therefore like to use this chance to let you, who are the next generation and who will be tossed into the midst of the upcoming 'legal innovation', know what transformations are likely to be seen in the legal world. I would like to use this opportunity to help you develop a deeper understanding of the concept of 'legal innovation', especially while the concept is still developing. That is why Professor Steffek and I planned this conversation series.

Our first guest is Professor Hiroto Koda. After graduating from the Faculty of Economics at Hitotsubashi University in 1982, Professor Koda joined the Industrial Bank of Japan. He served as the Deputy President and in other positions at Mizuho Securities Co., and he has been the Representative Director of the Innovation Intelligence Research Institute since July 2018. Professor Koda now independently conducts research and consulting activities, and based on that, he also plays an active role in education and research activities while, at the same time, serving as an external director at the Japan Investment Corporation and elsewhere.

As you can see from his career, Professor Koda has been engaged in system research related to financial system reforms, the financial Big Bang and other capital market reforms as well as FinTech and other innovation support. I would now like to invite Professor Koda to speak to us about Japan's position from his perspective.

**Koda:** As an introduction to the theme of 'legal innovation', I would like to talk about the perspective from which we should understand the relationship between 'economic and social innovation' and 'legal innovation' in the 2020s as Japan is facing a mountain of social issues.

## FIVE ISSUES IN JAPANESE SOCIETY

**Koda:** With the ongoing COVID-19 situation, it is undeniable that the environment surrounding Japan's economy has become more difficult than previously expected. Given this situation, the issues faced by Japan include an inability to respond to digitalisation; a delay in responding to digital transformation (DX), namely a change in business model in the light of digitalisation; and a contraction of Japan in general due to a decline in its population, especially outside the Tokyo Metropolitan Area. These issues are going to have a significant impact on Japan. In that sense, the question is how Japanese companies will set up and establish new business models. More than ever, companies must act with an awareness of Japan's social agenda and in a manner that serves globally linked themes such as carbon neutrality. Companies will thus face a major challenge in terms of how they can incorporate innovation. Today, I would like to talk about that awareness of issues in layperson's terms and use that topic to discuss the importance of the relevant legal aspects.

I would therefore like to discuss five issues in Japanese society of which we should be aware. The *first* issue is the increasingly harsh environment surrounding the Japanese economy, especially the prolonged effect of COVID-19, accelerating regional degeneration and a delay in DX. The *second* issue is whether Japanese companies can establish a new business model. The *third* issue is the direction of efforts by concerned parties to solve social issues. The *fourth* issue is how to link collaborations between industry, government, academia and financial institutions (regional financial institutions), which is one of our future directions, with digital solutions. Finally, the *fifth* issue is how to utilise Japanese human resources. I think these are the keys to innovation in future.

## THE FUNDAMENTAL PURPOSE OF THE CAPITAL MARKET IS TO INCREASE CORPORATE VALUE

**Koda:** First, I would like to illustrate how the development of the digital society is interrelated with the capital market. In capital markets, a company is listed and that company's share value is formed through trading by investors. If a company is listed, various investors will participate in transactions that have the legal character of so-called securities in a framework known as an exchange. Notably, it is a matter of course that companies need to increase their value. Figure 1.1 illustrates how to capture the concept of increasing corporate value in terms of the development of the digital society.

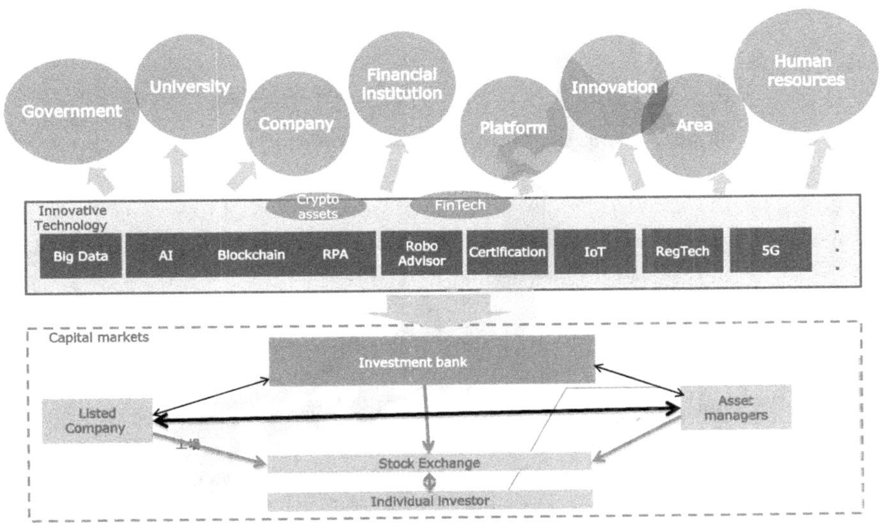


FIGURE 1.1 Digital society and capital markets

Figure 1.1 shows that the elements of innovative technologies in the middle of the figure such as artificial intelligence (AI), Big Data and the Internet of Things (IoT), which are hailed as the fourth industrial revolution, are interrelated through technological changes with companies and financial institutions that are the parties in the capital market as well as regions, workers and universities that are types of stakeholders in those companies. On this point, I would like you to be aware that it is extremely important to understand how to use new technologies in order to increase corporate value.

Elements that materially affect corporate value include changes in industrial structure, changes in management models and technological evolution. Addressing Japan's social issues or global social issues, which is the theme of today's conversation, is directly linked to increasing corporate value. Admittedly, how changes in industrial structure and technological evolution will increase corporate value has always been a debated issue. On this point, I would like to reiterate that linking social issues and corporate value has become a significant element in increasing corporate value.

In the light of this, I will split my lecture into four sections: (i) the post-COVID-19 era and Japan's social issues, (ii) circumstances surrounding Japan's capital markets, (iii) innovation and the venture ecosystem and (iv) digital strategies and innovation. The *first* theme is how to understand Japan's social issues in anticipation of the post-COVID-19 era. The *second* theme is what we should learn from Japan's capital markets in terms of increasing corporate value. The *third* theme is the relationship between innovation and the venture ecosystem from the perspective of innovation. Finally, the *fourth* theme is the need to consider the relationship between digitalisation and innovation, which has become extremely important during the COVID-19 pandemic. I will discuss these themes by starting with general concepts, and then, I will focus on specific issues.

## JAPAN'S ECONOMY IS LAGGING BEHIND

**Koda:** Figure 1.2 summarises the current major themes in Japan in the 2020s. As the global situation rapidly changes and a new industrial revolution and innovations take place, Japan has fallen behind considerably over the past thirty years. Japan, on the whole, is now faced with the question of how to catch up with the rapid advancements in the rest of the world.

As Japan suffers a rapid decline in its population, it is dealing with social and economic structural problems, including a labour market that has not yet been mobilised and an excess concentration of its population and industry in the Tokyo Metropolitan Area. There are also many structural issues on the company side such as a concentration of managerial resources in large companies, a failure to make full use of those resources in order to increase corporate value and continued excessive competition resulting in low profitability.

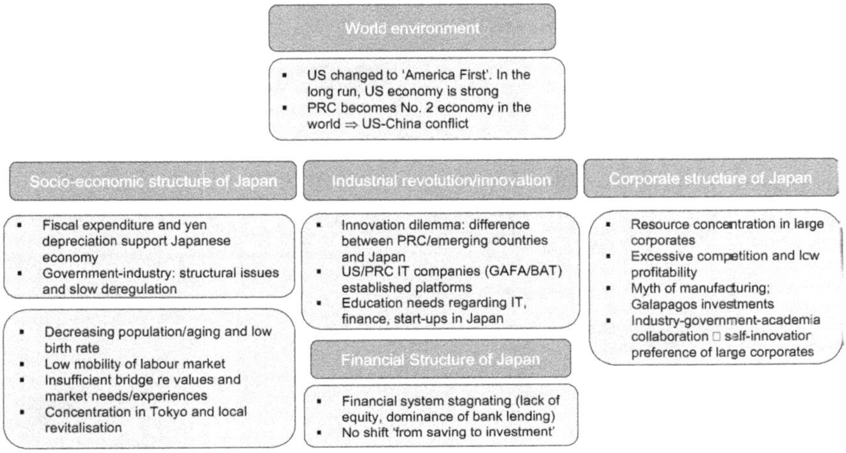


FIGURE 1.2 Major issues in Japan

At the same time, there are structural financial issues. These include a failure to shift from savings to investments based on the indirect finance system, and insufficient investment of equity funds as risk money. Without addressing this range of structural issues, Japan will be left behind by the rest of the world. The question now is whether Japan can take the pandemic as the final opportunity and what measures it can come up with. With this background, I would now like to look at the structural issues in each area while referring to related data.

## A FALLING BIRTH RATE AND AN AGEING POPULATION IS NOT AN ISSUE THAT IS UNIQUE TO JAPAN

**Koda:** As you are all aware, Japan is facing a problem with the ageing of its average population. The number of people aged 65 or older in 2020 was 36.17 million, which accounts for 28.7 per cent of the total population, and this number continues to reach all-time highs.[1] This number is expected to exceed 35 per cent in around 2050. As shown in Figure 1.3, this issue is not unique to Japan and it appears other major countries in the world will also have a very high ratio of elderly people. In such a scenario, the rest of the world will look up to Japan to see how it deals with an increasingly elderly population. In other words, Japan will be a trailblazer and the eyes of the rest of the world will be on it and its attempts to solve this social issue, as Japan's solution might be the solution for the rest of the world.

As a typical example, the population pyramid in Figure 1.4 shows that people aged 65 years or older will account for 38 per cent of the population in 2060. Accordingly,

[1] Ministry of Internal Affairs and Communications (23 September 2020); for details, see Figures 1.3 and 1.4.

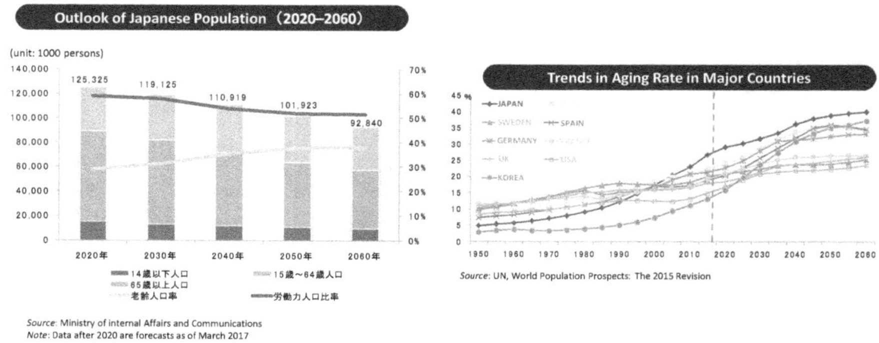


FIGURE 1.3 Declining birth rate and ageing population in Japan

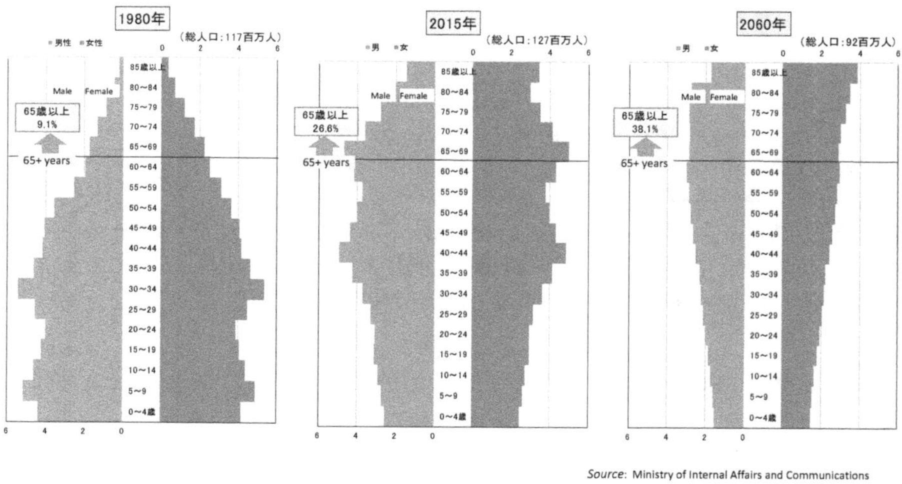


FIGURE 1.4 Population pyramid: rapid ageing in Japan

the initiatives that are taken in awareness of the long-term population pyramid will be closely linked to increasing corporate value. For companies, ageing is associated not only with a decline in domestic demand but also with the issue of the workforce. Specifically, companies must change their marketing approach and methods of reaching individual customers in response to the ageing of the population. It is expected that there will be a significant change in Japan from a growth-based model (a model without population decline) from 1980 to 2015 to a new model until 2060 (a model with population decline), which is a change engendering a need to innovate.

## SOCIAL ISSUES TO BE CLASSIFIED BY REGIONAL CHARACTERISTICS

**Koda:** Gaps between the Tokyo Metropolitan Area, which is overconcentrated, and other regional areas have caused various social issues. Both urban areas and depopulated areas have challenges of their own. Japan as a whole has issues such as labour shortage and various educational issues. We need to organise and classify them into issues that are to be addressed by the entire nation and those that are to be addressed by each region – taking a sensitive approach to solving them.

Looking at the shift in the productive-age population ratio for each prefecture from 2010 to 2020, Akita Prefecture has the largest rate of decline in its productive age (15–64 years) of over 20 per cent, followed by Hokkaido, Aomori, Yamagata, Fukushima, Yamaguchi, Tokushima, Kochi, Nagasaki, Miyazaki and Kagoshima, which each had a decline of 15–20 per cent. The rate of decline is extremely high in the Tohoku, Kyushu and Shikoku regions, highlighting the seriousness of the situation that has occurred in recent years. It is anticipated that this will continue to worsen, and it is increasingly important to address this issue.

Let us look at what will happen in the Tohoku, Kyushu and Shikoku regions, where the population is shrinking dramatically. It has been noted in discussions at study groups at the Ministry of Internal Affairs and Communications that it would be difficult to take advantage of scale and to maintain the status quo in areas such as education, healthcare, infrastructure and disaster prevention, including in terms of the labour force. This means that the essentials for people living in those areas, including education, disaster prevention and healthcare, will inevitably shrink. It is important to understand the gravity of this social issue. Our current way of life will be jeopardised in other regions too.

## REGIONAL SOCIETY ISSUES WILL BECOME WORSE AFTER THE COVID-19 PANDEMIC

**Koda:** As we look towards the post-COVID-19 era, it is said that there will be changes in lifestyles, corporate models and the paradigms of society, including an orientation towards a dispersed society. It thus begs the question as to what will actually change? These changes are already taking place and are related to various areas across society, including work style and logistics trends such as remote working and rearrangement of supply chains, and structural changes such as those pertaining to healthcare and employment issues. Although some of these changes will have a positive effect, they might, at the same time, intensify the social issues mentioned earlier that Japan is currently facing in the 2020s such as its ageing population and regional disparities. It might be possible to deal with those issues from a political perspective, but I expect there is a good chance that those issues as a whole will exacerbate in times to come.

In that sense, it is necessary to consider the social issues faced by Japan mainly in terms of (i) demography and economy, (ii) economy and industry, (iii) environment and energy, (iv) social systems and inclusion and (v) consumption style. With respect to these five typical social issues, depopulation is particularly serious. Additionally, global warming is an issue in the category of environment and energy that is expected to become more serious and needs to be dealt with. As for consumption style, a traditional mass-production and mass-consumption model has been replaced by a bidirectional model based on platforms. It will be necessary to use that system based on digitalisation while at the same time solving social issues. This will certainly require a legal response. It is thus necessary to quickly come up with responses and measures to address those issues. The social system based on the idea that 'no one should be left behind' is deeply related to the issues of economic and social disparities, which are also linked to issues such as changes in working styles and employment mobility.

As the workforce in Japan shrinks, there are a myriad of issues that require attention, including how working styles will change and how to structurally improve without delay employment mobility in an era where people live to be 100 years old. In other words, it is necessary to consider how to become aware of, how to respond to and how to solve social issues including all the issues discussed earlier.

## TO WHAT EXTENT CAN WE CHANGE THE OLD-FASHIONED STRUCTURE?

**Koda:** Figure 1.5 shows that Japan remains one of the countries in the world in which wages are proportional to the size of the company and the length of employment. This is because long-term employment at a large company was a considerably positive incentive when Japan had a growing economy. However, this might become a negative factor in future. While Japan's major corporations claim that their seniority-based pay system is being replaced with a performance-based system, in reality, many of them still have a seniority-based system. There is thus a need to make more drastic changes to that structure.

However, if there is a transition from a seniority-based pay system to a system based on professional merit, the social mechanism will be significantly altered, and solving the issues of disparity and building a safety net must take place

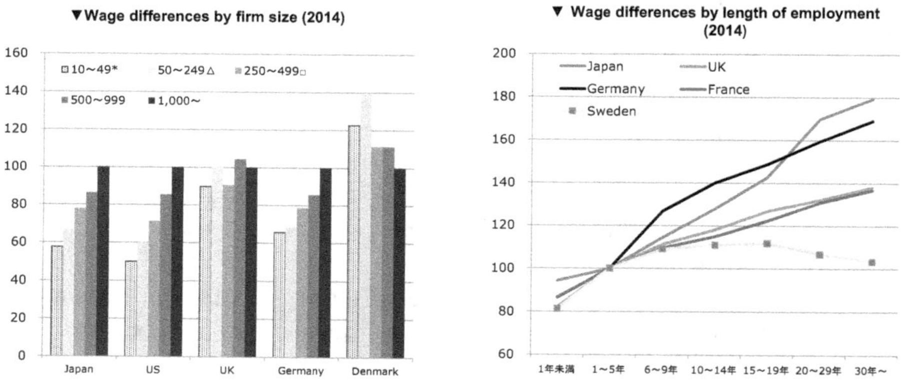


Sources: Japan: MHLW; US: Quarterly Census of Employment and Wages; Europe: Structure of Earnings Survey 2014

Note: Wage for 1–5 year employee: 100
Sources: Japan: MHLW; Europe: Structure of Earnings Survey 2014

FIGURE 1.5 Wage difference

simultaneously. Additionally, some believe that the declining workforce in Japan might be solved by improved productivity. In general, manufacturing is more productive, while retail and distribution as well as small and medium-sized companies are less productive. It is necessary to start making efforts such as saving labour using platforms or digitalisation as I mentioned earlier and at the same time confronting the accompanying social issues. Small and medium-sized companies are increasingly at risk of closure and discontinuance of business as their management grows older. Succession of business is also becoming an issue. I realise, as somebody in the financial industry, that during the COVID-19 pandemic, a much larger number of people are taking specific measures for business succession. We need to position this as a social issue and take measures accordingly.

## CAPITAL MARKETS AND CORPORATE VALUE

**Koda:** Till now, we have discussed the overall picture of Japan's social issues as well as specific examples pertaining to the same. Now, we will use data to examine the issues in increasing corporate value surrounding capital markets in Japan.

Figure 1.6 shows data comparing the market capitalisation of the top ten companies in the United States and those in Japan in 2007 (before the collapse of Lehman Brothers) and 2017, ten years later. The total market cap of the top ten companies in Japan in 2007 was at a level of 90 trillion yen and showed only a marginal increase in the subsequent ten years. On the other hand, the market cap of the top companies in the United States increased from 192 to 512 trillion yen within a span of ten years between 2007 and 2017. The reason behind this significant increase in the United States is the high growth potential of the tech giants known as GAFAM (Google – now Alphabet, Apple, Facebook, Amazon and Microsoft). As against the position in the United States, Japan's top ten companies are still

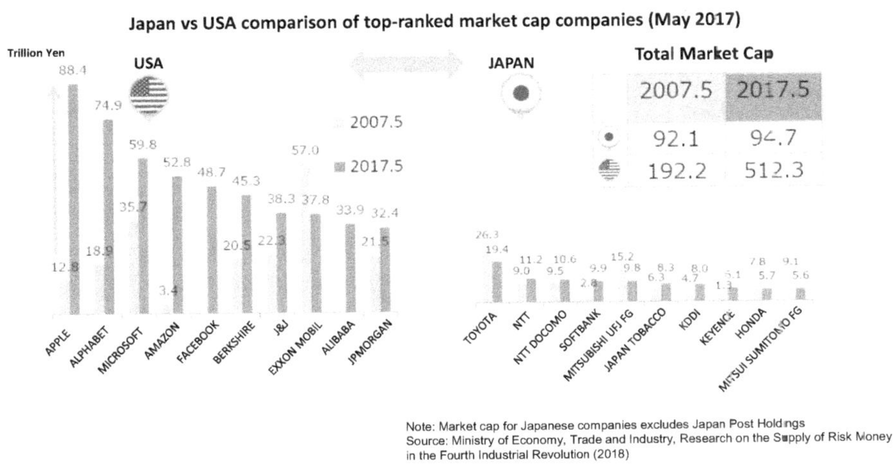


FIGURE 1.6 Japanese corporations today: market cap comparison

**1990**
World market cap ranking

| Rank | Company Name | Market Cap ($ billion) | Country /Region | Rank | Company Name | Market Cap ($ billion) | Country /Region |
|---|---|---|---|---|---|---|---|
| 1 | NTT | 1,639 | Japan | 21 | Kansai Electric | 309 | Japan |
| 2 | Industrial Bank of Japan | 716 | Japan | 22 | Long-Term Credit Bank | 309 | Japan |
| 3 | Sumitomo Bank | 696 | Japan | 23 | Tokai Bank | 305 | Japan |
| 4 | Fuji Bank | 671 | Japan | 24 | Mitsui Bank | 297 | Japan |
| 5 | Daiichi Kangyo Bank | 661 | Japan | 25 | Merck | 275 | USA |
| 6 | IBM | 647 | Japan | 26 | Nissan | 270 | Japan |
| 7 | Mitsubishi Bank | 593 | Japan | 27 | Mitsubishi Heavy | 267 | Japan |
| 8 | ExxonMobil | 549 | USA | 28 | Dupont | 261 | USA |
| 9 | Tokyo Electric | 545 | Japan | 29 | GM | 253 | USA |
| 10 | Royal Dutch Shell | 544 | UK | 30 | Mitsubishi Trust Bank | 247 | Japan |
| 11 | Toyota | 542 | Japan | 31 | BT | 243 | UK |
| 12 | General Electric | 494 | USA | 32 | BellSouth | 242 | USA |
| 13 | Sanwa Bank | 493 | Japan | 33 | BP | 242 | UK |
| 14 | Nomura Securities | 444 | Japan | 34 | Ford | 239 | USA |
| 15 | Nippon Steel | 415 | Japan | 35 | Amoco | 229 | USA |
| 16 | AT&T | 381 | USA | 36 | Bank of Tokyo | 225 | Japan |
| 17 | Hitachi | 358 | Japan | 37 | Chubu Electric | 220 | Japan |
| 18 | Panasonic | 357 | Japan | 38 | Sumitomo Trust Bank | 219 | Japan |
| 19 | Philip Morris | 321 | USA | 39 | Coca-Cola | 215 | USA |
| 20 | Toshiba | 309 | Japan | 40 | Walmart | 215 | USA |

**2018**
World market cap ranking

| Rank | Company Name | Market Cap ($ billion) | Country /Region | Rank | Company Name | Market Cap ($ billion) | Country /Region |
|---|---|---|---|---|---|---|---|
| 1 | Apple | 9,410 | USA | 21 | UnitedHealth | 2,431 | USA |
| 2 | Amazon | 8,801 | USA | 22 | Intel | 2,419 | USA |
| 3 | Google (Alphabet) | 8,337 | USA | 23 | Anheuser Busch | 2,372 | Belgium |
| 4 | Microsoft | 8,158 | USA | 24 | Chevron | 2,337 | USA |
| 5 | Facebook | 6,093 | USA | 25 | Home Depot | 2,335 | USA |
| 6 | Berkshire Hathaway | 4,925 | USA | 26 | Pfizer | 2,184 | USA |
| 7 | Alibaba | 4,796 | China | 27 | Mastercard | 2,166 | USA |
| 8 | Tencent | 4,557 | China | 28 | Verizon | 2,092 | USA |
| 9 | JPMorgan Chase | 3,740 | USA | 29 | Boeing | 2,044 | USA |
| 10 | ExxonMobil | 3,447 | USA | 30 | Roche | 2,015 | Swiss |
| 11 | Johnson & Johnson | 3,376 | USA | 31 | Taiwan Semiconductor | 2,014 | Taiwan |
| 12 | Visa | 3,144 | USA | 32 | PetroChina | 1,984 | China |
| 13 | Banc of America | 3,017 | USA | 33 | P&G | 1,979 | USA |
| 14 | Royal Dutch Shell | 2,900 | UK | 34 | Cisco Systems | 1,976 | USA |
| 15 | ICBC | 2,871 | China | 35 | Toyota | 1,940 | Japan |
| 16 | Samsung | 2,843 | Korea | 36 | Oracle | 1,939 | USA |
| 17 | Wells Fargo | 2,735 | USA | 37 | Coca-Cola | 1,926 | USA |
| 18 | Wallmart | 2,599 | USA | 38 | Novartis | 1,922 | Swiss |
| 19 | China Construction Bank | 2,503 | China | 39 | AT&T | 1,912 | USA |
| 20 | Nestle | 2,455 | Swiss | 40 | HSBC | 1,874 | UK |

*Source*: Weekly magazine 'Diamond' (August 2018)

FIGURE 1.7 Big change in industry structure after collapse of 'bubble economy'

made up of traditional large companies, and although some new faces such as Keyence and SoftBank have recently emerged, their market cap is still significantly lower than that of the US companies.

Figure 1.7 shows changes in the global top rankings in terms of market cap over thirty years from 1990 to 2018. Most of the top-ranking companies in 1990 were Japanese companies. But this situation altered drastically in 2018, when only one Japanese company, Toyota, appeared in the list, placed at the 35th position. Companies from the United States and China dominate this list with IT companies holding most of the top-ranked positions, and this trend is continuing.

The *Financial Times* published an article titled 'Prospering in the Pandemic: The Top 100 Companies', which listed companies in order of the absolute amount of increase in market cap from the start of 2020, when COVID-19 began to have a global impact, to mid-June.[2] The top five companies listed in this article were Amazon, Microsoft, Apple, Tesla and Tencent. The only three Japanese companies ranked in the top 100 were Chugai Pharmaceutical, Keyence and Daiichi Sankyo. It is therefore clear that Japanese companies are being left behind in terms of growth.

This trend can also be seen in the price-to-book-value ratio (PBR), a number obtained by dividing the stock price by the net asset value per share. The PBR is normally used as an indicator to determine whether a stock price is low or high. If the PBR is 1, the stock price has a value that is appropriate considering the net asset value. Figure 1.8 shows the PBR values for Japanese companies. As can be seen, over 50 per cent of Japanese companies have a PBR below 1. This means that Japanese companies are assessed by the market as having low growth potential. This

[2] 'Prospering in the Pandemic: The Top 100 Companies' (*Financial Times*, 19 June 2020) <www.ft.com/content/844ed28c-8074-4856-bde0-20f3bf4cd8f0> accessed 1 November 2023.

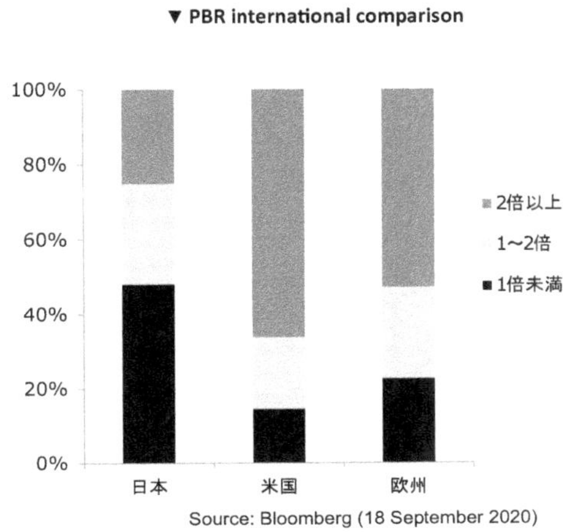


FIGURE 1.8 Price-to-book value ratio comparison: Japanese banks

is in contrast to the United States and Europe, where much fewer companies have received the same assessment.

## SOLVING SOCIAL ISSUES WILL LEAD TO INCREASED CORPORATE VALUE

**Koda:** In recent years, in addition to growth potential, the perspective of environment, society and governance (ESG) investment is becoming extremely important. More emphasis is being placed on ESG every year as institutional investors investing in equity give particular consideration to it while deciding on their corporate investments. In other words, increasing corporate value is directly linked to corporate activities aimed at solving social issues. This means that the capital market and social issues are perfectly linked to each other in moving forward towards a sustainable society.

For companies to address these social issues and promote corporate activities, it is essential to incorporate new 'innovation'. In Japan, there has been a gradual increase in investments in venture companies nationwide, and there has been a change in the erstwhile low supply of risk money and equity investments. This means that in terms of social agenda themes such as 'digitalisation and work style reform', 'maturity of society' and 'business succession', Japan must transform through equity investments or by taking risks with risk money and developing businesses. Traditionally, in Japan, risk money has not been circulated due to financial bottlenecks, which inhibited the growth of new companies. This status quo has finally begun to gradually change, and together with fund functions, Japan is undergoing change.

## IMPORTANCE OF THE 'VENTURE ECOSYSTEM'

**Koda:** Figure 1.9 summarises the current situation of risk money supply in Japan in comparison with China and the United States.

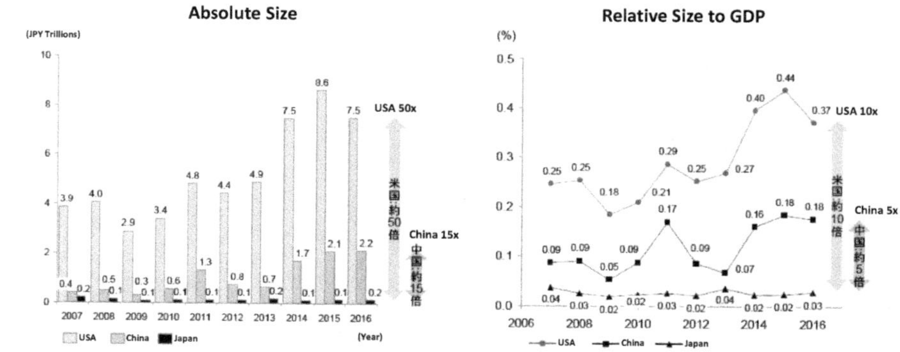


*Note*: Investments by VC only and excludes venture investments by companies
*Source*: Venture Enterprise Center, Venture White Papers 2017

*Source*: Ministry of Economy, Trade and Industry, Final Report on the Trend of the Global Economy and the Supply of Risk Money in the Fourth Industrial Revolution (2018)

FIGURE 1.9 Venture capital environment: comparison with China and the United States

The volume of risk money supply as venture capital (VC) in Japan is as much as around fifty times lower than in other countries. The difference compared to the United States is as much as ten times in relation to the GDP, while China has around fifteen times more risk money based on an absolute amount, which corresponds to five times more than Japan in terms of GDP. Representative countries promoting innovation with risk money include the United States, followed by Israel, India, China and Canada. Japan seems to have insufficient money circulating as risk money, given its economic size.

However, under the growth strategy adopted as per the Abenomics policy since around 2013, investments in these innovation areas have recently increased. The amount raised by venture companies, which was just over 100 billion yen around 2013, is currently around 500 billion yen per year. The fundraising amount did not decrease in 2020 despite the pandemic, remaining at a level of just below 500 billion yen. Accordingly, more money is being raised and is flowing in Japan. Despite this, the gap between Japan and other countries is actually widening because of a lack of speed of fundraising and insufficiency of volume.

Figure 1.10 shows the fundraising amount achieved by Japan's start-ups by sector in 2020. With the AI sector at the top, there are some emerging sectors, including Clean Tech, sharing economy and medicine. This shows that Japan has a wide area of venture investments and that the base of these venture companies advancing their efforts is widening in a variety of business areas.

## KEY TO GROWTH OF VENTURE COMPANIES

**Koda:** In fact, there are some venture companies in Japan that are achieving significant growth such as Preferred Networks, which is frequently mentioned as a

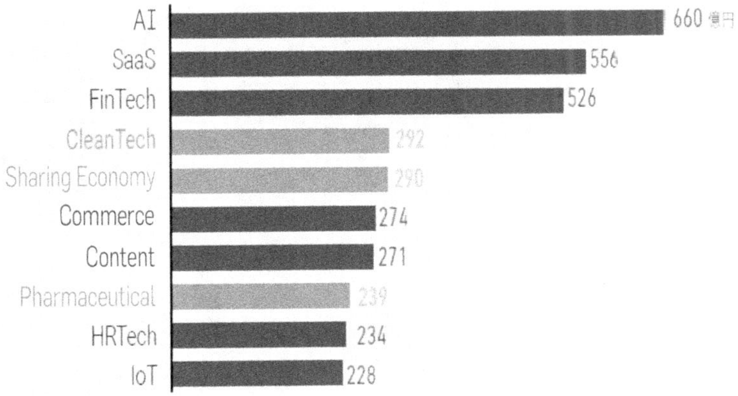


Source: Initial Japan Start-up Finance Report (2020)

FIGURE 1.10 Start-up company fundraising

representative AI company that was valued at 350 billion yen in 2020, and Spiber, which is a spin-out material company of Keio University that artificially synthesises tough and flexible 'spider silk' and has achieved a market cap of 100 billion yen. Although Japan has fewer unicorn companies valued at over 1 billion dollars than the United States and China, we are seeing gradual growth in Japan's venture companies.

In terms of promoting initiatives linked to changes in Japan's social and economic structure, which I highlighted earlier as regards solving social issues, important 'innovation' areas include healthcare, agriculture, regional areas and creation of communities and responses to labour shortages. This means that it is increasingly important to solve social issues using data platforms and digital technologies such as AI and IoT. Solving social issues means using key factors to follow up on solving issues that are detrimental to society. As many venture companies are based in Tokyo, it is also important to expand that base to regions other than Tokyo to promote regional expansion.

This also requires the establishment of a cyclical ecosystem, also known as a 'venture ecosystem'. As shown in Figure 1.11, venture companies need to overcome a variety of bottlenecks as they grow through the stages of seed, start-up, early stage and growth. Ideally, a venture company will grow with support from various professionals. To that end, it is extremely important, inter alia, to build a mechanism of financial support and industry–government–academia cooperation and to obtain support to secure human resources for venture companies.

Great results have been produced out of the 'venture ecosystem' in Silicon Valley, and that has been backed by the prevalence of cooperation between industry, government and academia. In Silicon Valley, academic institutions such as

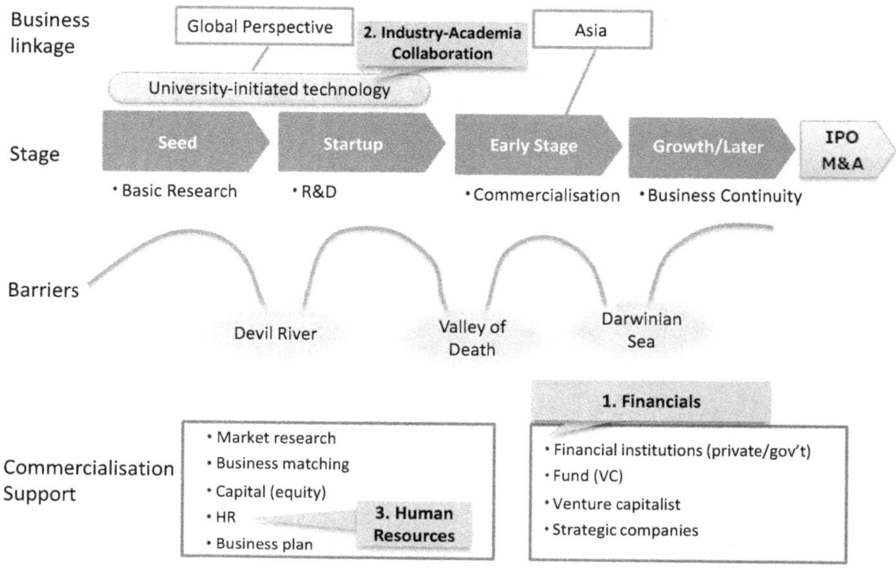


FIGURE 1.11 Building a venture ecosystem to support innovation

Stanford University and the University of California, Berkeley; major companies such as Apple, Amazon and Facebook; and also venture companies, lawyers, designers, accelerators, mentors and other professionals are part of a network that forms a cyclical 'ecosystem'. This is a big difference as compared to the situation in Japan. While Japan has also seen an 'ecosystem' gradually form in the Tokyo area as well as in the manufacturing industry in areas such as Kyoto and Osaka, there is still a large gap between Japan and other countries in this regard.

Figure 1.12 shows the correlation between Japan's entrepreneurial activity rate and VC investment versus GDP. In Japan, the ratio of VC investment to GDP on the horizontal axis and the entrepreneurial activity rate on the vertical axis remain 0.07 per cent and 5 per cent, respectively, which are positioned at the bottom left of the above figure and are lower than the world average. On the other hand, the ratio of VC investment to GDP and the entrepreneurial activity rate in the United States are both high, as depicted on the top right of the figure. Besides the United States, countries such as Canada and South Korea are also emerging, and the gap between them and Japan is widening. To put it differently, it is significant for venture companies to take an approach to solving social issues with agility. Accordingly, in the case of Japan, boosting entrepreneurial activities and the importance of risk money supply have to be highlighted. At the same time, large companies and mature companies are required not only to make efforts towards their own innovation but also to work on present corporate issues in a speedy manner through transformation such as business restructuring, selection and concentration. Initiatives to

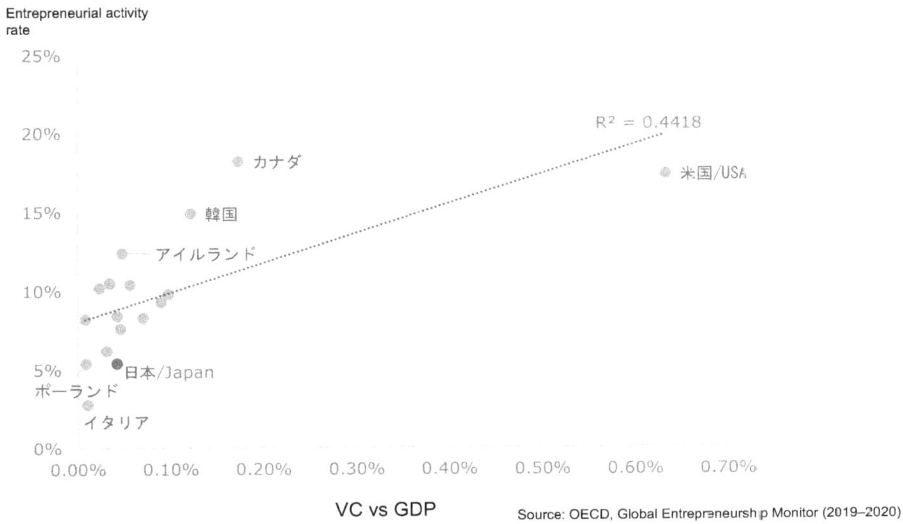


FIGURE 1.12 Venture capital investment and entrepreneurship

increase corporate value sustainably in the medium term, such as the Corporate Governance Code and the Stewardship Code, are rapidly underway, including on the investor side, indicating that large companies have started to change.

## DIGITALISATION AND INNOVATION

**Koda:** Finally, I would like to look at the relationship between innovation and digital strategies. In July 2020, when the COVID-19 pandemic was spreading, the Abe administration in its final phase issued the so-called big-boned policy (Basic Policy on Economic and Fiscal Management and Reform 2020) as a policy on economic and fiscal management in the light of the situation resulting from the pandemic. The aim of the policy was to push through reforms that would normally take ten years, featuring concentrated investment in digitalisation, regional revitalisation and strengthening investment in people and innovation. The contents of that policy are concise and precise, and I believe these initiatives are on the right track. There is no doubt that it is necessary and extremely important to politically push through reforms such as these.

Be that as it may, I am rather sceptical about whether Japan can push through reforms that normally take ten years. It will be imperative to associate such reforms with specifics, namely action plans, and to promote the same in a speedy manner. In that sense, it is essential to create a synergy between the government making efforts towards the digital new deal and the private sector accelerating corporate actions with an awareness of social issues. The government must cooperate with the private sector, and the private sector must rapidly create model cases. This must be promoted while keeping in mind how the government and the private sector can keep in step with each other, whether that can be advanced expeditiously and whether the private sector can change.

## FROM DIGITALISATION TO DIGITAL TRANSFORMATION (DX)

**Koda:** Speaking of digitalisation, we must take measures such as abolishing seals and dealing with electronic approval processes as a matter of course. This means digitalising such things using IT. The questions Japanese companies are facing now are whether it is possible to create new value using digital technology and create new products and services. Rather than digitalisation simply replacing existing analogue technologies with IT equipment and data, what is important is whether it is possible to shift to a business model that creates new profit and value based on digital data, i.e. DX. This depends on whether it is possible to create new products and services and new business models using digital technologies.

As per the results of a May 2019 questionnaire circulated by the Information-Technology Promotion Agency of Japan (IPA), an industry group, on the dissemination of DX in companies, around one-third of the responding companies used the term DX, and I am sure the term has become even more familiar since the pandemic began. When companies were asked what kind of DX they are currently working on, almost 80 per cent of the answering companies said that they were working to 'increase productivity by streamlining their businesses', which indicates that Japanese companies are good at 'streamlining'. That being said, for most companies, DX is still limited to the confines of just incorporating or replacing IT in their internal systems, and very few companies have used DX to make 'drastic changes to their current business models'. These circumstances make it difficult for Japanese companies to reach 'business creation' (digitalisation), which is the original aim of DX, or to develop 'new business models' or 'create services'. I believe this is the most significant bottleneck to 'digitalisation and work style reform' in Japan.

A major change is also taking place in the relationship between the market and the customers. In recent years, there has been a change to a customer model that is bilateral between customers as consumers and companies supplying products and services. At the same time, this market is also circulative around the axis of information provision and evaluation feedback, known as a platform. It is quite difficult, including in terms of mechanics, to suddenly adapt to a bilateral circulative model from a customer behaviour model in which customers act in line with a series of processes including recognition, selection, evaluation, purchasing and use for which companies provide products and services.

## MEASURES FOR A SOCIETY WITH ACCELERATING INFORMATION AND COMMUNICATIONS TECHNOLOGY (ICT)

**Koda:** I believe we have to be more serious than ever about how to use new technologies in addressing social issues. The Report on Roundtable Meetings on ICT Global Strategy for the Digital Transformation Age by the Ministry of Internal Affairs and Communications states, in relation to accelerating the implementation of ICT as regards social issues, that while Japan is experiencing changing values and an acceleration of technical innovation, it is essential for companies, the government, local governments, universities, academia and individuals to continue to undergo fundamental changes such as in their thinking, business approaches, systems and education.[3] The report indicates important directions such as promoting an understanding of ICT by upper management at companies and local government heads, top-down innovation reforms, support for venture companies and an 'agile' development approach to manufacturing, while at the same time constantly adjusting and improving products. This means that Japanese companies need to make adjustments to schemes with respect to which they lack capabilities in order to keep up with the rest of the world. Japanese companies must work to shift from a traditional linear-type 'pipeline business model' from manufacturers to business operators to consumers, to a 'platform business model' that connects manufacturers and consumers and generates value by 'producing' transactions.

## CAN JAPAN RESPOND TO PLATFORMERS IN TIME?

**Koda:** Japan is seeing platformers such as GAFAM growing rapidly in the digital market. Accordingly, the Ministry of Economy, Trade and Industry, with concern over issues including the competitive advantage and dominant position of these companies, launched the Cross-Sectional Research Group for the Fourth Industrial Revolution in January 2016. This research group examined three cross-sectional systems, 'competition policy', 'data use and protection' and 'intellectual property', conducted interviews with parties such as online business operators and electronic device manufacturers and revealed the actual situation at that time. The report stated that while there is concern that fair competition might be hindered, the question of whether those companies are in violation of the Antimonopoly Act cannot be discussed in general terms. Thereafter, on 18 December 2018, the Study Group on Improvement of the Trading Environment Surrounding Digital Platformers announced basic principles for the development of rules dealing with emerging platformer businesses, which has led to the subsequent development of

[3] Japanese Ministry of Internal Affairs and Communication Affairs, *Publication of ICT Global Strategy* (31 May 2019) <www.soumu.go.jp/main_sosiki/joho_tsusin/eng/pressrelease/2019/5/31_5.html> accessed 1 November 2023.

legal principles. Despite these advances, it is undeniable that Japan's examination and development of rules on digital platformers lag behind those of Western countries. Building a framework when innovators such as platformers emerge is important, and it is extremely important for the legal system to catch up with innovations in the future.

Finally, I would like to look at the importance of preventing regional degeneration as an example of various social issues, and the future sense of direction. For this social issue, it is important to take an extensive approach to regional co-creation. A regional ecosystem can be built by identifying social issues by region and examining how to solve them using regional strengths. One of the keys to creating a virtuous cycle is the role played by local financial institutions. Furthermore, evolving collaborations with universities and major companies will be extremely important to promote initiatives to solve regional issues. From this perspective, Figure 1.13 shows the possibility of these initiatives to leap forward through close cooperation among large companies, universities, start-up companies and VC funds. It shows the importance of an 'ecosystem' with universities serving as a hub. The creation of such a mechanism has become increasingly important.

To wrap up, the post-COVID-19 era will overlap with the introduction of drastic changes to Japan's economic and social structure, which will require new initiatives that are not an extension of Japan's traditional framework. To promote those initiatives, it is necessary to create innovation, use new technologies such as AI and Big Data, address social issues and advance various efforts. This means that not

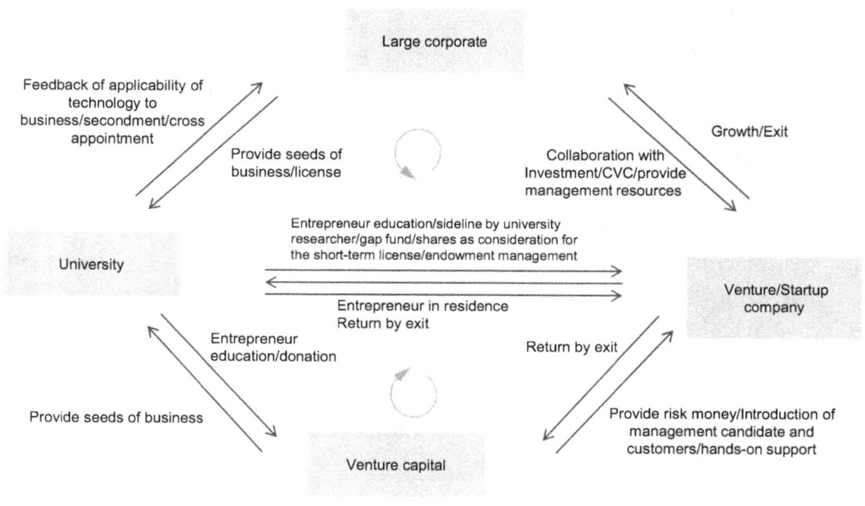


FIGURE 1.13 Innovation cycle of industry–academia collaboration

only companies but also the government, local governments and universities must structurally change as a nationwide effort. From the company's perspective, it is necessary to promote an approach to solving social issues using innovation and new technologies in order to enhance corporate value, which depends on whether a new, balanced, society-wide framework can be built. In doing this, various discussions on legal aspects will arise, so the legal side will need to promptly encourage changes in the social and economic structure to support these efforts while consistently working on building a new legal framework.

## QUESTIONS AND ANSWERS SESSION

**Sumida:** Thank you for your excellent presentation, Professor Koda. Does anyone have any questions?

**Student A:** You mentioned that venture companies are suitable to challenge businesses to address social issues. I think large companies such as trading companies have departments to study new business models, but are there any barriers for a large company to conduct their business in a way to solve social issues?

**Koda:** Large companies are indeed addressing major social issues head-on such as by producing products that discharge as little plastic waste as possible and by manufacturing electronic vehicles for decarbonisation. Large companies are naturally making an effort to expand their businesses while addressing social issues that affect their success.

Based on this, to answer the question of how large companies can proactively deal with social issues, I must say that it is limited to what they study internally or in their laboratories. In fact, it is also limited by companies engaging in closed innovation whereby they develop solely through internal research and development. Such closed innovation practised by large companies is well known to act as a bottleneck in an increasingly competitive global market.

On the other hand, the companies I mentioned earlier, such as Amazon and Google, engulf various start-ups in Silicon Valley by acquiring them through mergers and acquisitions (M&As). For instance, Google has acquired 200–300 companies through M&As in the past decade. They actively commercialise and incorporate the ideas of those start-ups. In contrast, large companies in Japan are not very good at that, and although they understand that open innovation aimed at inter-company creation is necessary, this actually acts as a bottleneck.

There is no doubt that innovation promoted by large companies to solve social issues and innovation independently promoted by venture companies are inseparable, but the actual situation in Japan is that large companies sticking to the tenet of developing innovations by themselves is acting as a bottleneck.

**Sumida:** You mentioned an important issue: open innovation versus closed innovation. Could you let us know your thoughts about what is important for a culture of open innovation to take root in Japan?

**Koda:** When a large company in Japan collaborates with a start-up to promote research that has been undertaken by the start-up, the laboratory side often turns a deaf ear, saying that the collaboration is meaningless because the laboratory did not succeed in that research. However, in recent years, large companies have become aware of the limitations of developing innovations by themselves and they have, for example, started to use the concept of 'Dejima'. Dejima was an island in Nagasaki in the Tokugawa era, and it refers to an approach where a certain area is prepared, funded and allowed to act freely, which is an approach to innovation that more companies are now adopting. If a huge elephant tries to do something by itself, it is difficult because it takes time and costs money and it takes ages to see any change. Companies have therefore started to take the 'Dejima' approach because they have found it to be effective. Nonetheless, whether they can catch up with the world standard by taking that approach at the current pace is a different issue.

**Sumida:** Isn't it right that Dejima was not open for trading with all countries? The ability to trade might have depended on whether there was a close connection with a certain country. The Dejima approach has a limitation in that sense – is this correct?

**Koda:** Yes, that is right.

**Sumida:** I see. Thank you. Does anyone else have a question?

**Student B:** With respect to the legal development you mentioned in the last part of your talk, the legal development in a digital area might involve matters that cannot be dealt with or that are beyond the knowledge of legal scholars or legal professionals at present. Could you please let us know if there are any agendas or efforts being made to deal with this issue?

**Koda:** The extent of the changes that need to be made in terms of the legal system will be determined by the progress of innovation and technology. Hence, the approach to be taken is to make preparations to a certain degree by following a 'reality-first' approach. Here, I would like to introduce the sandbox mechanism created in the United Kingdom and Singapore in areas such as FinTech. Sandbox, meaning 'play in the sand', allows an easing of regulations on matters that are difficult to deal with within the current regulatory framework, under certain conditions to find legal bottlenecks, and if that works to a certain extent, measures are taken to adopt the learnings in the legal system.

Japan also started to use this mechanism a few years ago in an attempt to implement deregulation and instantiation industry-wide. However, it seems that Japan has not been able to connect the fundamental need for changing its laws alongside these deregulatory attempts. It is necessary to make more innovative efforts such as broadening the range of attempts and giving an incentive to the private sector. I therefore think that it is worth increasing and promoting mechanisms like regulatory sandboxes.

On another front, amending laws is an issue of jurisprudence. That being said, it is difficult to instantly have more people who can discuss certain reform issues right away. This is Professor Sumida's area rather than mine, but it is related more to the aspect of how to educate lawyers and foster legal scholars.

**Sumida:** Thank you. We will have contributors from the Financial Services Agency in a later session, and they will talk about the sandboxes you mentioned earlier with some specific examples.

Now, Professor Koda, I would like to close this session. Thank you very much.

## DON'T BE A STRANDED GREAT WHITE SHARK

**Sumida:** Now I would like to take some time to talk a bit about the next session and then explain why I asked Professor Koda to talk to you today.

At the outset, I will give you the gist of the conversations on legal innovation that started today, and I would like to tell you the ideas that I put into this conversation series when I planned it. You are going to study law and go out into the world, so you should not be a stranded great white shark.[4]

As you are aware, a great white shark is the ultimate predator in the ocean, and it can smell blood from many kilometres away. However, what if the environment changes? Great white sharks are hyper-optimised for the sea, but a shark would just struggle if it were stranded on the beach. In other words, a great white shark, which has made the ultimate effort to be optimised and evolved, would be helpless if the environment changes. I do not want you to be like that. I want you to properly adapt to any new environment you encounter. That was my thinking when I planned this conversation.

Professor Koda gave a gentle but insightful indication on how to change legal scholars, and I was partly ready to receive that message because I actually feel a sense of crisis about that issue myself.

## ISSUES POSED BY '*ORE ORE* SWINDLES'

**Sumida:** In my career, I was initially attracted by consumer laws, and since I decided to be a scholar and entered this field, I have always studied consumer laws. At the end of the previous century, I spent all my time in the field of consumer affairs and provided support in studies and advice on that area.

Around 1995, when I was a postgraduate student, I visited an expert on consumer laws at the National Consumer Affairs Centre of Japan. When we talked about interesting recent issues, the topic of '*ore ore* swindles' – phone scams involving calls from people pretending to be relatives in distress – came up in the conversation. The name '*ore ore* swindles' has a nostalgic feel now, but that was around the time when that scam first appeared, and that was considered a new, strange and troublesome

[4] This is a metaphor from Andrew W. Lo, *Adaptive Markets: Financial Evolution at the Speed of Thought* (Mamoru Mochizuki and Toshio Chiba trs, Toyo Keizai 2020) 13.

problem. Then, the consumer law expert said: '*Ore ore* swindles are a pretty clear scam. What is the problem with that?'

When I heard that, I thought it was bad because even though that person was a hard-bitten consumer law expert with a great reputation, I realised that that person was obsessed with the idea that consumer law is a new, interesting legal issue that still has no clear answer in terms of interpretation and solving consumer problems.

'*Ore ore* swindles' is an easy-to-understand swindle in terms of the study of legal interpretation. The perpetrator tells a lie with the intent to deceive the other party, and the victim falls for the scam and sends money. From a legal perspective, it is evident that it is a fraud. In other words, this is a novel scam that uses psychological knowledge to throw people off the scent, which is beyond the border of a consumer issue that takes advantage of loopholes in terms of legal interpretation.

Of course, as you are aware, '*ore ore* swindles' have more variety now and it remains a serious issue known as 'special fraud'. Despite that, the consumer law expert inadvertently asked what the problem was, because that expert had a stereotyped image of consumer issues and could not appropriately respond to the emergence of a new type of issue. That was the moment when I realised that it is possibly a case not only with that expert but also with many other people in the field of jurisprudence.

This leads to the reason why I asked Professor Koda to give today's first lecture. In other words, I thought that, in order to accurately perceive the changes occurring in the legal field and make a forecast, it is necessary to have an accurate grasp of the changes that are occurring not only in the field of law but also in the economy and the current situation in Japan.

## SHOGI WORLD COEXISTENT WITH AI

**Sumida:** While talking about changes, I would also like to mention what happened in the shogi world. Shogi is a strategy board game for two players. It is now possible to play shogi games online because there is a complete game record database which records, inter alia, the situations of the game played. I heard that highly advanced technologies are now used in shogi software. We often see that AI and humans coexist in the gaming world, which is one step away from the real world, and Yoshiharu Habu, a shogi superstar, describes the recent situation in the shogi world as follows:

> Shogi players of the old times would be very surprised to see the recent shogi world. The changes are like from modern paintings to postmodern paintings. New moves are being created one after another, and popular taste is rapidly changing.[5]

[5] Yoshiharu Habu, *NHK Special Shuzaihan Core of AI* (NHK Publishing Shinsho 511 2017) 95.

Coexistence of AI and humans will be seen in many other areas including the legal world, so I cited Mr Habu's words, which I found very impressive, to give you an idea of the changes that are going to happen.

## DIFFICULTY IN DEALING WITH ACTUAL HUMAN BEINGS

**Sumida:** Getting back to our topic, what are the 'difficulties that are unique to law' and not to the shogi world? Let us think about the difficulties that would be unique to the legal world if what has happened in the shogi world also happens in the 'legal' world, i.e. if similar new digital technologies appear in the 'legal' world.

First, 'laws' actually deal with social and economic issues that involve real people, and they reflect, dissect and give legal solutions to issues that arise using the logic of law, or arrive at solutions if there is a conflict. This is very similar to the shogi world in terms of dissecting by logic, but the challenging part in the legal world is that it involves real people. In other words, a legal solution to a conflict will change real lives, and the more people that are involved, the more complicated the issue becomes.

Now we get back to the topic I mentioned earlier: do not be a stranded great white shark. It is essential that we always adapt to environmental changes; otherwise, it is likely that we will make mistakes when we reflect reality based on the logic of law, and that is the difficulty that lies in the legal world.

## AIMING TO USE THE LEGAL SYSTEM LIKE AN IMMUNE SYSTEM

**Sumida:** The other difficulty is that each judgment related to law is responsible for the operation of the legal system, which serves as the basis of social rules. At the same time, in the shogi world, game records are created from Mr Habu's games, and AI learns those records and creates new moves, which makes shogi players feel as if they are playing a game with the entire logic and thoughts created in the past by a human, and this might be a similarity between the shogi and legal worlds.

That being said, the law is a social norm because it reflects the reality and dissects it with logic. In interpreting and applying the rules of law responsible for the operation of the legal system, it is necessary to maintain consistency in the system and issue guidelines pertaining to the interpretation and application of law. As the term 'stability of the legal system' indicates, it might be necessary for the legal system to maintain consistency, properly reflect the relevant situation and, based on that, make appropriate judgments.

This operation is like that of an immune system, where life forms are always in contact with various external foreign substances but maintain themselves as a uniform system. Come to think of it, the legal system is in a way like a social immune system. It might be a perspective on how to avoid dysfunction of the system, but this is just an idea that has not been fully developed.

Having said that, if the consistency of the legal system is not maintained, social trust in the judiciary might be lost. For this reason, lawyers need to make appropriate judgements and take appropriate measures while dissecting the issues occurring in the rapidly changing world with the logic of law under the constraint of maintaining consistency in the system. To that end, I think we should appropriately use technology, and the awareness of this issue underlies this conversation.

## MISTAKES MADE BY VOLKSWAGEN

**Sumida:** I would like to introduce the case of Volkswagen as an example of the aforementioned legal issues. You might know about the scandal involving the use of fraudulent software at Volkswagen, a world-renowned company.[6] I will explain the events up to the trial using an example case. Plaintiff X bought a diesel-powered vehicle from car manufacturer Y, the defendant (Volkswagen in the real case), for 10 million yen. Y cleared the world's strictest environmental regulations in country A (the United States in the real case) and advertised its technological strength as having realised a reduction of environmental burden, good fuel efficiency, accelerating performance and durability at the same time. As a result, Y earned a great deal of trust in the market. Following this, however, it was discovered that for some time Y had installed in its vehicles a software that activates purification equipment to the fullest capacity during emission tests.

Many of you may know about this case as it was a major scandal. Some of Y's diesel vehicles emitted as much as forty times more pollutants than allowed during driving conditions, but the driving safety of such vehicles was not found to be problematic. However, the revelation that the scandal had occurred resulted in an across-the-board prohibition of activating purification equipment only during emission tests in the country in which X resided, and almost all countries by now. During that period, Y stopped manufacturing diesel vehicles with the problematic equipment, and the diesel-powered vehicle purchased by X is one of the discontinued models.

Following the revelations about this scandal, the representative director of Y announced his view in a press conference as follows:

> We are deeply distressed by the fact that a few engineers were involved in fraud, and we will do our best to restore trust. We are advancing the preparation for relevant customers to download, free of charge, a drastically updated version of the software at issue so that the software can fulfil its original function, and we will send a letter of apology and explanation in a few days.

[6] For literature in Japanese, see Hiroko Aoki, 'Overview of Volkswagen's Emission Gas Fraud Case' (2019) 11 Disclosure & IR 19; for an update, see the website of the law firm Dr. Stoll & Sauer: 'Latest News on the Emission Scandal' <www.dr-stoll-kollegen.de/news-urteile/abgasskandal> accessed 1 November 2023.

Subsequently, Y actually took these measures. Now, if X, who bought and used that diesel-powered vehicle, considers bringing a lawsuit against Y, what arguments do you think X would raise against Y? Would those arguments be accepted? Company Y came up with certain measures and showed their sincerity, but if that is not satisfactory to X, would a claim by X be accepted? What would you think if you were a judge in charge of this case?

## WHY DID VOLKSWAGEN RESPOND DIFFERENTLY IN GERMANY AND THE UNITED STATES?

**Sumida:** I cited this case as an example because Volkswagen adopted different responses in the light of the justice system of the country in which the dispute surrounding its actions arose. This difference in responses became widely known and caused heated discussions.

As you know, Volkswagen is based in Germany and sells vehicles all over the world. I intentionally revealed that country A where Volkswagen cleared environmental regulations is the United States because the United States has a unique justice system in which a class action suit might be filed or punitive damages or legal liability beyond the amount of the damage actually incurred might be imposed in case of a serious offence. However, X filed an action against Volkswagen in Germany, which is where many other Volkswagen users also sued Volkswagen, and this caused trouble later on.

Here is the cause of the problem. Volkswagen, which has an understanding of the characteristics of the US justice system, quickly offered a settlement in the United States as per which it would buy back the diesel-powered vehicles it sold. This was a safety precaution to avoid incurring a large amount of liability as a result of a trial. This precaution was, however, taken by Company Y only in country A, the United States, in the light of its extremely severe environmental regulations and rigorous justice system. On the other hand, the representative director of Company Y offered in Germany, its home country, to 'guarantee a free download of software'. Company Y thought those terms would be acceptable in Germany.

## SELLER'S CONTRACT NON-CONFORMITY LIABILITY

**Sumida:** I am going off track, but the Civil Code of Japan has been modernised recently, and among the amendments to the Civil Code or laws of obligations, which might be familiar to the students of the Faculty of Law, there have been significant changes to the rules concerning remedies available to purchasers under purchase and sale agreements. Contractual liability owed by sellers and determined as the sellers' obligation is now of extreme significance, and sellers are liable for contractual non-conformity. Roughly speaking, Japan has finally incorporated world-standard ideas.

The rules on purchase and sale agreements in Germany are not so different from the rules implemented in Japan in 2020, which, in binding the other party to the agreement through a remedy of specific performance, adopts more flexible terms rather than strongly adhering to the agreed terms of the right to demand performance.

For example, if you buy a book and find that a page is missing in that book, would you argue in court that the book does not conform to the contract and exercise your right to demand performance by asking the seller to give you a proper book? You do not have to. You could take more reasonable measures to deal with the situation. There are many other items that could replace that book, so it would be acceptable if a substitute item was provided or if the missing page was given so that the book conforms to the contract. These alternatives are available to the seller wherein they could take additional reasonable measures to make an arrangement to complete the contractual performance properly.

It is assumed that the view underlying the offer made by the representative director of Company Y was that 'fixing the bug of the defective software' was deemed as an option that would be equivalent to 'providing the missing page' so that it would be deemed that a reasonable agreement has been fully performed. In fact, a certain number of legal professionals in Germany initially regarded that offer in that way. However, in the current information age, it is not possible that the terms of the settlement offered in the United States would remain unknown to users in Germany. The anger of German consumers was, thus, fuelled by the company not providing benefits to the citizens of its place of incorporation.

Against this backdrop, the Federal Court of Justice, which is the Supreme Court of Germany, made an unusual decision that, despite the settlement having already been made, Volkswagen must accept a solution for Germany that is comparable to the one offered in the United States. In fact, up to that point, there had been various measures such as the EU Commission telling Volkswagen to make a decision that is balanced considering the settlement in the United States.

## AIMING TO USE THE LEGAL SYSTEM AS A SOCIAL IMMUNE SYSTEM

**Sumida:** It can be simply concluded that the confusion in the German judicial world over the scandals involving Volkswagen was under the control of political power, but I thought that it was an example in which the legal system worked as a social immune system, as I mentioned earlier.

In this age of information, with globalised economic activities, the justice system is required to play the role of a social immune system that adapts to environmental changes, and if people or society have less confidence in the justice system, it means that the justice system is not functioning properly as an immune system, which is something to be avoided.

In principle, judges can make their own decisions in accordance with their legal conscience as long as such decisions are in compliance with their own legal system and court precedents, without needing to refer to decisions or solutions adopted in other countries. This, however, at times might be a casual approach, and this is the issue that was raised here. The use of AI as a second opinion, as mentioned by Mr Habu in the shogi world, might also become necessary in the world of 'law'. I would like you to imagine what view you would take if you were involved in this kind of dispute.

## DIALOGUE WITH THE SPEAKER AFTER THE LECTURE

**Koda:** Thank you for the very informative introduction of your awareness of the problem. Speaking in broader terms, judicial reform was one of the major subjects promoted in the so-called national governance reforms during the Heisei era. That being said, it might be quite difficult to address legal system reform concerning business aspects. Although systems such as the intellectual property system have been organised to a certain extent, what perspective should be taken for more specialised areas, particularly regarding how to create a legal system as well as the accompanying dispute resolution mechanism?

**Sumida:** I would like to answer your question along the lines of consumer issues as that is the area I have been involved in. If we compare the manner in which human resources generating ideas as seeds for new rules are cultivated in Europe with the process of generating new ideas in Japan's consumer policies, I find a gap that is equivalent to the large gap found in the example of the 'venture ecosystem' you described.

We might have to give further thought to the vision that justice system reform was aimed at achieving. Although the legal system must cultivate an environment to adapt to and move ahead of those business changes, I am afraid that the cultivation of human resources that can create ideas has been lacking.

It has been common, of course, that young attorneys who have a keen awareness of the issue, throw themselves into policymaking, but at the same time, compared to the diversity of human resources in Europe, based on my observations and the status of studies that are the underlying basis of policymaking, there is quite a large gap. It might sound wild, but while policymakers in Japan are mainly the best and the brightest who have passed the national bar examination as soon as graduating from law school and have gone into the civil service for a certain period in their career, studies for policymaking in Europe are much broader-based and diverse in terms of the people involved. I think this affects factors such as the diversity and novelty of ideas and strategic strength.

Moreover, in terms of methodology for policymaking and studies, and in terms of self-discipline, Japan is clearly two steps behind Europe in that it starts making policy after examining European directives. It is far behind in terms of strategy. We need to work towards an environment in which we can more carefully nurture strategic moves reflecting the actual condition in Japan.

**Koda:** Certainly. Although Japan is considered a forerunner in dealing with various social problems such as depopulation and ageing, it has no forum for discussions on the framework of a legal system to solve such issues and to turn signs of change into a certain mechanism. No mechanisms are in place for open communication such as an 'ecosystem' to take integral measures before something happens, rather than reacting after the occurrence of the event, and this might be one of the major problems.

**Sumida:** That is right. From a desire to create such an environment, I described the students as great white sharks, and I feel sorry for that. But I dared to do that so that you can have an image of the problem.

Professor Koda, in conclusion, can you please give a message to future lawyers?

**Koda:** Thank you for this opportunity. As Professor Sumida says, this is a challenging issue, but we are now clearly in an era in which we must change or create something with an awareness of social issues. Each of you might take a different approach, but I think you should study while paying attention to how to overcome social issues. I hope you continue to challenge yourself.

**Sumida:** Professor Koda, thank you very much for your valuable and enjoyable lecture.

## CONCLUDING CONVERSATION

### *Professor Felix Steffek and Professor Mihoko Sumida*

**Sumida:** The most difficult question in planning this conversation series was how to start it. Various state-of-the-art issues will be discussed in the following sessions, but I encourage all the students to not just 'watch' those discussions but view the topics as important issues related to their future and experience dialogues with the guests. I also wanted to develop my thinking of what 'legal innovation' is together with the students rather than defining that at the beginning. To that end, I wanted to start the conversation series by sharing awareness of why legal innovation is necessary. The question, however, was how to substantiate that.

Professor Hiroto Koda used a wealth of statistical data to clearly present social issues Japan is facing and the approaches being explored to solve those issues. What impressed me was his comment that, as the global situation has rapidly changed and a new industrial revolution has taken place over the past thirty years, Japan is now being asked the question as to what measures it can come up with. Japan has a number of structural problems, including rapid depopulation, excessive concentration of population in Tokyo, low employment mobility, a lack of utilisation of managerial resources concentrated in large companies, a failure to move household assets from savings to investments and a low supply of risk money. Professor Koda repeatedly emphasised that we should find a way to work out business models that will contribute to solving those social issues.

Moreover, Professor Koda even gave us an important homework assignment. He asked us to substantiate legal innovation and not just to use slogans, and to think about the legal environment that is necessary to achieve legal innovation.

**Steffek:** The United Kingdom is also facing social challenges. Brexit and the aftermath of COVID-19 are examples of the issues that need to be dealt with from a legal aspect. However, the UK judiciary is actually taking those social issues as an opportunity to intensify DX and is advancing reforms. Sir Geoffrey Vos, who is leading those reforms, can be said to be the role model of a legal innovator in the United Kingdom today.

**Sumida:** Someone who is pursuing an approach to solving social issues in concrete terms in the world of justice! That is great. Can you tell me more about him?

**Steffek:** Sir Geoffrey Vos is a judge with the second highest rank in England and Wales. He assumed the office of Master of the Rolls, President of the Civil Division of the Court of Appeal, in January 2021, where he is responsible for the deployment and organisation of the duties of judges in the Civil Division and also presides at court in that division, often handling the most complicated cases involving civil and family law issues.

Sir Geoffrey has boundless energy. He is a member of the UK LawTech Delivery Panel and has served as the chief coordinator in the announcement of the panel's legal statement on cryptoassets and smart contracts in November 2019. He also promotes London as a global hub for dispute resolution, leading activities to promote the use of technology in judicial administration and dispute resolution.

**Sumida:** A leader of judges for justice system reforms! I am boundlessly curious about him. What specific vision does Sir Geoffrey put forth in leading justice system DX?

**Steffek:** Sir Geoffrey views the civil justice system as a vital part of our economic infrastructure and says, 'Digitisation is essential to modernise the infrastructure, and create a system that allows our businesses and individuals – national and international – to perform economically at their best without impediment and delay to the vindication of their legal rights.'[7]

**Sumida:** The civil justice system as an economic infrastructure. That is a great angle!

**Steffek:** I completely agree with you. Sir Geoffrey used the following metaphor: 'If multinational corporations chose not to export their goods to the UK because our ports built in 1745 were too shallow, we would deepen them or build new ones. Lawyers and judges alike sometimes fall into the trap of thinking of the system of

7 See <www.lawsociety.org.uk/topics/civil-litigation/sir-geoffrey-vos-speech-at-the-launch-of-the cityuk-legal-services-report> accessed 1 November 2023.

justice as something free-standing. It is not. It is an essential part of our economic infrastructure.'

**Sumida:** So the justice system is like a port.

**Steffek:** As a specific example, an online settlement system service (Online Civil Money Claims [OCMC][8]) was launched in 2018 that allows people to make monetary claims, which previously were unlikely to be actually collected despite an immense amount of effort and cost, up to a value for £10,000 online, free of charge, without the need for third-party involvement, and the system is expected to bring enforcement online. Sir Geoffrey says that the service was implemented based on the idea that we must try to create an ubiquitous streamlined online civil justice system to ensure that what is properly owed in all areas is paid promptly without the delays that the present systems allow.

He explains the reason for that as follows: small disputes are as important as big ones in economic terms. Big businesses can generally survive if the resolution of their litigation is delayed by the court process. Small businesses often cannot. An efficient digitalised and online civil dispute resolution process will be of huge value to our economy. It will ensure that individuals and small and medium-sized enterprises (SMEs) are paid what they are owed and can continue to trade. It will reduce unnecessary personal and corporate insolvencies and enhance access to justice.

**Sumida:** What an energetic statement that is enormously persuasive! What are the conceivable types of disputes that a digitalised streamlined online civil dispute resolution process will deal with?

**Steffek:** The very title of the lecture given by Sir Geoffrey in June 2021 was 'Recovery or Radical Transformation: The Effect of COVID-19 on Justice Systems'.[9] As a radical transformation indicated exactly by the title, reforms of the dispute resolution 'systems' themselves are underway in addition to changes to the justice system operation 'methods' such as remote hearings. Sir Geoffrey's vision is to build online funnels within the coming years. He concluded, 'the vast bulk of civil disputes, and possibly the vast bulk also of employment, tribunal and private family disputes are amenable to a streamlined online dispute resolution process' and that 'the speed of that process – even if there are still face-to-face hearings in the most difficult cases – will allow the parties to spend less time and emotional energy agonising over their disputes, and more time concentrating on their economic or personal lives.'

**Sumida:** Thank you for wrapping things up by describing the legal innovations that will be realised by using technology.

This was a great start to the lesson on how to be a legal innovator!

[8] See <www.gov.uk/government/case-studies/online-civil-money-claims-service-ocmc-acting-on-feedback> accessed 1 November 2023.

[9] See <www.judiciary.uk/announcements/speech-by-the-master-of-the-rolls-at-the-london-school-of-economics-recovery-or-radical-transformation-the-effect-of-covid-19-on-justice-systems/> accessed 1 November 2023.

## QUESTIONS FOR FURTHER THOUGHT

- What will be needed to address and move towards resolution of the structural issues faced by Japan's society and economy, large companies and finance in the 2020s?
- How will Japanese companies be able to establish a new business model?
- Which Japanese companies can realise the efforts to solve social issues, large companies or venture companies?
- Does Japan have an environment in place that is necessary to nurture human resources to make innovation happen?
- What contributions are specifically required from lawyers in the efforts to solve social issues? What skills are necessary for that?
- Assuming that humans and AI are able to coexist in the shogi world, do you think the same will also happen in the legal world? What are the difficulties that are unique to the legal world?
- What is Japanese society expecting from legal innovation?
- What legal innovations do you expect to be working on in ten and twenty years' time?

# Conversation 2

## Dispute Resolution Transformed by Technology

ABSTRACT

This conversation explores how technology changes the way disputes are solved. The focus is on the impact of artificial intelligence. After reporting on a competition, in which lawyers and an artificial intelligence competed to accurately predict the outcome of disputes before the UK Financial Ombudsman, the speaker explains how artificial intelligence is practically used in dispute resolution. Such use cases include the production of information, the creation of focused analyses, the finding of decisions and the generation of communication. The speaker then presents research projects using artificial intelligence to predict dispute outcomes in the courts of different countries. The conversation also addresses the ethical questions arising from different use cases of artificial intelligence in conflict resolution. In conclusion, the potential of artificial intelligence to improve access to justice is identified together with the ethical challenges that need to be addressed.

| | |
|---|---|
| *Speaker* | Felix Steffek |
| *Moderator* | Mihoko Sumida |
| *Comments* | Kazuhiko Yamamoto, Masato Fujita, Keisuke Takeshita and Hiroaki Yamada |
| *Concluding Conversation* | Felix Steffek and Mihoko Sumida |
| *Questions for Further Thought* | Felix Steffek |

### AI VERSUS PROFESSIONAL LAWYERS

**Sumida:** The second session will be on 'Dispute Resolution Transformed by Technology'. I would like to ask Professor Felix Steffek to begin his presentation following his self-introduction. Thank you very much.

**Steffek:** It is a great pleasure to be here with you today. I am very grateful to Professor Mihoko Sumida for arranging this amazing course. It has been a great pleasure working with you, Mihoko. I am also very grateful for the excellent translation provided and for the colleagues and external visitors to be here. It is great seeing so many of you in this virtual setting.

My name is Felix Steffek, as Professor Sumida has already mentioned. I am based at the University of Cambridge, Faculty of Law, and I am the Director of the Centre for Corporate and Commercial Law. My interests are in dispute resolution, but also in corporate finance and corporate insolvency. Most recently, I have engaged with LawTech, also referred to as legal technology, particularly with artificial intelligence (AI) in dispute resolution. The latter is also the topic of my contribution to this session. In this contribution, I will focus on civil and commercial dispute resolution. I will not cover criminal law and particular public law issues.

How do I use the term 'AI' in this lecture? There are many definitions, but a very brief and rough-and-ready definition would be technology trying to make intelligent choices. When I use the term 'AI', I have in mind machine learning, in particular deep learning, and natural language processing (NLP). Later, I will give you an example of how it works, and I hope that it will also help you understand what AI in law means.

Here is a brief outline of what I will talk about. To start with, I will give you a report on the Case Crunch Lawyer Challenge. It was a competition that students from the University of Cambridge, Faculty of Law, had staged. It was really interesting, so I thought I should tell you about it. Then, I will provide some background information on this competition. I will explain how the students used AI in the area of law. Following this, I will report on current research. I will refer to studies on the use of AI in dispute resolution so that we get an understanding of the field and where the research stands at the moment. Then, I will move on to discuss some use cases. In other words, I will talk about how AI can be employed in the practice of law. Then, I will discuss three essential issues. *First*, I will address the issue of bias that concerns many people as regards the use of AI; i.e. AI perhaps makes the same mistakes as we have made in the past. *Secondly*, I will deal with the issue of transparency because law and legal decisions have to do with transparency. For example, in court, we do not only hear the result but also want to know why a judgment is made. *Finally*, I will bring these issues together to raise more general ethical considerations. I will investigate the ethical advantages and disadvantages of using AI in dispute resolution.

Let us start. What you see in Figure 2.1 is some key information on the Case Crunch Lawyer Challenge. As I mentioned earlier, I will report on this project that was conceived by students at the University of Cambridge. What happened? In October 2017, they organised a competition between an AI and real lawyers. You can see that this was already some years ago. Later, I will talk about the advances in AI and law that have happened since then. At the time, these students were really at the forefront of developments. What was this project about? There were four

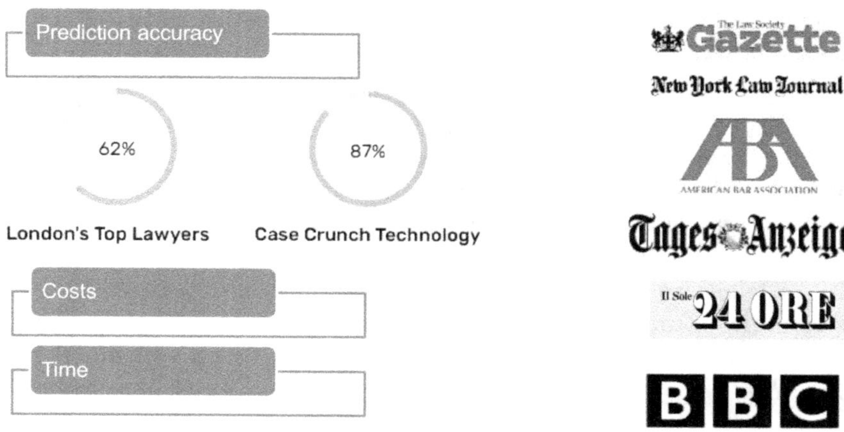


FIGURE 2.1 Lawyers vs Case Crunch technology

students. They had programmed an AI to predict the outcome of cases. Their idea was to test how good their AI was by asking lawyers to compete against it. Both the AI and the commercial lawyers would predict the outcome of cases. The challenge was to predict more cases correctly. In the end, more than 100 lawyers participated. They were all very good commercial lawyers, mainly based in London.

What was the specific task? The task was to predict real cases that the Financial Ombudsman Service had to decide in the past. The Financial Ombudsman Service is an ombudsman service for the financial services industry. At the time, there were many cases concerning Payment Protection Insurance (PPI). This is an insurance product that enables consumers to insure repayment of credit if the consumers, i.e. the borrowers, become ill or disabled, lose their job or face other circumstances that may prevent them from earning income to service the debt. In the past years, such PPI was widely sold by banks and other credit providers as an add-on to a loan or an overdraft. However, consumers often felt that they did not need this insurance and that banks or financial institutions had pushed them to buy this product. Later, they wanted to get rid of it, saying that they were mis-sold such PPI.

Everyone taking part in the competition, the AI coded by the students and the more than 100 commercial lawyers, received real cases from the Financial Ombudsman Service. Of course, they only got the facts. They did not get the outcomes, i.e. the decisions that the Financial Ombudsman Service had taken. Based on these facts that describe the case – how the consumer bought the product, what the consumer was told and so on – both the AI and the lawyers had to predict whether the consumer applying to the Financial Ombudsman would win or lose the case.

The facts of thousands of cases were put on a website, and the lawyers could log in and look at these facts. Then, they could take all the time they wanted and could consult all the material they wanted, including both online and offline sources.

Then, they had to click a button to predict whether the consumer would win or lose the case. In other words, the lawyers had to predict the decision of the Financial Ombudsman Service. This way, the lawyers made more than 750 predictions. So, the lawyers were quite active, and there were a large number of predictions by them. The AI did the same. After all predictions were made, everyone attended a conference in London to learn about the results. To make sure that this was a fair competition, there was a technical judge who inspected that everything was fair in terms of technology and that no one had an advantage. There was also a legal judge to make sure that the competition was fair in terms of legal matters. I had the privilege to serve as the legal judge. I can assure you that it was a fair competition. No one had an unfair advantage over the other. In Figure 2.1, you can see the result of the competition.

The lawyers achieved a prediction accuracy of 62 per cent. That means that in ten cases, they predicted about six correctly and four wrongly. The AI, the students called it Case Crunch Technology, had a prediction accuracy of 87 per cent. This is close to 90 per cent, which roughly means that in ten cases, the AI was correct nine times and got one case wrong. Hence, the competition resulted in a win for the AI. Put differently, the AI was better in predicting the outcome of PPI cases than the lawyers.

After revealing the results, the participants at the conference in London also had a discussion on what these results meant. In the discussion, the issues that were raised concerned costs and time. For each case, a lawyer would probably take one hour (at least) to work on it. Quite likely, there would also be other staff in the law firm working on the case, which would probably result in a three-figure fee to be paid by the consumer in British pounds. On the other hand, the AI, once it is set up, which comes with costs, would do the calculation and the prediction in a fraction of a second. Depending, of course, on the number of cases, the AI would incur fewer costs than the lawyer's firm would charge.

So, it is worth noting that the discussion at the conference did not only concern the accuracy of the prediction but also the costs and the time involved. Of course, the main issue at the conference was the result of the competition, and this concerned the accuracy of the prediction. The discussion at the conference also concerned what this might mean for the future. A further question that was raised concerned the amount of time one needs to invest to get information on the law and what the costs of this are. This concerns both the AI and the lawyers – both need to acquire information on the law before they can render their services.

We were quite happy to see that the results of the competition were reported all around the world. On the right side of Figure 2.1, you can see a selection of journals and news providers that reported on this competition. I will come back to that later and tell you a little bit more about what the British Broadcasting Corporation (BBC), said on their website. I think that the wide media coverage and interest show that people are interested in the future of justice.

## WHO WOULD YOU LIKE TO ASK FOR LEGAL ADVICE, A HUMAN LAWYER OR AN AI?

**Steffek:** As Professor Sumida intends this event to take the form of a dialogue and I very much like this idea, I have a question for you. Imagine you had a dispute concerning PPI, as was the case in this competition, with your bank and you considered an application to the Financial Ombudsman Service. However, you would be interested in knowing whether it is worth going to the Financial Ombudsman Service, investing your time and perhaps your money. You want to know whether you would be successful. Who would you ask?

I will provide you with three choices, but you can also make up more choices if you have another opinion. Would you ask: (A) a human lawyer, (B) the Case Crunch AI or (C) a human lawyer who uses the Case Crunch AI?

**Student A:** I would like to consult both, a human lawyer and the AI, so I would choose option C. The reason for this is that I have concerns about the diagnostic results of AI alone. I am not yet familiar with AI, and I would like to know information surrounding the results, such as why these diagnostic results were obtained and what rulings have been made in the past. Such information is not available in the AI's diagnosis. That being said, I just saw that the AI had a much higher percentage of correct answers, so I would like to benefit from both.

**Student B:** I would choose only the AI, option B. The reason is the cost hurdle. There are enormous legal fees involved in asking a human to give their advice. Accordingly, I would be happy with the AI alone, as long as it is accurate, and I would be able to rely on it to prepare my decisions.

**Sumida:** Are there any other voices with different opinions? Would anyone opt for option A, i.e. only consult a human lawyer?

**Student C:** I would prefer to ask a human lawyer, option A. I learned from a professor at my university that law has a social function and intervenes to support people who tend to become emotionally involved in a dispute. Such intervention can come in the form of a lawyer, a third party. The lawyer will aim to reach a social solution while also calming the emotions of the respective parties. I agree with that very much. When you are faced with the need to use insurance due to a contingency, such as loss of employment, you may have a lot of emotions and may not be satisfied with the situation. As a party, you may feel uneasy about whether you can make a good enough claim by pitching it to AI. Instead, I feel that if I ask a trusted lawyer, they will be able to adequately get my point across. This is the first reason for choosing option A.

Secondly, I do not know from what perspective the accuracy of the AI's prediction is measured. There might, perhaps, be aspects that are not correct in the assessment by the AI even if the assessment is in your favour. For instance, an AI might suggest that you are entitled to claim insurance benefits, even though in reality you have a very weak case. Hence, I think that asking a human lawyer is not necessarily a negative course of action.

**Sumida:** So, we have had a lot of opinions. Felix-san, would you like to respond?

**Steffek:** Thank you very much for your opinions. These were perfect answers because you covered the relevant issues. Often, we concentrate on accuracy first; we look at the facts and want to predict the future. In addition, you mentioned the issue of costs. This shows that while we desire perfect justice and predictions as an ideal starting point, in practice, we ask the question what this will cost. Sometimes, we will accept a less-than-perfect service because the costs of a perfect service would not be justified for the specific case at hand. This applies, in particular, to cases with a low value. There are also further considerations. The last comment emphasised the human side of justice. Justice concerns not only cold facts but also emotions. Taking all answers together, I think you have covered the relevant issues.

Interestingly, the fact that we had voices for all three options shows us that different people want different things in justice. There may be people who are only interested in the result. They say, 'I want the money back and that is all.' For other people, dispute resolution is rather an emotional process. They have anxieties or they are angry; they want to express that in the process of solving their dispute, and they want to express it to a human. Different people want different things in dispute resolution, and it is for them to decide. This is why your answers are all good answers. There is no wrong answer because it is your wish. Different citizens have different wishes. This reminds me of my little son, Max. He is four years old, and he came back yesterday from kindergarten and said, 'Daddy, people are different and they want different things.' And that is how it is.

However, we also have constraints. Such constraints set limits to our wishes. We only have a certain number of resources, and when you go to court, it can be a zero-sum game, i.e. there can only be one winner and the other party will be the loser. In reality, we cannot always have it our way. This is why we need the law and lawmakers to make choices, which wishes to grant and which wishes to deny. This is the background of what we are discussing today.

## CREATING LEGAL PREDICTION TOOLS

**Steffek:** Now, I would like to explain how the team behind the Case Crunch Challenge organised their project and how they used AI. It all started with a dataset. They went to the Financial Ombudsman Service and asked whether they could have a dataset of cases that were decided in the past. The Financial Ombudsman Service decides hundreds of thousands of cases every year and provided the team with a large dataset. The Case Crunch team decided to concentrate on cases concerning PPI and not deal with other cases. Each case had the same structure. The first part provided the facts, and the second part the decision of the Financial Ombudsman Service. As there are many PPI cases in the United Kingdom, the dataset was quite big. There were around 100,000 cases in the dataset. The team then took 10 per cent of these cases, i.e. 10,000 cases, and created a training dataset with these cases. They used NLP to classify these 10,000 cases as cases where either the consumer wins or loses. To give you an example, the team used an algorithm according to which if the last sentence of the decision contained the phrase 'not successful' or the word 'unsuccessful', then that case was classified as 'consumer loses'. This shows that already at the stage of creating the training dataset, they used computer algorithms. This was necessary because it would have been too tedious to classify all 10,000 cases by hand.

You can imagine the result of this algorithmic classification as a big table where in one column, i.e. in one cell for each case, you have all the facts, and in the second column, you have a 'yes' or 'no' as regards the outcome. 'Yes' means the consumer wins, and 'no' means the consumer loses. These two pieces of information, facts and outcome, are linked to the relevant case, identified by a case number. After the training dataset was constructed in this way, the Case Crunch team used a neural network, which is a form of AI, to learn which factors in the facts would determine the outcome, i.e. whether the consumer's application to the Financial Ombudsman Service would be successful or unsuccessful.

Thus, this is where AI comes in. The neural network is an algorithm that trains itself. You do not have to do anything except wait until the training process is concluded. Essentially, one provides the algorithm with the relevant information – in this case, the facts and the classification as 'win' or 'lose' – and the neural network will then, by trial and error, determine which factors within the facts determine the outcome. During the training process, the AI makes predictions. These predictions will be very arbitrary at the beginning. It will start with the facts of one case and arbitrarily predict the outcome. Let us assume that the consumer, in fact, won this case. If the AI predicts a win, then it sees the factors it considers as confirmed. If, however, the AI predicts a loss and then realises that the prediction is wrong, it will go back and try to understand what factors are relevant for losing. The AI does this process again and again for all 10,000 cases in the training dataset. The higher the number of cases the AI can learn from, the better the predictions can get.

At the end of this learning process, the AI gets better and better through trial and error and can connect factors in the facts with the expected outcomes. This process of learning which factors are relevant (and which are not) is not something that the human influences at that stage. Instead, the neural network, of which you see a representation here in Figure 2.2, does it independently. The input layer in the figure is the facts, the output layer is win or lose, and the circles in between are the factors which the AI determines to be contributing to whether a case will be won or lost.

The relevant factors are determined and weighed by the AI itself. It is not the human creator who does that. It is the neural network that does it. Notably, since it is the AI determining the factors, the human creators and users do not always know what the AI uses as factors to determine whether the consumer will win or lose. This is called the 'black box' effect. Due to this effect, humans have problems understanding which factors are relevant for the AI, particularly since the AI looks at a large number of factors. Additionally, as shown in the figure, the connections between the factors are quite complex. They are often so complex that it is difficult for humans to fully understand the weight of each individual factor for the final result.

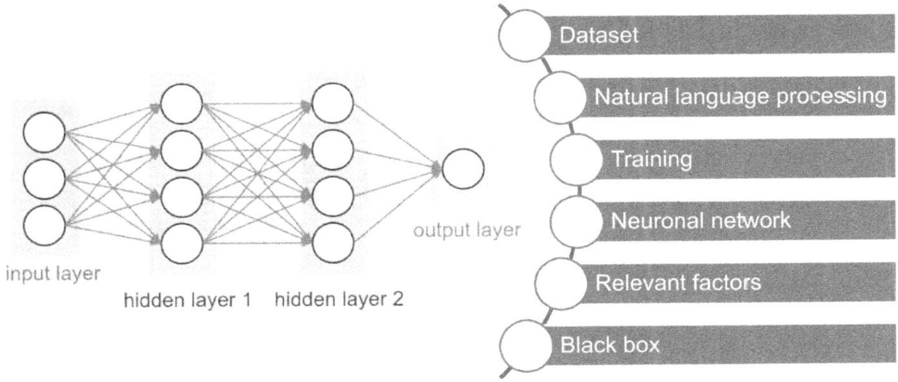


FIGURE 2.2 Artificial intelligence at work

At the end of the training, the AI is ready to look at new cases. This is when the Case Crunch competition started. After the AI had been trained on 10,000 cases, it would then – in the competition – get the facts of a new case and predict the outcome, i.e. whether the consumer would win or lose. At this point, the AI had a prediction accuracy of 87 per cent as I reported earlier. In other words, it would reach the correct prediction in 87 per cent of the cases. This is an example of how AI can be used to predict the outcome of a dispute resolution procedure such as ombudsman proceedings and court litigation.

## LEGAL AI: WHERE DO WE STAND?

**Steffek:** Let me provide you with an overview of some of the existing research and literature on using AI to predict the outcome of cases. In these projects, the fundamental approach is often the same, mirroring the methods that I have just explained. Researchers take a dataset, train an AI and then apply the trained algorithm to a new case where the AI does not have the result but will predict the outcome. The result is then compared to what the judges or the ombudspersons decided, and the precision of the prediction is calculated. There are more studies than I can present today. I picked some from around the world to give you an impression of where research currently stands in this field.

I will start with the paper by Katz et al. published in 2017.[1] They looked at the US Supreme Court. This research project had 28,000 decisions in the dataset. An important question concerning such datasets is: 'What exactly is the information contained in a dataset?' In Figure 2.3, I refer to this as the basis of the research project. This particular research project only had meta-factors in the dataset. What are meta-factors? 'Meta-factors' refers to abstract information on the case and excludes the specific facts of the case. For example, this research project used the following meta-factors: *First*, what is the circuit of origin of the case? In other words,

[1] Daniel Martin Katz, Michael J. Bommarito II and Josh Blackman, 'A General Approach for Predicting the Behavior of the Supreme Court of the United States' (2017) 12(4) PLoS ONE.

| Authors | Year | Dispute body | Basis | Decisions in dataset (rounded) | Precision (rounded) |
|---|---|---|---|---|---|
| Katz et al | 2017 | US Supreme Court | Meta-factors | 28,000 | 70% |
| Sulea et al | 2017 | French Supreme Court | Facts | 126,000 | 96% |
| Long et al | 2018 | Chinese civil law courts | Facts, law, applications | 100,000 | 80% |
| Bull & Steffek | 2018 | UK Financial Ombudsman Service | Facts | 100,000 | 87% |
| Chalkidis et al | 2019 | European Court of Human Rights | Facts | 11,500 | 90% |

FIGURE 2.3 AI prediction precision and dispute resolution

where does the case geographically come from? *Second*, what is the legal area of the case? Is it commercial law? Is it criminal law? Is it public law? And so on. *Third*, what is the type of the petitioner? Is the petitioner an employee or is it the State? *Fourth*, what is the type of the respondent? Similarly, is it a corporation, is it an employee, or is it the State? And *fifth*, what is the ideology of the lower court? Is it a liberal court or is it a more conservative lower court? It is important to remember that in this study, the AI did not have access to the facts. It also did not have access to the law. It only had access to meta-factors. But still, the AI showed a precision of 70 per cent in predicting real cases that were decided by the US Supreme Court.

The next study by Sulea et al. concentrated on the French Supreme Court.[2] They had a bigger dataset. The research team had 126,000 cases, and the dataset in this research project contained facts, but not law. Even though the AI only had the facts of the case, it achieved a very high precision of 96 per cent; i.e. in 96 per cent of cases, the AI was correct in predicting the decisions by the French Supreme Court.

Next, moving on to a Chinese study looking at Chinese civil law courts, Long et al. published a paper in 2018.[3] They again had a pretty big dataset of around 100,000 cases. In this project, the dataset contained not only facts but also information on the law and applications. 'Applications' refers to the petition, i.e. what the petitioner wanted the court to decide. The AI in this project achieved a precision of 80 per cent.

Furthermore, Bull and Steffek's paper reported on the Case Crunch Lawyer Challenge.[4] This study was conducted by Ludwig Bull, who will speak tomorrow, and Felix Steffek, which is me. In this paper, as I mentioned earlier, we received a dataset from the UK Financial Ombudsman Service. Our dataset contained around 100,000 cases, and only the facts of these cases were included. The AI did not have

2 Octavia-Maria Sulea and others, 'Predicting the Law Area and Decisions of French Supreme Court Cases' (4 August 2017) arXiv:1708.01681v1.

3 Shangbang Long and others, 'Automatic Judgment Prediction via Legal Reading Comprehension' (18 September 2018) arXiv:1809.06537v1.

4 Ludwig Bull and Felix Steffek, 'Die Entschlüsselung rechtlicher Konflikte: Der Einsatz künstlicher Intelligenz zur Ermittlung von Entscheidungsfaktoren der Konfliktlösung' [2018] (5) Zeitschrift für Konfliktmanagement (ZKM) 165.

access to the law. The precision, as I explained earlier when reporting on the Case Crunch Lawyer Challenge, was 87 per cent.

Finally, Chalkidis et al. published a paper in 2019 focusing on the European Court of Human Rights (ECHR).[5] They had a smaller dataset of 11,500 cases, again containing only the facts. They achieved a prediction precision of 90 per cent.

What can we learn from these studies? First, it is interesting to see the variations in precision. We also get an idea of the number of cases contained in the datasets currently used for such studies. Further, it is quite impressive to see that AI has achieved high prediction precision in many studies, even though it did not get any information on the law. This is quite surprising because, as lawyers, would we not think that the law is essential in predicting the outcome of a case? I am very happy to discuss these issues later if you are interested.

## IS THE USE OF AI IN DISPUTE RESOLUTION A GOOD THING?

**Steffek:** Now I would like to involve you again by asking a question. I would be very grateful again for your answers. My question takes the form of a statement, and I would like to know whether you agree or disagree with the statement. The statement is as follows:

> It would be good if citizens and businesses had access to AI services predicting the outcome of dispute resolution procedures such as court litigation, arbitration and ombud schemes.

What is your opinion?

**Student D:** Access to AI services predicting the outcome of disputes will have a positive impact, of course, but there is a concern that the number of lawsuits may drop a little. I have learned recently that Japan has a low litigation rate compared to other countries, and that is a problem. One of the reasons for this is that the Japanese legal system tends to make it rather easy to predict the outcome of litigation. People tend to give up on their cases before they even start to sue, thinking that their case will probably not be successful. If the number of lawsuits is reduced, it may have the negative effect of reducing the use of the court system and isolating people from legal participation. At the same time, I think that it would be very innovative and useful if it meant that people could anticipate the result of legal procedures, at least as a reference. I would say that I agree to a certain extent, rather than completely agreeing with the proposition.

**Student E:** I have the same opinion and agree to a certain extent. The reason why I do not fully agree is that I am concerned that if the results are shown in advance by AI, it may cause claims as to why the actual results are different from them. On the other hand, from the citizen's and company's point of view, I believe it has both positive and negative aspects. It certainly makes it easier to plan future actions when damages occur. They will be able to foresee to some extent how much they will have to pay.

5 Ilias Chalkidis, Ion Androutsopoulos and Nikolaos Aletras, 'Neural Legal Judgment Prediction in English' (5 June 2019) arXiv:1906.02059v1.

**Steffek:** Thank you – again, you have identified important questions. Applications of AI – as the studies I have presented show us – are good, but they are not perfect. None of the projects achieves a prediction accuracy of 100 per cent. Hence, the question arises: 'What if the AI is wrong?' Your answers also show that you have started thinking about how the world would change if we already knew the outcome of the dispute resolution processes. Would we still go to court? If we knew the outcome in court, then perhaps we would come to an amicable solution to the dispute even before that. Knowing the outcome of the dispute resolution processes would be quite a fundamental change to our societies, our businesses and our relationships. This would also mean that we knew the law, i.e. the legal consequences of our actions. Would it not be great if we all knew the law and the legal consequences that our actions will have? Is there any value in people not knowing the law? These are interesting questions that have been raised by you, and the advances in applying AI to the law make these questions practically relevant.

## THE ROLE OF AI IN LAW

**Steffek:** Figure 2.4 presents the BBC website and how it reported the Case Crunch Competition.

The BBC raised the same issues that you have raised so far. The heading of the website says, 'The robot lawyers are here – and they're winning'. In other words, the journalist tells the audience, 'Look, here are robots that are more capable of predicting case outcomes than lawyers. What does this mean for the human element in justice? Which role should humans play?' Before we discuss the human element, I will introduce you to further use cases of AI in law. We first need to know how AI can be used in legal services before we can fully discuss ethical issues.

FIGURE 2.4 The robot lawyers are here – and they're winning

So, how can AI be used in practice? One important point I want to make is that AI can be used on different sides. As shown at the top in Figure 2.5, decision-makers can use AI, i.e. judges, arbitrators and ombudspersons. On the other hand, as shown at the bottom, parties and their advisors can also use AI. The implications are quite different depending on whether a judge uses AI or whether a party uses AI. This is something we need to distinguish when we discuss the desirability of AI applications in the legal domain.

What can AI be used for? It can be used to improve three areas, namely information, analysis and decisions. I would like to give you examples of such use cases. Some of these examples are quite pedestrian and probably uncontroversial, while others are advanced and highly controversial. The fact that using AI in law is sometimes not controversial but sometimes very controversial reminds us that the ethical considerations will depend on the specific use case.

How could a court use AI to improve information? A judge could use AI to find relevant cases in the case database. The judge might be interested in determining what other courts have decided in similar cases, and AI could be used to improve the database search. Or, to give another example, courts could use AI to extract relevant evidence from submitted documents in cases where there are thousands of pages of submitted documents. Again, AI could be used to improve the information available to the court.

How could a court improve its analysis? Courts could analyse past decisions and try to find out whether it has been biased in the past, e.g. by overemphasising certain characteristics of the claimants. How do we do that? Conceptually, it is quite simple. You set up an AI to predict the outcome based on past decisions, and then, you take out one type of information, e.g. the identity of the claimant, and see whether this influences the prediction. This will help you understand whether the identity of the claimant will affect the results. You make a first prediction where the AI has information on the claimant, e.g. age, gender, nationality and whether it is a corporation or a consumer. Then, you ask for a second prediction, but you take this information away from the AI, i.e. you remove it from the dataset. If the

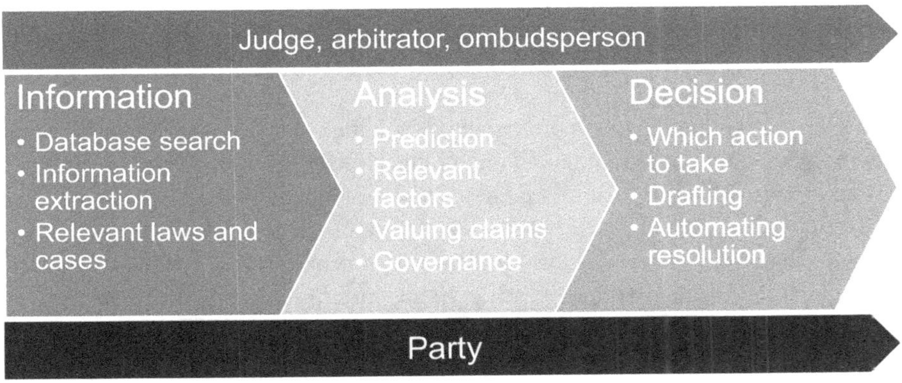


FIGURE 2.5 AI use cases for courts and parties

outcome is different, then it seems that the identity of the claimant may be relevant. Of course, the law applies equally to all, and the identity of the petitioner should generally not be relevant. The law should be administered the same way. If such an analysis of past cases, however, reveals that the identity of the petitioner is relevant in past judgments, it means that there may have been bias in the past. Courts could learn from it and improve current and future decisions.

Third, decisions: for example, you could ask an AI to double-check decisions or get support in drafting decisions. I would like to emphasise that when I describe what AI might do, I am not commenting on whether this is a good or a bad idea. I am only telling you about the possibilities. I say what is feasible. I am not saying that we should do it or should not do it. That is another topic we need to discuss.

How can parties use AI? Parties can use it to identify relevant case law. Advisors can find cases that are similar to the one they are dealing with. In addition, to improve their analysis, they can predict the outcome of going to court or another dispute resolution institution. They can predict the costs of taking a case to court. They can predict how long a case will take in court. As regards decisions, parties or their advisors can ask the AI to help them decide whether to bring a claim to court or to sell the claim. As shown in Figure 2.5, you see 'access to justice' as a theme. I think that many use cases of AI can contribute to making law more accessible. This concerns, in particular, the perspective of the parties.

## EVALUATING AI FROM A BUSINESS MANAGER'S PERSPECTIVE

**Steffek:** I would like to hear your opinion again. How would you decide in the following scenario?

> If you were the director of a large company, would you use AI for the conflict management of your company? Would you think that it is helpful for you to use it or would you not use it?

**Student F:** If I were the manager of a large company, I would want to use AI for conflict management. If you are a large company, you are likely to find that devoting human resources to a single lawsuit often interferes with your core business. For example, if you are managing an insurance company, you often have to call an external lawyer for litigation and pay them to attend to the case. By employing AI, you can manage the dispute more efficiently. I believe this would allow us to solve the problem without the reputational harm created by litigation. I think it would be useful to use AI for two reasons: efficiency and reputation.

**Student G:** I would like to defend the position of not introducing AI. The disputes that large companies have to deal with are likely more complex than, for example, the PPI case mentioned earlier. In the current social climate, there is a risk that society will criticise companies for using AI. In other words, until AI is used in various places and citizens are fully accepting AI, it may be difficult for society to tolerate the use of AI by large companies for such dispute resolution. As regards complex cases, I would not use AI since the possibility of mistakes that humans would not make cannot be ruled out.

**Steffek:** Thank you for your excellent contributions. This is a practical question, and you are raising important practical matters. The first comment points to the efficiency advantages that using AI might have. If automating certain legal tasks by way of AI is cheaper than paying someone to do it, then businesses are rational to use AI. This assumes, of course, that the results the AI offers are of the same or better quality. The same logic applies to use cases where AI supports human decision-makers. If AI saves costs or produces better results, then it may be a commercially wise decision to employ it.

The second comment, however, reminds us that AI – at this point in time – might not be able to contribute to all types of tasks. This comment points to very complex cases and doubts that AI is ready to meaningfully contribute to such cases. This is a correct and important point. Currently, the applications of AI in law are quite specific, and there is no AI application in existence that could replace human legal experts in every case. In summary, it depends on the specific task that is to be performed, whether an AI could replace humans in the performance of such a task and, if so, at what cost.

## HOW TO SOLVE THE BIAS PROBLEM

**Steffek:** As mentioned earlier, I would now like to address bias. Bias is a major issue with AI in law, and there are a number of sources for bias. It may be that the dataset has gaps, or there may even be mistakes in the dataset. Perhaps past court decisions were wrong. In such a case, AI will learn from those wrong decisions. Or the algorithm has mistakes and produces wrong predictions. Maybe it chooses the wrong factors, labels the wrong text or is based on a faulty logic. If an algorithm predicts the court outcome correctly in 80 per cent of the cases, it is wrong in 20 per cent of the cases. Or the humans ask the wrong questions to the AI.

What can we do to avoid such mistakes? An important point that I want to make here is that there are technical solutions to bias and there are legal solutions. As lawyers, we may think that law needs to come in and solve the problem of bias, but experts in AI and NLP are also working on solutions. Technical solutions might be to get more data or to de-bias data. De-biasing data concerns, in particular, cases where there is bias in past decisions. Researchers are working on algorithms that help remove bias from data.[6] Legal solutions, on the other hand, may involve the

[6] See for example Manish Raghavan and others, 'Mitigating Bias in Algorithmic Hiring Evaluating Claims and Practices' (21 June 2019) arXiv:1906.09208; Chalkidis, Androutsopoulos, and Aletras (n 5); critically, Hila Gonen and Yoav Goldberg, 'Lipstick on a Pig: Debiasing Methods Cover Up Systematic Gender Biases in Word Embeddings but Do Not Remove Them' (9 March 2019) arXiv:1903.03862.

- Sources of bias
  - Dataset: gaps, mistakes, bias
  - Algorithm: labelling, coding mistakes, choice of outcome
- Solutions to bias
  - Technical: dataset (more data, less biased data, de-bias data), algorithm
  - Legal: rights and obligations
    - Negative impact v optimal outcome
- Bias in existing dispute resolution systems
  - AI can detect bias in existing dispute procedures
    - Evidence evaluation, decisions
  - AI can provide consistency checks

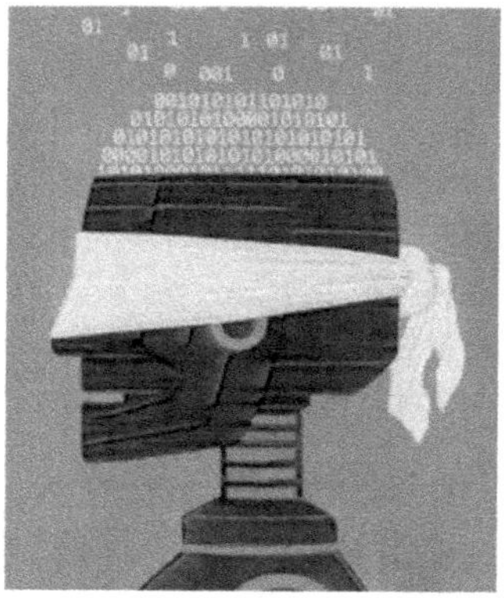

FIGURE 2.6 Bias

establishment of rights and duties to remove bias. The point that is important here is that there are technical solutions and there are legal solutions. The choice we need to make in specific use cases is whether it is better to apply a technical solution, a legal solution or both.

Looking at the bigger picture, we also need to ask what we would like to achieve as regards the content of AI predictions. Are we interested in optimal outcomes, or are we interested in avoiding negative impact? Often, lawyers focus on avoiding negative impact, but ultimately, I think, AI is a tool to get optimal predictions. Achieving optimal outcomes and avoiding negative impact are not always the same thing, even though an optimal prediction, of course, avoids unwarranted negative impacts. My last point about Figure 2.6 is that existing systems are also not perfect. But AI can help us and courts, for example, to find mistakes or biases in past decisions. This perspective raises the issue of what we compare AI applications against: current practice (which is not always perfect) or optimal outcomes?

## THE REMAINING CHALLENGES TO TRANSPARENCY

**Steffek:** Moving on to transparency brings us to the black box problem that I introduced earlier. It is a technical problem – to start with. When using a neural network, we do not even know what factors the AI uses to achieve its prediction. It is also an ethical problem, since justice is not just about the decision but also about the explanation of the decision. We know this from the way law is taught at university. In the classroom, when discussing legal cases, we do not only ask what the result is and who wins, but we also ask why and discuss the reasons for the outcome. This explanation is part of justice. The same applies to court judgments. They do not only contain the result but also contain the reasons for the result. This is another real-world example making it tangible that justice is not only about the outcome but also about explaining the outcome to those affected by the result.

If AI only tells us the result, that is not the same as justice as there is no explanation. Again, there are technical solutions to the black box problem. Researchers and businesses are working on explainable AI, i.e. they are developing applications that not only predict the outcome but also provide an explanation as to why this outcome is likely. For example, there are research papers using AI to generate explanations.[7] Such explanations can take the form of the reasons for a judgment or the form of a list of reasons, for example, the applicable statutes and existing cases a court might refer to because they are similar to the case at hand.

As with bias, there are also legal solutions, which can be to require transparency of the algorithm. Another legal approach might be that the parties agree on an algorithm. There are already court cases where parties have agreed on which algorithm to use, and that was a good, consensual solution to the black box problem. Similar to the solutions to bias, the question is whether we use AI to mimic what humans would do or whether we use AI to provide explanations that are better than the explanations humans can provide. To give you an example, let us assume that the average number of reasons for a decision in a first instance court usually provided in a judgment handed to the parties is five. In other words, the parties to a dispute receive five different explanations for the decision of court in the text that is handed to them. Let us also assume that courts provide a qualitative (but not quantitative) explanation of which reasons are more important than the others. Now assume that an AI would be able to generate at least ten or even twenty reasons for the decision. Assume, in addition, that the AI could rank all of these reasons and attribute a percentage figure giving their relative importance in the case. Which type of explanation would you prefer? The qualitative explanation based on five reasons provided by court or the quantitative explanation based on ten or twenty reasons provided by the AI?

## USING AI IN COURT

**Steffek:** This brings me to my last question taking the form of a statement again. The statement is as follows:

> As a party I would welcome if the judge deciding my case uses AI to check the judgment (after it is written) and considers amending the judgment if the AI diverges.

In other words, would you like the judge to first decide and then look at the AI and, if the AI decides differently, the judge to check whether they have made a mistake? Would you prefer this to be court practice, or would you prefer the traditional, AI-free approach?

7 See, for example Federico Ruggeri and others, 'Detecting and Explaining Unfairness in Consumer Contracts through Memory Networks' (2022) 30 Artificial Intelligence and Law 59.

**Student H:** I am against using AI in such a court setting. I think judgments should be written by humans due to the human and societal aspects of justice.

**Student I:** I would prefer that AI is used to check judgments and that judges would reconsider their decisions if the AI came to a different conclusion. This is similar to DNA testing, and if there is a technical and scientific basis, then AI should be used to check judgments.

**Steffek:** Thank you very much for your opinions. I am glad that you voiced different opinions as they show the challenge we face: 'How much human involvement is needed for a court decision to be just?' First of all, your answers confirm that different people want different things. The court system and its regulation need to respect this. In this specific case, the solution could, perhaps, be a rule in the procedural code saying that the use of AI to check decisions already taken is only allowed if both parties consent. The question I asked also addresses the point of how good – in the sense of correctness – humans and algorithms are in making legal decisions. Research shows that both humans and algorithms can suffer from bias when determining legal outcomes. It is also worth noting that there is a lot of development in the quality of legal applications of AI. We will also see that the way in which people consider the use of AI will change over time. This tells us that there is no right answer for all people at all times, but that our answer will depend on a number of elements, such as the quality of AI and human decisions, the way in which such decisions are presented (e.g. whether they are properly explained) and individual perceptions of justice.

## REGULATING AI IN DISPUTE RESOLUTION

**Steffek:** I will conclude with a few thoughts on ethics. AI can improve access to justice. However, despite the advantages provided by AI, there are risks as well. Using AI in dispute resolution is not straightforward, and there is no one-size-fits-all approach. I do think that AI will lead to us using law more to create legal relationships ex ante and less to litigate ex post. This is a good thing because people should know about the consequences of law before they act and not be surprised by the legal consequences later. In the future, we will see more people using technology to understand their legal position before they take action, instead of not understanding legal consequences, then being exposed to a problem later on, going to court and getting a surprise decision. AI will allow businesses and consumers to have a better idea of the law before they make decisions.

Ultimately, it is the interests of citizens that should guide lawmakers, and I think your answers today have shown that there are different citizens who want different things. This is quite a challenge for lawmakers. However, to solve this challenge, we can use existing experience and knowledge. This concerns procedural law, for example. It is not new to us that resources are constrained and that decisions are not always optimal. It is not new that we must find a balance between finding the truth in court and having constraints in terms of time and resources. Human rights will guide us as regards using AI in law. Procedural rights and principles, too, can guide us. Consumer law can also help us navigate this new field, dealing with situations where one party might have access to AI information and the other might not.

Nonetheless, I think that AI will not just be plugged into the existing justice system, but it will fundamentally transform our legal systems, including legal dispute resolution. I would like to end by saying that in a research project between the University of Cambridge and Hitotsubashi University, we are looking at developing a 'Guide for Regulating Artificial Intelligence in Dispute Resolution'. In this project, we will try to give answers to the questions raised today. I am now at the end of my presentation. It was a great pleasure to have a dialogue with you, and I am very grateful for your opinions. I would like to hand back to Mihoko, and I am very interested to hear what the commentators and further discussion will bring.

## WHY JAPAN HAS NOT STEPPED UP ITS USE OF AI

**Sumida:** Thank you. Professor Felix Steffek leads the team at the University of Cambridge investigating AI in dispute resolution. Professor Kazuhiko Yamamoto is the leader of the mirror working package at Hitotsubashi University, and he is a maestro in civil procedure law. I would like to ask Professor Yamamoto to comment on Professor Steffek's presentation.

**Yamamoto:** Thank you very much for your very valuable talk. I completely agree with Professor Steffek's concept of utilising AI in dispute resolution. As you mentioned earlier, if parties can access the dispute resolution results predicted by AI, they will be able to resolve their own disputes by, for example, settling them voluntarily, which will result in lower dispute resolution costs and will be beneficial for the parties. It would also be good for society as a whole, as it would allow courts, a valuable resource, to focus on more difficult disputes or more important cases.

However, the preconditions for the use of AI in justice probably differ from one country to another, and what is done in one country will not immediately become possible in other countries. As I see it, there are some differences between the United Kingdom, other Western countries and Japan. I would like to focus on two points.

The *first* issue is the number of court decisions and out-of-court disputes, including those that are known as alternative dispute resolution (ADR), that can serve as the basis of a dataset. Figure 2.3 shows a list of research projects conducted in Europe, the United States and other countries, and the datasets range from 10,000 to over 100,000 cases. In Japan, however, there are generally very few cases of dispute resolution in the public sphere, and more often than not, these cases are resolved in the form of settlements, which are not necessarily public.

Suppose, for example, that you wanted to conduct an AI analysis of a medical lawsuit. In Japan, there are about 800 lawsuits per year for accidents and errors that occur in the medical field. Furthermore, medical lawsuits have a relatively high rate of settlement, with only 200–300 cases resulting in a judgment that is publicly available. If one were to create a dataset as available in other countries – spanning between 10,000 and 100,000 cases –, it would take more than thirty years to collect 10,000 cases and more than 300 years to collect 100,000 cases. That is the current situation in Japan.

The Financial Ombudsman, researched by Professor Steffek, was also established in Japan about ten years ago, modelled after the British example. In Japan, the Financial Ombudsman functions through an organisation called the Japanese Bankers Association, which handles around 100–200 cases per year. The basic policy of financial ADR is to try to resolve disputes with banks through discussion, rather than through court proceedings. As a result, about half of these cases, between 50 and 100, are settled. Therefore, it would take more than 1,000 years to collect 100,000 cases as in Professor Steffek's study.

In addition, in the case of ADR, the Japanese Financial Ombudsman generally does not disclose the details of the cases, as the parties involved very strongly request for the cases to remain confidential. These cases are not accessible to the public. The same applies to many other ADR institutions, e.g. arbitration institutions. Against this background, my first point is that there are limitations in Japan in terms of creating legal datasets.

## CIVIL LAW VERSUS CASE LAW JURISDICTIONS

**Yamamoto:** The second problem is the nature of the legal rules. In Anglo-American law, say, common law countries such as the United Kingdom, where the law is originally based on case law, rules are analysed from the point of view of what exactly is different in each case. This is probably the type of rule system that is familiar to AI analysis.

In contrast, Japan is a country based on a civil law system and codified law. In other words, the system is such that when there are certain legal requirements, certain legal effects will follow clear articles of law. The predictability of the outcome of dispute resolution here is mainly based on such rules. There has been a handful of research in Japan on what kind of legal requirements lead to what kind of legal effects and how to code them into AI such that if certain facts are present, certain legal effects will be produced. In other words, I think we are moving towards coding legal rules rather than analysing actual cases.

Of course, in Japan, too, there are no clear rules regarding, for example, the calculation of the amount of damages. Thus, in the case of traffic accidents, research that analyses precedents and cases as to the damages awarded has been conducted. I understand that this has been done, but I have the impression that this has been the exception in a rule-based system such as the Japanese. These are some of the differences between Japan and the United Kingdom. However, I believe that the situation in Japan is changing and that it is changing rapidly.

Regarding the first issue of the number of cases in datasets, there is currently a project underway, led by the Ministry of Justice, to make all judgments available in the form of open data. If this is achieved, there is a possibility that at least such judgments could become the basis of datasets for AI analysis. Even though there is the problem of the small number of judgments themselves, I think we will still be able to collect quite a lot of data.

Alternatively, in the ongoing project to digitalise civil litigation, it is being discussed whether all court case records should be converted into electronic data and whether in some cases online access should be allowed. If this can be achieved, there is a possibility to utilise not only the judgments but also the litigation records that form the foundation for the judgments as a dataset.

However, there are certain hurdles to these projects in Japan. Regarding the conversion of judgments into open data, there is a strong need to anonymise the parties involved. Currently, AI is used to remove names from case records. However, many parties in Japan may hesitate to go to court if all related case data will be available on the internet.

Similarly, criticism has begun to emerge against the idea of allowing internet access to the litigation records mentioned earlier, as it may result in an infringement of the right to a fair trial. From this perspective, it seems that in Japan, public perception is different in some respects from that of other countries in the West. I believe that this issue is closely related to developing datasets for conflict resolution.

## THE CHALLENGE OF UNLOCKING THE BLACK BOX

**Yamamoto:** Regarding the second issue of a civil-law-based system, I think that rapid changes are taking place. With changing social conditions, rules need to be as flexible as possible, and as I mentioned earlier, there is a move towards developing rules that can respond to changes in society by stipulating general clauses, using abstract concepts. In such a legal system, it is important to understand what factors judges specifically consider when applying such general rules, clauses and requirements, how they weigh the relevant factors, which factors they consider important and which factors have less relevance. When applying more general rules, there needs to be clarity on which factors are important and which are not so important. AI can contribute to this.

It is not easy to manually analyse the weighting of different factors in such cases, but I believe that the 'hidden layer' described in Professor Steffek's Figure 2.2 can provide new insights for analysing such rules. This is also related to the issue of transparency in AI, which Professor Steffek mentioned at the end of his talk. If the weight of such factors can be analysed, it will be of great significance to the parties concerned, to the judges who will make decisions based on them and to the legislators who are responsible for developing the rules. Hence, I have great expectations for this project, and I hope that the students who will be responsible for the future will look at jurisprudence from a new perspective. The relevant discussions will be very meaningful.

**Sumida:** Thank you very much. Today, we also have a member of the Ministry of Justice with us, Counsellor Fujita. Counsellor Fujita, I would like to ask you to contribute your thoughts.

## CAN JAPANESE LAWYERS ACCEPT AI?

**Fujita:** My name is Fujita and I am from the Civil Affairs Bureau of the Ministry of Justice. First of all, Professor Steffek, thank you very much for your very interesting talk on AI. I would now like to make a few comments, including from the perspective of a civil judge, although I myself am currently working for the Ministry of Justice and have been involved in IT in the judicial field. I am a practitioner, so I am in a position to lose my job as AI advances, which is a prospect I am not very keen on (laughs). Despite that, I believe it is a meaningful project that meets the needs of the times, and I would like to give a practitioner's opinion.

I would like to talk about three perspectives that I feel should be considered in relation to dispute resolution when new technologies, including AI, emerge, in the light of the current situation in Japan. The first concerns the technological potential of AI; the second investigates the mindset of the lawyers who are in a position to use it; and the third focuses on the public's acceptance of the services enhanced by technology and the security of the users.

Regarding the first point, the technological potential, in recent years, the potential and usefulness of using new technologies, including AI, has steadily increased in the legal sector, such as for contract verification and legal research. Many researchers and practitioners have become interested in this field. As a recent trend, the implementation of various service offerings, including those offered by start-up companies, is also progressing in Japan. There, apart from infrastructural aspects such as the small amount of data available in Japan, restrictions and difficulties in terms of technology are not much heard of. In the legal services sector, it can be seen that more advanced use of technology is possible, at least from a technical point of view. In the case of Japan, the challenges faced by the customer side, the lawyers and users, may instead be greater.

On the second point, concerning the mindset of lawyers as regards AI, I was joking earlier when I said that as a lawyer, I do not want AI to take my job. I personally think that human lawyers and legal AI can coexist well with an appropriate division of roles. Currently, in Japan, I have the impression that many lawyers want to use IT and AI as tools to assist and streamline their work but are afraid that it will replace them in their role as a lawyer who thinks and analyses. I think this fear is unfounded.

Why do Japanese lawyers have such an attitude? There are two possible causes – first, the traditional working style of Japanese lawyers. Japanese lawyers often go through several stages of listening to the client's story, analysing it, relating it to legal texts and precedents, drawing conclusions and seeking solutions while managing the client's expectations. The process is often carried out in several stages, moving back and forth between the lawyer and the client. It can be said to be a process that is tailored to the individual client and the dispute. Such a process, even if not consciously arranged, is likely to be a highly individualised approach. This creates the impression that such a service cannot be replaced by something automated or mechanical.

The second cause is rooted in the nature of the legal profession. Japanese lawyers may hesitate to prioritise convenience when it comes to the core of their legal services. This is because convenience often entails some risk. In Japan, there are very strict institutional rules and restrictions on the provision of legal services by persons who are not qualified as legal professionals. This practice has long been entrenched in the system. It is a tradition to which lawyers, judges and other legal professionals have been exposed. They all resolve legal disputes with high ethical standards and personal responsibility. They take pride in providing legal services themselves as skilled experts, without relying on external technology, such as AI.

Against this background, discussions concerning the use of IT and AI in the justice sector often raise the question of who is liable in the event of a technical fault or unexpected malfunction. Even if AI makes an obvious mistake due to unintended information processing, most lawyers are probably comfortable with the position that lawyers are not exempt from the risks and liabilities associated with the use of AI. The risk aversion of Japanese lawyers may be one of the reasons why the use of AI in the legal system has not progressed.

## WHAT DO USERS WANT FROM DISPUTE RESOLUTION?

**Fujita:** The third perspective concerns us as the users of the legal system. It is necessary to rethink how the parties involved in a dispute can feel satisfied with the resolution of the dispute. Japan has traditionally been said to have a strong 'sense of superiority', i.e. the public authorities are considered great, and they are thought to protect the common people. In an emergency, people want to rely on absolute authority. In legal disputes, a certain expectation and trust seems to have been placed on specialists such as lawyers or on having disputes resolved through the open, official authority of courts. Even if it takes some time and effort, such an open and clean resolution is considered to be a good thing.

However, recent changes in social conditions and technological developments have changed the situation of disputants. Looking at e-commerce and contracts on the internet between individuals, we wonder whether our traditional idea of judicial resolution of disputes through experts is always the right thing to do or whether it is the best way for all parties to gain a sense of satisfaction. Many people might rather prefer a more convenient and quicker resolution. As Professor Steffek said, it may be that many people will now prefer a resolution service that can be obtained easily and free of charge on the internet, rather than having to spend money and time consulting a lawyer. We have to rethink what good dispute resolution means for the parties concerned. From our point of view as practitioners, it may be necessary to change the mindset a little and to take an approach to dispute resolution that is easier and excludes emotional conflicts as well as the individuality of the case to a certain extent. Also, we should consider the possibility of closed solutions, such as private ADR, rather than public, rights-based solutions, such as court litigation. We should also think about a more open and transparent approach to dispute resolution, rather than a face-to-face solution. Furthermore, I wonder what kind of effect chat-based rather than face-to-face interactions will have in the future. There, seemingly contradictory interests, such as convenience and due process, will have to be reconciled and balanced.

One final point – as Professor Yamamoto mentioned earlier, the Ministry of Justice and others have in recent years begun to make concrete moves towards the digitalisation of court procedures and the application of open data principles to judgments. Given the time constraints today, I hope to talk about this at length if an opportunity arises later. To conclude, in Japan, judicial innovations are still on their way, in the process of being developed, and in this context, I listened to today's discussion with great interest. Thank you very much.

**Sumida:** Thank you very much for your valuable comments. Professor Steffek, would you like to respond to the Japanese side's comments?

## CITIZENS ARE AT THE CENTRE OF JUSTICE

**Steffek:** Thank you very much, Professor Yamamoto and Counsellor Fujita. These are very interesting and thoughtful points. I would like to concentrate my response to give us more time for discussion and thus would first like to comment on Professor Yamamoto's ideas that I found very fascinating. Professor Yamamoto raised the issue of the number of cases needed in the training dataset. I think that is, indeed, a very important point. Currently, AI research is also looking at whether good results can be produced with a lower number of cases in the dataset. The existing research papers tend to use datasets with many cases because such datasets are more likely to achieve better results. But I think we will see in the future whether, for example, a few hundred cases that cover a certain area can also produce good results. Research is not concluded as regards this issue. Listening to Professor Yamamoto, this will be quite important for jurisdictions such as Japan where there are not so many cases available in the legal system.

I would also like to comment on Professor Yamamoto's point where he said that in civil law systems, the law plays a bigger role, whereas in case law systems, as in Britain, court judgments are relatively more important. That is true. In the research project carried out with Hitotsubashi University, we will have an opportunity to compare the application of AI to Japanese law and English law. I expect that we can gain important insights from this comparative research, and I am very grateful that we have this research collaboration between the two institutions.

Thank you very much, Counsellor Fujita, for your very interesting thoughts and comments. I very much agree with the point you made that most practitioners expect that AI will supplement but not replace them. It seems to me that the situation in the United Kingdom and other countries is similar. Concentrating on tasks such as database research, providing advice, developing innovative contractual solutions, etc., is more helpful than only asking whether technology will replace human lawyers or not. The more granular focus on tasks is more precise. I also think that we can learn from past technology and how it has transformed the legal profession. How have computers changed the legal profession? What impact have email and the internet had on the legal profession? Technology has always transformed the legal profession, but it has never replaced lawyers. Computers and email have not replaced lawyers, but they have changed the way in which lawyers provide their services. That is why I think that this conversation series is a great opportunity for us as participants, since, as Professor Yamamoto said, we can learn and adapt to new ways in which law is applied. I think that, say, in ten or twenty years, legal services will look fundamentally different from what we see today. I also think your point, Counsellor Fujita, of helping people to develop trust in technological advances is very important. We need to look at the people and what they want. It is for the people to say, and that is the beauty of justice. It is about the people and the citizens and their wishes. But of course, not all wishes can come true, and this is the challenge we face.

**Sumida:** Thank you very much. Professor Takeshita is a member of the project who is also tuning in today. Professor Takeshita, would you like to add something?

## CRITICALLY EXAMINE YOUR OWN COMMON SENSE

**Takeshita:** My name is Takeshita and I am based at Hitotsubashi University. Thank you very much, Professor Steffek, for a really excellent lecture. I specialise in private international law, and I am interested in AI in relation to the use of online dispute resolution (ODR) in international dispute resolution. In the light of Professor Steffek's lecture today, I would like to comment on the significance of the use of AI in jurisprudence.

Dispute resolution prediction by AI has considerably overturned the conventional method of decision-making applied in Japanese civil jurisprudence. Although there are various types of AI, the AI for dispute resolution prediction introduced by

Professor Steffek inputs only facts and predicts the resolution of disputes as an output. Usually, if you make legal judgments in Japanese civil jurisprudence, as Professor Yamamoto mentioned briefly, you apply legal norms that combine legal requirements, *Tatbestand*, and legal effects. You determine in a step-by-step manner whether the legal requirements have been met, and then you conclude whether the claim is finally upheld or not. It is a very interesting point to skip all those legal judgments and let the AI learn and come to a conclusion in a way that links the facts and the conclusion.

It is interesting that in one study reported by Professor Steffek, AI has only learned from meta-factors, which is not an approach used in the normal application of the law. Furthermore, based on the results of the Chinese project, it appears that better results are achieved when only the facts are input rather than the AI having access to both facts and the law. I also thought that this was very interesting.

I would like the students to think about the following: if an AI that learns only facts and conclusions can predict dispute resolution more accurately than a human being who carefully applies the law, what is the application of the law then good for? Personally, I think that the significance of using AI's dispute resolution prediction ability is to critically examine the ideas of jurisprudence that we consider common sense. We can then see whether the application of law that we are undertaking is really the correct way of going about it.

There can be a real diversity of ideas in jurisprudence, and AI-based dispute resolution prediction will force people to reconsider the ideas in jurisprudence that you think are common sense. Nevertheless, as Professor Steffek pointed out, AI decisions still have a black box problem, i.e. that it is not directly revealed as to why a given solution is reached.

It is indeed a black box situation, where AI predicts a conclusion of conflict resolution with a high probability of being 'right', but the users do not know what the reasons or underlying factors are. In relation to this point, what I would like students to bear in mind is that if a certain meaning is to be given to AI prediction, including whether it is 'correct' or not, it still has to be done by a human being. For example, if the parties to a dispute demand an explanation for the outcome of the dispute resolution, there may of course be the possibility of an AI that automatically creates an explanation, as Professor Steffek mentioned. For the time being, however, a human hand will still be required to provide an explanation. In other words, the process of interpreting and applying the law that we are engaged in could be said to be exactly such a process of explanation and understanding, whereby it is assessed whether the human interpretation and application of the law is appropriate, when confronted with the results of dispute resolution presented by AI. Critical examination must be carried out, including the predicted results of AI learning from human-initiated cases, and it seems to me that it is still only humans who can do this.

Furthermore, AI basically learns from cases that have been judged in the past and predicts dispute resolution. It, thus, still may need human hands to realise a developed interpretation of the law. I believe that the significance of research in this field for the time being is to make efforts to ensure that humans properly understand the meaning of dispute resolution predicted by AI and to utilise this in human justice, as Professor Sumida also talked about the 'coexistence of AI and humans' in one of her previous classes.

**Sumida:** Thank you very much. Felix, would you like to say anything after listening to all those comments?

## CO-EXISTENCE WITH AI REFINES HUMAN INTELLIGENCE

**Steffek:** Yes – thank you very much, Professor Takeshita. You mentioned that the research papers I have presented show that approaches where the AI had access to only the facts produced results with high precision. I think we could spend a whole session discussing all these papers and why they achieved a higher or lower precision. Such precision also depends – often quite substantially – on data pre-processing. In some of the existing studies, in particular, studies that I have not presented today, the question arises whether the facts already contained signals from the judges about what the outcome would be. Hence, the AI may actually have found clues in the facts about what the outcome would be. This would not be desirable because, ideally, we would want facts in the datasets that do not indicate the outcome.

To conclude, on the one hand, we realise that AI is not perfect. There are no AI applications in law with a prediction accuracy of 100 per cent. On the other hand, the question is whether the existing justice institutions, e.g. courts, are always 100 per cent correct. Some cases go to appeal and are overturned, so it seems that not all decisions by courts are perfect. The question then is how we can use AI to make justice better and avoid the risks that AI brings. Thank you very much, Professor Takeshita, for your insightful comments.

**Sumida:** Would anyone like to speak? Professor Takeshita also raised some issues with the students, and if anyone was inspired in any way by today's discussion, I would be very grateful if you could tell us if you have changed your mind.

**Student J:** Yes, thank you very much for today. I am mainly studying statutes on a daily basis, but I was reminded of the importance of case law. It seems that the process of drawing conclusions in AI is based on case law, so I will put more effort into the same. It is just a brief impression, but thank you very much.

**Sumida:** In the previous session, I was talking about an analogy, i.e. that the coexistence of humans and AI has been realised in the world of shogi, Japanese chess, for a while now, and that what is happening in the world of shogi will, to some extent, also happen in the world of law. In the shogi world, amazing tactics are developed by AI through a process completely different from that of humans. The royal road of tactics, in which it had been said that 'whoever masters these tactics will win the shogi world', has lost against new moves developed by software. The world of shogi and go in Japan is a leading example of humans improving their intelligence while coexisting with AI. Japan is at the stage where research such as that introduced by Professor Steffek today is still in its infancy, but shogi is a world of professionals that is familiar to Japanese people.

## DIFFICULTIES IN PROCESSING JAPANESE LEGAL DOCUMENTS WITH AI

**Yamada:** Artificial intelligence covers quite a wide field of research. Famous applications are in the areas of robotics and gaming, including chess and shogi. Also, fundamental studies such as search, inference and machine learning are important. Among AI research topics, NLP is an essential field in AI and law. Natural language refers to the language we humans use. NLP is a field of research to develop technologies that allow computers to process human language. NLP aims to save human effort by, for example, analysing large amounts of documents efficiently by computational tools or generating sentences by computers. Typical applications include *kana-kanji* conversion (Japanese input method), machine translation and document retrieval. In the context of Japanese legal NLP, the judgment retrieval system has been the most widely used application. However, now that the scope of application of NLP in the legal field is expanding, as we see, the 'legal tech' concept has become more and more popular in recent years. The application of NLP to the legal field has become a field in which many research institutes and companies are working worldwide.

## CHALLENGES IN PROCESSING LEGAL DOCUMENTS WRITTEN IN JAPANESE

**Yamada:** In NLP research, the target of studies is text data. As English and Japanese are different languages, NLP systems developed for each language are also different. Most of the NLP systems are developed in English, and there are fewer Japanese studies than English ones. When it comes to legal NLP, this tendency is more remarkable. Is it difficult to create a system for the Japanese language, especially in the legal domain? Actually, we can utilise NLP techniques developed in other languages (often in English) even for the Japanese legal domain.

Most of the methods proposed in recent research are data-driven, i.e. they involve learning patterns based on the collected data, rather than rule-based methods, which process according to predefined rules. In data-driven methods, input sentences are divided into words (or similar units such as morphemes) and converted into computer-processable representations by assigning a numerical representation to each unit. Thus, in subsequent stages of learning and reasoning, the differences between languages are not a critical barrier in transferring techniques from one language to another. Even if a method is initially developed for English, it can be used for Japanese as long as enough Japanese data are available for learning. We cannot guarantee that every system developed for English can easily be adapted to Japanese without any issues. Still, the principal methods can often be transferred and utilised for different languages. Therefore, the unique characteristics of the Japanese language are not critical obstacles.

What about the uniqueness of the legal domain? Does it hinder the application of NLP? There are differences between linguistic expressions used in everyday life and those used in legal documents. For example, the vocabulary used in news documents naturally differs from that used in contracts. These differences can be resolved in a similar manner as the differences between languages if enough data in the legal domain are available for learning.

However, there might be technical issues caused by the characteristics of the Japanese legal system and legal documents, which are more complex than simple differences in vocabulary and expressions. There are many areas where research and development must be conducted. Nevertheless, some of the issues can be solved by applying existing NLP technology where sufficient data are available.

## LEGAL NLP AND DATA AVAILABILITY: OUTSIDE JAPAN

**Yamada:** Due to data availability, legal NLP research is more popular abroad than in Japan. In the legal domain, judgment documents are more readily available in electronic and machine-readable formats in the United States and the United Kingdom, whose justice systems are based on the common law. They are far ahead of the Japanese legal system. The machine-readable format refers not just to an electronic version of a document but to a format of data authored in a structure that allows a computer to extract and process its contents easily.

The Caselaw Access Project (CAP) in the United States has published a database containing all precedents in the United States published up to around June 2018, which is not simply scanned data in PDF format but data available in a machine-readable format.[8] In Europe, case data are also easily accessible through the EUR-Lex[9] and ECHR websites.[10]

These publicly available datasets help apply NLP technology to the field of law. For example, a language model called BERT,[11] which has been widely used since

[8] Caselaw Access Project (Harvard Law School) <https://case.law/> accessed 1 November 2023.

[9] <https://eur-lex.europa.eu/> accessed 1 November 2023.

[10] HUDOC: European Court of Human Rights <https://hudoc.echr.coe.int/> accessed 1 November 2023.

[11] Jacob Devlin and others, 'BERT: Pre-training of Deep Bidirectional Transformers for Language Understanding' (11 October 2018) arXiv:1810.04805.

2019 for its performance and versatility, was adapted to the legal domain in 2020,[12] using data from CAP and ECHR. Better data availability enables rapid development and application of NLP in the legal domain. Data availability is also crucial in terms of experiments and evaluation, as well as the reproducibility of research.

## APPLICATIONS OF NLP AND DATA AVAILABILITY IN JAPAN

**Yamada:** Various applications of legal NLP have already been implemented in Japan. As a support tool for legislation and administration, the Japanese Ministry of Internal Affairs and Communications provides the e-Legislative Activity and Work Support System (e-LAWS), studied by Nagoya University's Toyama Laboratory.[13] e-LAWS provides consistent support from the drafting and deliberation of bills to their publication on the web. The system stores legal data in a machine-readable and unified format. Thus, it is also a source of open data in the Japanese legal sector. In the field of corporate law, NLP has often been used in contract analysis and drafting. Corporate law work, which is based on text-based records such as contracts or agreements, would be a good target for NLP applications. Recent advances in NLP technology and the rise of needs in corporate digital transformation have made legal NLP applications more popular.

On the other hand, in Japan, NLP applications for documents related to courts (e.g. judgments) appear to be less advanced than abroad. There is a wide range of possible applications for legal NLP in this area, e.g. in improving judgment retrieval systems, pseudonymisation of court decisions and automated summarisation. However, we need the documents to be publicly available in a machine-readable form. Currently, only a small number of judgment documents are available on Japanese court websites, and a machine-readable format has not been employed. Compared to the previously mentioned examples, such as the CAP project and the ECHR, it is much harder to obtain judgment document data in Japan.

If the data are unavailable, it is difficult to conduct even basic experiments using the existing technology before developing advanced systems and methods to reflect the characteristics of the Japanese legal system and documents. In order to discuss the benefits, challenges and concerns that new technologies such as NLP and AI will bring to the judiciary, it is necessary to evaluate their possibilities through actual research and development. To this end, the first step is improving the availability of the data, ideally as open data. In Japan, discussions are underway to make civil judgments open data.[14] This should be achieved as soon as possible.

[12] Ilias Chalkidis, 'LEGAL-BERT: The Muppets Straight Out of Law School' (6 October 2020) arXiv:2010.02559.

[13] <www.kl.itc.nagoya-u.ac.jp/index_e.html> accessed 1 November 2023.

[14] <www.jlf.or.jp/wp-content/uploads/2021/04/pt-houkoku20210325.pdf> (in Japanese) accessed 1 November 2023.

## CONCLUDING CONVERSATION

*Professor Felix Steffek and Professor Mihoko Sumida*

**Sumida:** Professor Steffek, the man behind this series of conversations, appeared on stage to start the discussion. The discussion got off to a great start with the students actively speaking up. The issue of 'technology changing conflict resolution' is at the heart of our joint research project between the University of Cambridge and Hitotsubashi University. Thank you very much for sharing your insights.

**Steffek:** It was a great experience to exchange views with the members of the research project and the Japanese Ministry of Justice, and, of course, to interact with the Japanese students. I have never taken a class like this before, but if I were a student, I would definitely enjoy it (laughs).

**Sumida:** I totally agree with you on that (laughs). I was pleasantly surprised by the engaged responses of the students to my bold attempt to turn a challenging piece of research into an educational programme for the next generation. I thought that Figure 2.5 was very innovative. It clearly shows the world view that the use of AI in dispute resolution can qualitatively improve the information, analysis and judgment of both 'fair and neutral decision-makers' and 'disputants', and this will lead to the realisation of 'access to justice for all' for the society as a whole.

**Steffek:** Certainly, the message of the session was that we wanted people to understand that there are myriad ways in which AI can contribute to improving access to justice, and I certainly consider Figure 2.5 very important. It shows that the first contribution of AI to dispute resolution concerns 'information': AI can improve the quality of the collection and retrieval of legal information by, for example, locating relevant and significant legislation and case law. Secondly, AI can improve the quality of the 'analysis': it can assist with the examination of available information and provide the factors that may lead to a favourable or a non-favourable outcome in dispute resolution. Thirdly, AI can assist in 'decision-making': not only can AI be used in the decision-making process, but it can also assist in the drafting of judgments. Public and academic debate often revolves around this third area of innovation specifically because it is both the most glamorous and morally challenging. The contribution of AI to the acquisition and analysis of information may be modest, but it is very important for the practice of dispute resolution.

I also wanted to show that there is a use case for AI not only for neutral decision-makers such as judges, arbitrators and ombudspersons but also for parties to undergo a more effective and efficient dispute resolution. Thus far, it is private parties, often commercially based actors, who have used AI to manage disputes. The slow adoption of AI by neutral decision-makers is not surprising given that the use of data and algorithms by authorities is far less accepted than in the private sector and raises difficult ethical questions.

**Sumida:** The research project currently involves AI researchers to develop a predictive tool for resolving civil disputes, and in the second half of the research project, you plan to develop ethical guidelines for the use of AI in dispute resolution.

**Steffek:** It is important that lawyers are also familiar with technology and discuss it together with AI researchers. Some of the well-known risks and challenges of using AI include the risk of bias in predicting results and the issue of transparency in understanding the factors taken into account by AI – the 'black box problem'. The solutions to these problems lie in both technology – improvements in data and algorithms – and law – the imposition of rights and obligations. Lawyers in particular need to be aware that not all risks require legal solutions. For example, research is underway on de-biasing data and on explainable AI technologies that provide better transparency.

AI has great potential to improve access to justice, but its risks need to be understood and managed. The final and deciding factors are the 'interests of the citizen', which must be kept at the centre of measures undertaken by legislators, while taking into account human rights, procedural rights and research on the balance between the benefits and challenges of AI.

**Sumida:** I would like to focus on the word 'justice' in access to justice for a moment. In Japan, 'access to justice' seems to have been associated with a rather specific idea, such as support for law enforcement overseas, or even within Japan, legal advice in areas affected by large-scale natural disasters. However, if you think about it, the idea of using technology to spread the understanding of law in civil society and to 'realise justice through law' is not unique or special. It should be a normal issue for us, and I feel that the world has realised this again after the pandemic.

**Steffek**: I was happy to see that both Professor Kazuhiko Yamamoto and Counsellor Fujita of the Ministry of Justice were very welcoming to the idea of improving access to justice by introducing AI. As Counsellor Fujita stressed, the key is to ensure the public's trust in the judiciary. This may include dealing with cases where the AI has made incorrect predictions. For example, we may need to consider a new appeals mechanism.

**Sumida:** The last point is a very interesting one. In Japan, there is a consumer group litigation system that allows unspecified consumers to sue for their interests. Should we consider an AI screening version of such a system?[15] In the Netherlands, a human rights group sued to stop the use of an AI algorithm to detect welfare fraud by pointing out its bias.[16] Nevertheless, I am very curious about who identified the

[15] This direction is proposed by Souichirou Kozuka, Governance of AI Development and Use (in Japanese), NBL 1150, p. 31 (2019).

[16] Jenny Gesley, 'Netherlands: Court Prohibits Government's Use of AI Software to Detect Welfare Fraud' (*Law Library of Congress*, 13 March 2020) <www.loc.gov/item/global-legal-monitor/2020-03-13/netherlands-court-prohibits-governments-use-of-ai-software-to-detect-welfare-fraud/> accessed 1 November 2023.

problem with AI algorithms in the Netherlands and how they established the issue. And why were human rights organisations able to request an injunction against the algorithms? This is another area that needs to be researched.

As data scientist Cathy O'Neil says, it is very difficult to identify AI problems and challenge them in court.[17] I also mentioned consumer group litigation because in a Japanese society where the internet has become so widespread, most people are now considered to be 'consumers' of online platform services. There seems to be an opportunity to take consumer protection as a starting point. On the other hand, the insights from the Netherlands story cannot be ignored. If we are to connect the two, there is a need to radically and significantly upgrade the concept of consumer protection. First of all, the concept of the interests of consumers who are harmed may need to be reconsidered. For instance, it might be problematic if there are data scientists among those supporting collective litigation. There are likely to be many other issues, which we will continue to consider.

## QUESTIONS FOR FURTHER THOUGHT

- What would a world look like, in which everyone has access to dispute resolution outcome predictions? How would dispute behaviour and management change? What would be the effect on commerce or on consumers? Would this be a better or a worse world?
- What are the consequences if not everyone has access to dispute resolution outcome predictions? Do parties today have the same information available before going to court?
- Should all court decisions be publicly available for everyone at no cost? Should certain elements of the judgments (such as names) be deleted or anonymised before making them available?
- What is special as regards decision-makers, i.e. those deciding on the outcome of dispute resolution such as judges, arbitrators and ombudspersons, using AI? Does the administration of justice require a human decision-maker? What is the difference between AI being used before and after the human decision-maker comes to a conclusion?
- Does the use of AI by decision-makers hinder the development of the law as AI learns only from past judgments?

17 Cathy O'Neil, *Weapons of Math Destruction: How Big Data Increases Inequality and Threatens Democracy* (Kubo Naoko tr, Crown 2016).

# Conversation 3

## The Entrepreneur's Perspective on Innovation

ABSTRACT

This chapter aims to understand the entrepreneurial perspective on legal innovation. How do those who create legal innovation make the services and products that improve the way law is used? The conversation centres on topics such as passion for innovation, identifying needs for new products and services, dealing with failure, keys to success in the market, innovation networks, regulatory approaches to innovation and innovation in the financial services industry. The chapter also considers aspects of innovation that are particular to legal services. Among them are the creation and availability of legal datasets for the application of artificial intelligence and the transferability of legal innovation to other jurisdictions with different laws.

| | |
|---|---|
| *Speakers* | Ludwig Bull, Holli Sargeant and Wojtek Buczynski |
| *Moderators* | Felix Steffek and Mihoko Sumida |
| *Concluding Conversation* | Felix Steffek and Mihoko Sumida |
| *Comments* | Ryutaro Ohara and Yuya Ishihara |
| *Questions for Further Thought* | Felix Steffek |

INTRODUCTION

**Sumida:** Let us start the third session on 'The Entrepreneur's Perspective on Innovation'. I deliver the baton to Felix.

**Steffek:** A very warm welcome to everyone. Today, we are looking at legal innovation from the entrepreneurial side. We will have three speakers. First, we will listen to an entrepreneur. Then, we will hear about PhD research projects, looking at aspects of the use of artificial intelligence (AI) in the commercial world.

It is a great pleasure to welcome Ludwig Bull. He is the CEO of CourtCorrect, a LawTech start-up based in London. Yesterday, I told you about the Case Crunch Lawyer Challenge. Ludwig Bull was one of the people responsible for making that happen. In addition to his entrepreneurial activities, Ludwig also engages in research and teaching. In particular, he is a research partner of the joint research project of Hitotsubashi University and the University of Cambridge on 'Legal Systems and Artificial Intelligence'. We invited Ludwig to tell us about how he innovates law as an entrepreneur, and we are very grateful that he accepted our invitation. Ludwig, please, the virtual floor is all yours.

**Bull:** Thank you, Felix. Good evening. I am Ludwig Bull, the founder and CEO of CourtCorrect. I was interested in technology when I was at university and studied programming on my initiative. I am now twenty-five years old, and three years ago, while studying law at university, I started to learn programming because I was interested in exploring the mathematical properties of legal theory using quantitative methods. As I read large numbers of cases and papers every day at university, I thought that more could be done with AI. However, there was no useful dataset that could be used in this context. Data are essential for the use of AI, but there was no dataset. So, I decided to create a tool to find and collect legal data from the internet. That became the database of my first start-up, from which I created many AI applications. By the way, did you see the Lawyer Challenge reported on the BBC?

**Sumida:** Yes. Last time, Professor Steffek gave us an overview.

**Bull:** The Case Crunch Lawyer Challenge is based on the dataset I created. Datasets are probably the most important thing in AI. For example, when you want to establish a legal technology start-up, datasets are going to be really important. Am I right in thinking that obtaining legal datasets is a bit difficult in Japan?

**Sumida:** Yes, that is correct. In Japan, legal datasets are available on a commercial basis. Courts have also created datasets, but none of them covers all decisions. The percentage of represented cases is quite low. The datasets available are limited to judgments that contain important issues. So, they contain only a selected collection of relatively complex cases.

**Bull:** That is a bit of a problem, because you always need a sufficient amount of data. By the way, my major was law, not technology. But when I wanted to study law with AI, I did not know enough about technology, so I decided to study programming online while studying law at university. For example, Stanford University has a very good online course on programming and another on AI. It was hard during that period because there was just so much to study, but learning is fun. Even if you do not know about an area, for example, technology or programming, there is a lot of information on the internet, and if you are willing to learn, there are many good online courses. The knowledge you need is not hard to find with such courses and resources. In fact, it can be an enjoyable experience.

Going back to entrepreneurship, when we were looking for data to use for AI, we found a large legal dataset, but it was unorganised and not very user-friendly. So, we built an AI system to organise the data. For example, we let the AI read the legal cases in the dataset and extract the lawyers' names. It turned out to be a really good dataset allowing good-quality predictions. As a result, the creation of this dataset led to the start of the business. Three years have already passed since then, and the dataset is still active. We also use it in research projects at the University of Cambridge and Hitotsubashi University. It is very useful for innovation, and we plan to continue using it in the future.

## PASSION

**Bull:** Many law firms and research projects now use legal datasets, but two years ago, I was the only one using it. I am really happy for the dataset to have grown. I believe that the most important thing in my work is passion. Passion made me start my own business, and I am still working with passion. That is why I love my job.

At the same time, in my start-up, I experiment a lot. Every day, everything, is an experiment such as with the dataset collection. Feedback on experiments becomes really important because start-up work is always an experiment.

If you are thinking of starting a business, passion is the most important thing. Find something that you are passionate about. Follow your passion and start your start-up. If you have passion, experimentation and a lot of feedback, you can create innovations. The beginning is passion.

In my case, I started my first company with a friend. We grew the company by creating a dataset and providing that dataset to law firms. Then, we proved the technology and certainty of the technology in a competition. That was the Case Crunch Lawyer Challenge. As Felix explained in the last session, this challenge created a competition between lawyers and our AI.

The challenge resulted in us getting new clients. We had a very good reputation. But in fact not many companies approached us. The reason was that our service was quite expensive. The licence fee for one year was €40,000, which is about £35,000. It was so expensive that it became unaffordable for many people, especially individual users. This was not the way I wanted to go. I wanted to bring technology to all citizens. However, it was difficult to change the direction of the company, so I started another new company, CourtCorrect, of which I am now the CEO.

## TWO KEYS TO BUSINESS SUCCESS

**Bull:** When CourtCorrect was set up, one of my friends and business partners was against it. His view was that a small number of customers was fine. Such differences in business policy are common in start-ups. My friend and I had different visions of the company, and our opinions remained divided. I think passion and ideas are important drivers to overcome such differences in opinion and keep the business going.

At the same time, running a business requires a vision. When you set up a new company, it is often small at first, with one or two colleagues, if any, and often you are alone. The vision you want to achieve through your company is really important, as this is what motivates you to keep running it. Vision is the shape of the future You cannot create innovation without a vision.

In my first company, my friends and I did not have the same vision. The company was born before we had a vision and grew very quickly, partly because the way we used technology to solve problems was simple and straightforward. But I wanted to develop the business true to my passion, so I started a new company. Although the start of the second company was more difficult than the first, it is now growing well.

CourtCorrect is a robot lawyer that functions as a search engine like Google. People are now researching WhatsApp and Telegram issues for improved data protection. Our search engine scanned WhatsApp's legal documents, summarised them into a clear explanation and uploaded them. For example, end-to-end encryption is a key feature of WhatsApp's secret chat, but experts found that its privacy policies are actually the same as before. Users can search CourtCorrect to find new privacy policies and learn about legal information.

We also have a lot of user information and have understood essential trends. For example, users are very much interested in the issue of the United Kingdom leaving the European Union and digital problems connected to services such as WhatsApp and Facebook. They search for these issues and related words very frequently.

Many users are now searching for legal issues on robot lawyers, and we provide legal explanations as clearly as possible to help them understand. The number of searches has reached one million, and we are very pleased that we are helping so many users through our legal services.

There is a term in the United Kingdom called 'access to justice for all', and that is what we are trying to achieve. Many people in the United Kingdom do not ask for a lawyer because they consider lawyers to be expensive and they perceive law as a bit scary. They do not really understand law. It is probably the same in Japan. This perception of law is really not a good thing. Law is important for everyone. My dream is to use new technology to teach everyone about legal issues. That is my passion. Now that I can do that, I really enjoy it. I think using legal technology to teach people law is a good idea. Do you have any questions so far?

## A GROWTH CHALLENGE FOR AI LAWYERS IS THE LACK OF DATA

**Sumida:** Could you please raise your hand if you have a question?

**Student A:** Yes, thank you. You referred to a giant dataset which you found fun to study. While using the dataset to study, are there any cases that left a deep impression on you?

**Bull:** We made a lot of interesting discoveries while analysing the dataset. For example, when you analyse the judgments, you discover the characteristics of the judges in charge of the cases. For example, US Supreme Court judges use language grounded in morality and ideology. Perhaps these judges are less fond of doctrinal arguments. We are always looking at new cases, and there are new cases and new legislation coming out all the time. It is really a challenge to exactly know what the law is at any given point in time.

I was also surprised that the dataset-based AI reached a prediction accuracy of 70–80 per cent. Artificial intelligence is already really good.

We have analysed 400,000 cases over the past five years. We have also extracted the names of the lawyers from all 400,000 cases and analysed the results. The results include the number of cases litigated, won, lost, withdrawn etc. We can, for example, identify the success rate for each lawyer. It was an interesting analysis, but it was not well received by all lawyers.

**Student B:** What was the most difficult part of creating an AI lawyer?

**Bull:** Current robot lawyers using AI are at a basic level. They can answer simple cases quickly and accurately, but when the circumstances become more complex, they start to struggle. Human lawyers have a wide range of work; some of them are legally complex and difficult, while others are simple and easy to understand. At present, we are using robot lawyers to do these simple but time-consuming and labour-intensive things. This will probably change in the future, since AI will certainly grow and get better if it is allowed to learn.

Human lawyers have a lot of work to do: they read documents, talk to clients and negotiate contracts. Today's robot lawyers can read documents in datasets but cannot really talk to clients. Until AI evolves a bit more, what we can currently handle are basic text-based tasks.

What AI needs to grow is training data. The problem is that there is a lack of these data. There are a large number of law firms in the United Kingdom, each of which has its own record of previous court cases. There are enough data, but they are not being shared. If such data could be collected and used as training data, AI would see tremendous growth. I started studying law and AI a couple of years ago. Between then and today, technology has progressed rapidly. I am sure that legal technology will continue to grow, and we will be able to do things that seem impossible now. So, I recommend studying AI and technology.

**Student C:** You mentioned that you gather a lot of information on the internet, but how can you gather accurate information on case law when the information on the internet has some variation in credibility?

**Bull:** Information obtained on the internet is indeed not always reliable. That is a really good observation. That is why I used a public source and built the dataset based on information created by the government and courts. Hence, we have a good-quality dataset.

**Sumida:** Is it official information?

**Bull:** Yes, it is. But there are also problems with 'official data'. There are 400,000 court cases. It is quite probable that there are still small mistakes in the data provided by official sources. Whenever you use information, you need to check the source and make sure that the data are correct.

## DIFFERENT LAWS, BUT THE CONFLICTS REMAIN THE SAME

**Sumida:** The following question was asked in the chat: 'I have a lot of respect for Ludwig because he uses many languages and is well versed in both law and technology, while I am just trying to understand the differences between the laws and systems in Japanese, English and my mother tongue, Vietnamese. When you are expanding CourtCorrect's services to foreign markets by making them multilingual, do you see any challenges in customising them to other languages and other countries' legal systems?'

**Bull:** Laws are rooted in a country's culture and history and are country-specific systems. Laws in the United Kingdom and France are different, and laws in Japan and Germany are not the same. Yet, everywhere in the world, the roots of conflict are the same: shopping, insurance, crime, etc. The legal systems may be different, but the essence of the problem is the same. In legal innovation, the focus is on the essence of the problem.

Artificial intelligence can understand Vietnamese, Japanese, German and English, of course. However, it needs data to understand these languages. The same applies to services. If you want to create a legal technology application in Vietnam, you need data in Vietnamese. Once the data are ready, it is quite straightforward to expand to other countries around the world. If we have an opportunity, we would like to experiment in Vietnam.

## EXPERIMENT, EXPERIMENT, EXPERIMENT!

**Bull:** In fact, we are now experimenting because our clients have found new problems. Experimentation is the most important part of entrepreneurship. Passion and experimentation are really important. Innovation is always based on experiments. We listen to feedback and then create a new product.

At CourtCorrect, we talk a lot with our clients and users. That is really interesting and fun. We learn a lot. The difficulty here is that – while it is very important to listen to feedback in order to innovate – sometimes the feedback is not correct and misrepresents the problem. In such cases, the entrepreneur needs to act a bit like a doctor. What I mean by this is that the entrepreneur has to 'examine' the feedback like a doctor. People see symptoms. The entrepreneur's job is to find the disease. The user tells you the symptoms, but you have to find the cause. This is my story.

## ENGINEERS ARE ESSENTIAL FOR MODERN ENTREPRENEURSHIP

**Bull:** For those interested in starting a business, I would like to talk a little about founding a company. In today's world, an essential part of starting a business is software engineering. In my case, I did my own software engineering. Most of my work was not professional lawyering but engineering. If you are going to start a legal technology business with a friend who is a computer science student, tell them a lot about your vision. If you plan to do it on your own, do as I did and study through an online course. Engineers and vision – those are the most important things.

In my case, I became an engineer myself, but I did not have enough time to talk about my vision with my business partner. If partners do not have the same vision, even if the business runs well, there can be problems running it. Misalignment of vision can be a big problem. So, talk to each other about your vision, as you can never have enough of it.

Actually, getting started is really easy in the United Kingdom, where there is a government online portal that you can access, and it only costs £14 to set up a company. What about Japan?

**Sumida:** A procedure that can be completed online has recently been launched, but it involves a notary public for the certification of the articles of association. The notary system in Japan is a measure to prevent corporations from being misused for money laundering and other criminal activity. However, it is possible to found a company online.

**Bull:** Starting a business is very easy nowadays, with low costs, but the real start is creating and selling a product. That is the real beginning. Once you have finalised your product, you have to find clients and get them to buy your product. It can be fun, but it can also be difficult.

And if you and your friends start a company and create a software product, do not be satisfied with the finished product, but rather keep trying to improve it afterwards. The way to do that is to listen to feedback from clients and users. That is really important. Constantly listen to feedback and keep improving, and when the product is even better, you have probably grown. Always look at the product, talk about it and keep improving it. Do not be afraid to put in the time and money to do that. Thanks to this, CourtCorrect has grown.

Investor funding can help your company or product grow faster. If investors give you more money, you can focus on research and experimentation without having to worry about the cost of experimentation, which may allow you to grow faster. However, investors in start-ups also expect a return and want to see a return of ten times their investment in roughly five years. Entrepreneurs need to let investors know that their business is worth it. This is what it means to talk about the future that must be realised – to talk about your vision.

By the way, have you heard of Airbnb? It is a popular company. Here is the material Airbnb prepared for investors in its first presentation. Let us take a look at a few things. First of all, in the introduction, vision is emphasised. Airbnb's innovation is to use a platform to offer cheaper accommodation to guests and money to hosts. Here is a new vision, a 'share culture' that hotels have not been able to cover so far. In its first presentation, Airbnb presents its original product and demonstrates that the market has huge potential. The latter is important for investors who aim for ten times their investment in five years. Now, Airbnb has grown into a very big company within an $80 billion rental market.

## GROWTH IN THE TECHNOLOGY INDUSTRY

**Bull:** Finally, let us talk about the technology sector market as a whole. Technology is becoming more and more important every day and is growing faster than ever. Take the capital expenditure of giant technology companies. Amazon, for example, has almost tripled their technology expenditure in the last few years to 32 billion USD. In 2020, the COVID-19 pandemic started, but it had very little impact on the technology industry. This also applies to my company. CourtCorrect is a technology company, and the pandemic did not create real business problems for us. Technology is very important for all sorts of business.

Take another example. The share price of Alphabet, which owns Google, Waymo, and YouTube, has strongly grown since the start of the pandemic. Compare this with the struggling growth rates of IAG, which owns British Airways, over the same period. You can see how much more growth there is in technology companies.

Technology will become even more important in the legal sector. It will be really important for lawyers, judges, engineers, everyone. It will be used everywhere in the legal world. Without an understanding of technology, it will be difficult to understand the legal world.

There are strong companies in Japan. Have you heard of Vision Fund? Vision Fund is a Softbank fund, the biggest start-up fund in the world. It has a capital of more than 100 billion USD. Some of the most interesting start-ups that the fund has invested in are Airbnb and Uber. Masayoshi Son, the CEO of Softbank, has a great vision. I think he is a genuine investor.

That is all I would like to say today. Please, everyone, more than ever, learn about technology, whether online or at university. Technology will be an essential part of the world of the future.

## DON'T INNOVATE FOR INNOVATION'S SAKE

**Steffek:** Thank you, Ludwig. That was great. I noted one sentence that you said. You said, 'My dream is to use new technology to teach everyone about legal issues.' When you said this, I wondered whether we are doing the same thing at the end of the day, the two of us, just in different contexts: you in business and I at university. I really enjoyed your presentation taking the perspective of the entrepreneur.

Now, it is time to move on to Holli Sargeant. It is a great pleasure introducing her. Holli is a PhD student at the Faculty of Law of the University of Cambridge. Before coming to Cambridge, Holli took her undergraduate education in law and international relations at Bond University in Australia and then worked as a solicitor at Herbert Smith Freehills. There, she was seconded to the Australian Human Rights Commission to contribute to the Human Rights and Technology Project. Holli will be so kind to present some ideas, insights and questions from her PhD, and then, we will have an opportunity to ask questions. Holli, over to you.

**Sargeant:** Good morning to all of you. Thank you so much to Professor Sumida and to Professor Steffek for inviting me to give a brief overview of what I am researching for my PhD. Hopefully, this offers you some interesting insight following Ludwig's presentation about how you can explore different areas in a variety of different ways.

By way of introduction, I did my undergraduate studies in Australia. I did a double degree in law and international relations, especially focused on human rights. In my final year, I went to Singapore, which is where I really discovered the importance of law and technology exploring the LawTech sector, which is currently a booming sector in Singapore. I spent a year there and was able to see some of the challenges that Ludwig outlined with a lot of start-ups in trying to find their vision, but also solving important problems for lawyers, rather than just innovating for the sake of innovating.

I then moved back to Australia, where I started private practice as a trainee with Herbert Smith Freehills. I spent a lot of time practising law in relation to digital technology. There are many businesses, whether mining companies or banks, that are spending a lot of time bringing their teams up to a stronger technology focus in their business irrespective of whether they are a traditional technology company or not. All these experiences came full circle when I was seconded to the Australian Human Rights Commission and worked with them to draft a report on how technology actually impacts human rights. That was a huge undertaking, and it took us across a lot of different sectors and a lot of different types of work, which was a very interesting exposure. This experience led me to want to explore this at an academic level to be able to dig deeper and spend some more time teaching myself some new skills.

Against this background, I am interested in developing the bigger research question of how law should adapt to AI. What I am trying to find through this research is what the shortcomings of the current regulation are and what the areas are that do not need to be changed because law can be neutral to technology. But there are other areas of law that may be inconsistent and not prevent harms when we look at different economic and human rights interests. I wanted to spend my PhD research with a broader approach and use a lot of different research methods. You may or may not have come across some of these methods already in your undergraduate studies. I have picked three key ones that I wanted to explore, and I will walk you through some of the logic of this.

The first method is working through an economic analysis. Artificial intelligence systems exist in a unique marketplace where you have a lot of different relationships. As Ludwig described, data are important, and data sometimes come from the company or sometimes from elsewhere. Sometimes consumers are direct customers of your company, and sometimes they are more tangentially connected. I wanted to look at that network of relationships and analyse where outcomes are optimal and where they are not. I have a visual which I think can be helpful to understand it. I use economic analysis to show where there may be impacts on human rights or, perhaps more broadly, on some of these liberal democratic norms, such as access to justice and other important values.

Where we highly value personal interests in privacy and autonomy, we want these to be protected even where there is an economic incentive to do otherwise. This is where a normative analysis comes in. Finally, I use these prior methods to inform an analysis of the role and the application that positive law currently has to AI. My PhD research looks at these issues more broadly and investigates how law currently works and how it might need to change.

## BALANCING ECONOMIC BENEFITS AND HUMAN RIGHTS

**Sargeant:** To understand the intersection between law and AI, it is helpful to understand the various actors involved in designing and deploying AI. This network of actors is what a lot of people call the digital economy. I am a visual person, so I hope that Figure 3.1 is a helpful way to try and conceptualise some of the connections and relationships that you have in this new and emerging marketplace.

Figure 3.1 presents the most relevant stakeholders. You have corporations that each have people involved with significant interests and roles to play. You have people such as shareholders, managers, board of directors and creditors. In relation to start-ups, you might have a different set of stakeholders as Ludwig mentioned as well. You have investors who advise companies in particular directions, and then you have people like Ludwig who are the founders, who have their own set of interests that are a bit different to your normal employee within a big company.

Then, when you work through the system, you start to see that there is a difference between companies that supply AI, whether they develop it themselves, or outsource it, and the buyers of AI systems. I have pulled out some of these key relationships in Figure 3.1 to try and really dig into what the behaviours and interests are across these parties and how we analyse them.

Let us take an example where you have a start-up that has its founder who, obviously, believes in its vision and wants to push it in a particular direction. You have employees who help develop and build the AI system. And then, of course, you have other economic stakeholders such as investors, creditors and managers. They might build this piece of software and then sell it to a buyer, which here, as an

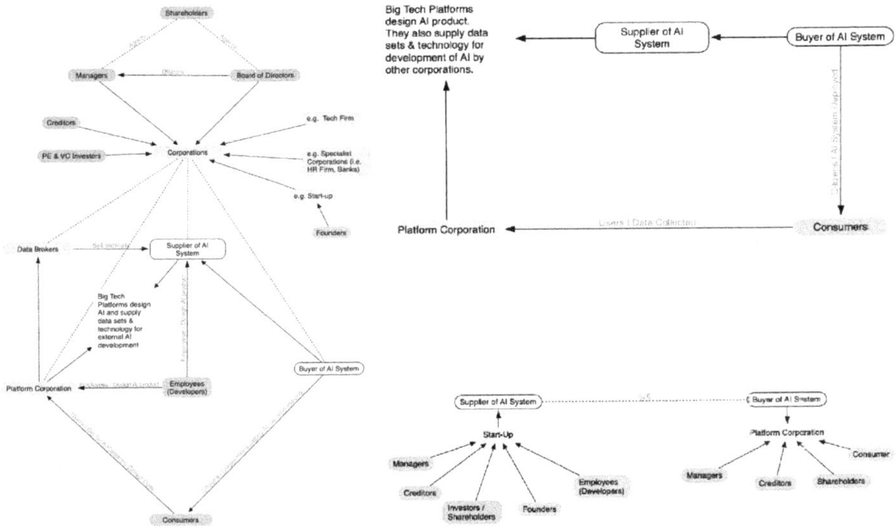


FIGURE 3.1 Network of relationships and interests

example, might be a big platform corporation – such as Alphabet or Softbank or one of the other big tech companies which we have talked about today. They have their own separate managers, creditors and shareholders, and then, of course, they have their customers, who might be either a direct purchaser of the product or another company, which is a commercial client.

In looking at these relationships, I want to explore what the different interests and behaviours are and the way that the actors use the information that is available to them, the way that they contract privately. In other words, I undertake an economic analysis of the relationships involved. I then aim to connect these insights to how the economic behaviours of these actors might infringe on the human rights interests of the consumers or other individuals that are connected to these transactions. That is what I am trying to do with the exploration of different methods. Human rights, if we think about it, are interests that we protect because we value them highly in a way that we say that one cannot achieve an economic outcome to the detriment of human rights. What I am trying to show through this analysis is the importance of achieving an optimal outcome where both the start-up and the big tech company achieve their goals, but not in a way that affects the human rights of their consumers or other individuals whose data they might be or who are users of these systems.

Following these two pieces of analysis, I plan to look at the way law currently works, whether there are sufficient legislative frameworks in different countries, whether we can just rely on the protections under contracts and private ordering or whether we need recommendations about the way we regulate these kinds of relationships. I hope, in the end, to bring together policy-based recommendations or principles that will guide lawmakers as regulation emerges in this unique set of relationships. It is a challenging exercise to bring together all of these really interesting considerations.

It is hard to bring all these ideas together into a short presentation, but I hope that this sparks some interest in you and gives you a few ideas to think about in relation to law and AI.

## MAKING LAW ACCESSIBLE TO VULNERABLE GROUPS

**Steffek:** Thank you very much, Holli. You mention access to justice as a human right or procedural right. Applications of AI, for example, that Ludwig mentioned, impact human and procedural rights in two different ways. On the one hand, access to justice gets cheaper, so more people have access to justice. On the other hand, AI is currently limited and has trouble answering very complex questions. Thus, while more people have access to justice as it gets cheaper, the quality differs. Currently, the advice that some LawTech applications provide is not very well tailored to the specific question at hand. Rather, more generic legal advice is provided. Hence, on the one hand, access to justice is provided to more people, but on the other hand, the quality provided may be somewhat lower. I find that a fascinating aspect of your research.

**Sargeant:** Yes, absolutely. Access to justice is very important and very interesting, and as you say, there is only so much you can deliver with technological solutions, such as a chatbot, when people have really complex legal challenges. Hopefully, technology does at least start to bridge barriers in some ways.

**Steffek:** I am sure you are aware of the saying that 'Access to justice is open to everyone like the Ritz.' If you have the money, then you will get fantastic advice, but not everyone can go to the Ritz. Thank you very much again, Holli.

We are now ready to move on to Wojtek. Wojtek is an AI regulation consultant during the day, and at night, he becomes a PhD student at the University of Cambridge. He is currently working on regulating AI as regards investment management. Wojtek, we are looking forward to your presentation.

## SHOULD THE FINANCIAL INDUSTRY BE REGULATED?

**Buczynski:** *Moshi-moshi*, good evening, everyone. It is a pleasure and an honour to be here. Many thanks to Professor Sumida and Professor Steffek for the opportunity. My name is Wojtek Buczynski and, as Professor Steffek kindly introduced me, I live a double life. During the day, I work as a financial technology and regulation consultant, and at night, I am a PhD student researching ethics and applications of AI in financial services. I have always had an interest in law, probably because my mother is a lawyer. My PhD is quite interdisciplinary because I look at several disciplines and my supervisors come from different disciplines as well. For my current project, I am looking at the AI regulations for financial services, more specifically in my industry, which is investment management.

My project mainly has a commercial focus. I am looking at the regulatory landscape of AI in financial services, specifically in investment management. We have all heard about the great promise and great excitement of AI in various industries. Financial services is one of the industries that is very optimistic about AI and has a lot of hopes pinned on it. However, one of the challenges is that there are no clear regulations regarding AI, and as you probably know, in financial services we are quite sensitive about regulations since the financial crash of 2008. So, there is this uncertain situation in which it is not clear what regulations apply or if any regulations apply at all. This lack of clarity is a challenge for implementation, and therefore, AI is not implemented as much as it could be because there are concerns about regulation. This is where my work steps in, hopefully.

My work has three primary angles. First, I am looking at the existing regulations. Some of them you may have heard about – GDPR for privacy, MIFID II for investments and a couple of others specifically for investment management. I am also looking at a number of proposed regulations. Currently, there are about fifteen proposed regulations worldwide that pertain to AI specifically in financial services or investment management. Interestingly, Japan, which is stereotypically seen as a hyper-technological and very innovative country, is not one of the countries currently proposing regulation. The Japanese regulator, the Financial Services Agency, does not actually have any publication or consultation on AI in financial services – at least not yet. However, there are about fifteen regulators worldwide that have published regulation proposals for AI in finance. The more original part of my work is to identify the different themes that emerge from the existing and proposed regulations. I am interested in establishing, for example, whether there are a lot of common themes. I will also try to propose, from my own perspective and my own experience, what should be included in a comprehensive regulation of AI in financial services. Possible topics are, for example, transparency and explainability.

## WHAT IS NEEDED TO CLARIFY THE REGULATIONS

**Buczynski:** Figure 3.2 shows the regulatory themes that have emerged so far from my research. Some of them may look familiar to you. There are topics such as transparency, explainability and security. All of these issues are relevant within the context of the financial services industry, but you can see that almost all of them are quite universal and applicable to other industries as well. There is a lot of interest and focus on skills in financial services because there is a huge lack of skills in technology in general, and even more so in AI. In particular, there is a dramatic shortage of skills in AI in financial services. As a result, regulators are interested in and concerned about making sure that people who use AI actually understand AI. The more you investigate regulatory themes, the more you identify. Globally, we have approximately ten to twenty regulatory themes that are emerging from different jurisdictions. One aspect that is spoken a lot about in AI, regardless of the industry, is AI ethics. Discrimination, bias and racism are other important themes as we see

FIGURE 3.2 Regulatory themes

some very unfortunate examples such as AI that favours white males or conversely that is much worse at recognising black or female faces. There have also been some unfortunate cases concerning discrimination in recruitment.

**Buczynski:** However, I want to draw a very clear distinction between regulations and ethics. They are often mixed together in one bag, but they are actually different things. Ethics is about values, our own sense of right or wrong. Ethics can concern universal values, the things that we share and the views that we share regardless of our cultures or our religions. Regulations are different. Regulations are about what the State tells us we should do and what we should not do. There will be some overlap between regulations and ethics, but I want to maintain a clear distinction between the two and focus on regulations.

We do have some existing technology regulations in financial services, for example, on the cloud outsourcing side, or a little bit on cybersecurity or technology risk sides. It is challenging to regulate technology because it moves so fast, but it can be done. I focus on regulations in my work because there is already a lot of research out there on AI ethics in different industries and it is very good. However, there is very little or, perhaps, no work focusing on regulations in financial services. This is the area which I would like to explore and hopefully the gap that I would like to fill.

Now, since this is a conversation series for students and we are all students, I think that there is a huge role that academia can play in this field, not just in financial services, but generally as regards AI regulations because AI is huge and very interdisciplinary. If only the industry, whether it is financial services or another industry, shapes AI, then there will be limits in terms of coming up with regulations. If we just have the relevant regulators trying to regulate, they will do their best, but they may sometimes lack the subject matter expertise because, particularly with AI, it is very complicated and fast-moving. So, this is a great area for academia to step in and add a lot of value with benefit to the industry and ultimately to society. It is really important that academia is consulted on regulations and also that academics proactively seek engagement. We are quite fortunate that we are beginning to see that. In financial services, we have academics consulted by regulators, and I think it is the best practice to follow internationally to make sure that regulations are not developed without subject matter experts.

This is all I had for this brief presentation. I am also a part-time blogger, so you can see my blog under https://wbuczynski.com. I blog about technology and, particularly, AI. If you have any questions or comments, you are welcome to get in touch with me.

## COORDINATING GENERAL AND SECTOR-SPECIFIC REGULATION

**Sumida:** Mr Buczynski, thank you very much for your interesting presentation. Let me ask you a question. Tomorrow's session will include a discussion on corporate governance and AI governance. I am also a member of the AI governance expert group, and I wonder how to improve the relationship between corporate and financial governance on the one hand and AI governance on the other. This concerns regulating AI issues in the context of financial regulation and risk regulation in the context of AI governance. It seems to me that there is a vertical division by industry. Artificial intelligence governance has a strong connection with human rights issues and data governance, but it is difficult to know how to relate it to finance. In Japan, these aspects are not yet well connected. How are you trying to coordinate AI governance and financial regulation?

**Buczynski:** I think the answer is that we should have a couple of levels of regulation. We may need some general regulations on AI that are universal. These would be more along the lines of principles and ethics, such as human rights, human centricity, avoiding bias and ensuring fairness. They should be imposed on all industries, not just financial services. Against the background of these overarching sets of rules that apply universally, you can have an additional smaller set of rules that apply to specific industries. We should have very specific and very detailed regulations, for example, for the autonomous car industry to make sure that self-driving cars are safe.

We should have a similar set of regulations for financial services. These regulations should be much more focused and specific to the industry. They should relate to the areas that are more finance-specific, such as data governance, transparency, advertising and marketing. This combination of general rules applicable to everyone and sector-specific rules based on the nature of a given industry is the way that I see it work.

Artificial intelligence governance in finance may be new, but governance in financial services is not new. It is a matter of taking what we already do in financial services – in compliance, in legal and generally in management and governance – and applying it to AI.

**Sumida:** Thank you. Is there anyone who would like to ask the next question?

## HOW SHOULD DATA CONFIDENTIALITY BE HANDLED?

**Student D:** For AI development, it was said that massive data are indispensable, and I think that the challenge is the same in Japan as well. Public information is first collected. Based on publicly available information, AI is trained. I think that is the process. But is there any private information, say, for example, a B2C company may have their undisclosed information or law firms may have some undisclosed information, too? Such private data are another source of information, and I wonder what kind of initiatives are now being rolled out to make use of such data.

**Sumida:** Ludwig, could you answer this question please? Have any efforts been made to collect private, rather than public information, to upgrade the datasets?

**Bull:** That is a good question. We have so far relied on public data, but client data can be used as well. However, client data can only be used within the system of that client. Different clients have different systems, and they do not share their information with other people. So, private data can be used, but that information cannot be shared with other parties. In future, ideally speaking, law firms should be able to share anonymous data. That will allow quicker development of AI.

**Sumida:** Would someone like to ask the last question?

**Student E:** I have a question for Holli. If a private company runs an AI system regarding law, then there will be risks. Is there a way to manage such risk if LawTech is provided by private businesses?

**Sargeant:** That is an excellent question, and it is one that is up for a lot of debate and is dealt with differently in different jurisdictions. To practise law, you need to have certain qualifications, which is generally your admission to the legal practice of whichever country you are in. In some jurisdictions, governments have started to expand the definition of practising law. In the United Kingdom, service providers can provide some legal services under the regulatory board, which is slightly different to other jurisdictions. The United Kingdom and Singapore, where there are big LawTech industries, have expanded the rules to allow for start-ups and AI systems to engage with the law. I think that is very interesting, and I hope that this offers some protection, but I think there will need to be a lot more work in this area to offer the necessary protections for these types of generic delivery, AI delivery of legal services.

**Sumida:** Thank you very much, Holli. It has been a great session joined by three young presenters. They have been a great source of inspiration for our young students. They have taken up interesting challenges. Thank you very much for your participation this afternoon. With this, I would now like to officially close the session today.

## CONCLUDING CONVERSATION

**Steffek:** I very much enjoyed the contribution by Ludwig Bull, explaining the entrepreneur's perspective on using technology to improve access to law. For me, his emphasis on the passion for one's work and having a vision for what one aims to achieve stood out.

**Sumida:** I was very impressed by Ludwig's vision. I was particularly impressed by the fact that he left his first company, which had grown enough to be viable, to start a new one with the determination to innovate access to justice through technology. This vision includes the common good, which is much more than just 'making money for ourselves'. This is why Ludwig has fully committed to our research project, while at the same time making his company CourtCorrect a successful business.

**Steffek:** Interestingly, Ludwig has said that the core of his business is teaching people law. This is a very thought-provoking statement because it is generally believed that law is taught in universities and colleges. The statement indicates that there is a market for legal education in the everyday lives of citizens. It also raises the interesting question of which market actor is best placed in which situation to teach citizens and businesses law.

**Sumida:** It is all about creating new markets. As a Japanese organiser, I would also like to point out that Ludwig conducted the session in Japanese, without simultaneous interpretation. As a German, he speaks German and English, of course, but also French, Chinese and Russian! His view is that the roots of legal problems in people's daily lives are the same and that they stay the same across borders. When lawyers look at the laws of other countries, they tend to look at the differences between countries because they start their comparison with the 'legal system'. His idea of starting with the 'problem' was innovative.

**Steffek:** I agree. I also found Ludwig's statement that two things are important to be innovative as an entrepreneur – to keep experimenting and to listen to others' opinions – very interesting. I am fascinated by the process that entrepreneurs use to innovate. Ludwig further cautioned that feedback is sometimes incorrect. In essence, he said: 'If a patient complains to a doctor about a symptom, it does not necessarily mean that the symptom is the problem. Rather, like a doctor, you have to find the disease.'

**Sumida:** According to the socialisation, externalisation, combination and internalisation (SECI) model theory of Ikujiro Nonaka and Hirotaka Takeuchi, the key to achieving sustainable innovation is to turn knowledge into wisdom, turn practical knowledge into flexibility and create a 'place' for creative interaction. Wisdom is not merely logical. Wisdom is not just logical knowledge, but tacit knowledge at a higher level, enabling us to 'see the essence of things'. I think the metaphor of the doctor is a perfect expression of this. And I took the repeated 'experiments' as a dynamic SECI spiral driven by flexibility, the very 'wisdom' that is useful for practical use.[1]

**Steffek:** I strongly agree with Ludwig's argument that 'data availability' should be improved. He believes that one of the main challenges for future progress is the availability of data. This is not, strictly speaking, an AI issue, but a data issue. In future, he hopes, AI will be able to answer more complex questions than at present. I think it is important for governments to understand that they can play an active role in supporting the start-up and research community by providing an attractive ecosystem. Supporting the availability of legal data is a key element of such an ecosystem.

**Sumida:** Our collaborator, AI researcher Dr Yamada of the Tokunaga Lab at the Tokyo Institute of Technology, makes the same point, and in Japan, the Ministry of Justice is taking the lead in considering this issue.

The focus of the next generation of AI researchers was also very innovative.

**Steffek:** Holli Sargeant is interested in how the legal framework should be adapted to achieve optimal results in relation to the development, use and deployment of AI systems. An important part of her analysis is to look at the different actors

[1] Ikujiro Nonaka and Hirotaka Takeuchi, *The Wise Company: How Companies Create Continuous Innovation* (OUP USA 2019) 9, 103.

and their relationships: suppliers of AI systems, their investors, data brokers, platform companies, buyers of AI systems, consumers, etc. Mapping these relationships is essential to understand whether AI systems are useful for society. In particular, we need to track how the interests of private equity investors affect the products that LawTech start-ups develop.

Wojtek Buczynski has used his experience of working in the investment management industry to conduct research that seeks to regulate in a very fast-moving sector, while protecting clients and consumers and not inhibiting technological progress. We look forward to hearing his suggestions for improving the beneficial use of AI applications in this area.

**Sumida:** The students were very excited and inspired by the new role models who appeared in this session. At the same time, there are also some young people in Japan who are daring to take up the challenge of LawTech. Two young experts have been working with us on our research project and they have contributed the following comments.

## COMMENTS

### *Expectations for the Use of Machine Learning in the Legal Field*

**Ohara:** The move to use machine learning in the legal field is no longer a temporary bubble, but an irreversible trend. Today, legal services such as 'AI-based contract checking' are being offered on a large scale. In the near future, the use of machine learning in the legal field will become commonplace.

Machine learning uses large amounts of data as training data, learns abstract patterns of facts and rules that can be read from the data and predicts results by applying these patterns to new cases. This way of prediction is precisely the kind of analysis that legal professionals do every day. Since the amount of data that a human lawyer's brain can learn is limited, machine learning, which can learn from a much larger amount of data at a much faster rate than humans, can be expected to make more accurate predictions than human lawyers can.

One area where machine learning is expected to be used is in the prediction of the court's judicial decisions. Predicting how a court will decide on a specific case is not easy, even for legal professionals. However, legal professionals can predict to some extent what the likely outcomes will be by referring to past court precedents. It is difficult for those who do not have legal knowledge to make such predictions. For example, in civil cases, those who are parties to a legal dispute must spend a considerable amount of money to obtain an attorney's opinion in order to take a fight to court. Often, people give up on filing a lawsuit because they believe that the benefits of filing such a suit are not worth the legal fees. Although access to lawyers has become easier today than it used to be, there are still many cases where parties give up because they cannot find an affordable lawyer. From this perspective, the cost of litigating a case in a court is often still too high for the parties involved.

If models that have learned from a large number of past court precedents through machine learning can predict the court's judicial decisions at a level close to that of lawyers, even those who do not have legal knowledge will be able to predict the benefits and costs of filing a judicial claim (or responding to a claim against them). This would make it easier and significantly less expensive than it is today to ascertain the costs and benefits of disputes. If the other party understands that it is clear that they will lose the case based on machine learning predictions, there is no need to fight the case in court, and the dispute may be concluded or resolved without both parties incurring the costs of going to court.

This would greatly reduce the litigation costs for both parties and greatly improve accessibility to judicial services by the courts. Such initiatives also contribute to the Sustainable Development Goals (SDGs), which have become a guideline for action by governments and private companies.

### *Challenges to Overcome*

**Ohara:** The 'Legal Systems and Artificial Intelligence' project, of which the editor of this book, Professor Mihoko Sumida, is the project leader, is attempting to predict judicial decisions using machine learning. At this point in time, the project is still in the process of constructing the prediction model of machine learning. I will describe some of the technical challenges that must be overcome in order to use machine learning to predict judicial decisions. I was not familiar with machine learning before participating in this project, and what follows in this section is only what I consider to be possible issues from the standpoint of a legal practitioner.

First, especially in Japan, there is a high hurdle in obtaining data on court cases. The data, which are provided by courts and are accessible to all, contain much fewer court cases than the datasets provided by private companies, and the amount of data obtainable from open sources is still insufficient for machine learning. In Japan, the government and the Japan Federation of Bar Associations are currently discussing the conversion of court records into open data. We hope that this will be done promptly.

Second, the nature of the data used for learning in the legal field is quite unique, in that they include sentences written in judicial decisions, which are different from those used in everyday life and thus require special consideration. For example, a single sentence in a court case can be extremely long. It is thought that sentences become long in order to make them as unambiguous as possible while taking into consideration the arguments of both parties. It will be a challenge to learn the exact meaning of such special sentences via machine learning. Additionally, not only court cases but also legal writings consistently use unique terms. Whether a model of machine learning can accurately learn certain 'rules' peculiar to such legal writing seems to be another issue to be addressed.

Third, attention must be paid to the handling of data from the Japanese Court of Appeals and the Supreme Court. Since the Court of Appeals and the Supreme

Court examine the judgments of the lower courts, the data of the lower courts must also be included in the learning process; otherwise, the learning will not be accurate. Since the Japanese Court of Appeals uses expressions such as '[t]he following decision is revised from line X to line Y on page Z of the original judgment' and takes the form of revising only a part of the judgment of the lower court, the judgment text of the Court of Appeals itself does not provide a complete picture. Instead, it needs to be checked against the language of the original judgment of the lower court. How to handle data from the Court of Appeals and the Supreme Court, which have such special characteristics, is, hence, an issue to be addressed.

Fourth, studying court decisions alone does not allow us to take into account social circumstances that are not included in the court's decision but have an impact on the court's decision. For example, if the parties are a giant corporation and an individual consumer, the court may tend to rule in favour of the individual consumer. In a type of case that has attracted social criticism, the court may make a harsh decision against one of the parties. Legal professionals would make predictions based on such out-of-court circumstances, but there are technical challenges in how to make machine learning learn about such out-of-court circumstances.

However, none of the above issues are technically impossible to overcome, and they will probably be overcome through repeated attempts at prediction.

## HOW TO DEAL WITH NEW TECHNOLOGIES

**Ohara:** There is a concern that new technologies such as machine learning will take away the work of lawyers. In fact, there will be fields in which the use of machine learning will make it possible to eliminate the need for human involvement. For example, tasks such as reviewing routine contracts (e.g. non-disclosure agreements) may no longer be a job of lawyers.

One example of technology that has had a significant impact on the work of lawyers is case databases. I was told by a senior lawyer that before the advent of databases, he used to stay in the library all night and search through every published casebook to see whether there was any relevant case as regards the matter he was handling. Now, thanks to case databases, we can easily search by keywords in an instant, and we do not need to spend the night in libraries. For lawyers, the amount of time required to research precedents has been greatly reduced, and the amount of time chargeable to clients has decreased. There is no doubt that the efficiency gains in operations have more than outweighed the downsides.

The use of machine learning has a far broader and deeper range of applications than case databases. However, it is no different from databases in that it is just one of the useful tools that lawyers will be able to employ. The question is how to deal with new technologies such as machine learning.

The use of machine learning in the legal field is still in its infancy. It is an area where lawyers and machine learning experts are working together to create something new, confronting the challenges they discover. Out of simple curiosity, I jumped into a project to predict judicial decisions using machine learning, even though I was a lawyer with no prior knowledge of machine learning. As a result, I am constantly stimulated by discussions with the diverse members of the project, who have the courage to boldly solve difficult problems without fear of failure. The attempt to decipher court cases from the perspective of machine learning has also led me to reconsider the depth of decisions of courts. This concerns, for example, the fact that there are many issues in which judges seem to avoid providing clear judgments. In today's society, where new technologies, not limited to machine learning, are rapidly penetrating globally, it seems to me that being actively involved in areas created by new technologies will broaden the scope of a legal practitioner's activities. The more colleagues are willing to dive into this new world, the more enjoyable discussions can be had, and the better new things can be created.

Regarding the concern voiced at the beginning of this section that the use of machine learning will take away the work of lawyers, if machine learning reduces the time required for tasks that were previously done manually, then lawyers will be able to devote their time to more creative work. For example, even if machine learning reaches the same level of accuracy in predicting judicial decisions as legal professionals, it will not eliminate the work of litigation lawyers. If the opposing party makes similar predictions, there will be more phases in which victory or defeat will depend on the strategies of litigation lawyers than there are now. Using machine learning predictions, it may become easier to strategically avoid arguing certain issues and focus on those that have a chance of winning.

I think the best way to deal with new technology is not to passively accept it but to think ahead and take advantage of it.

## APPLYING MACHINE LEARNING TO LAW

**Ishihara:** Some years have passed since the 'Third AI Summer', and many systems have been applied and introduced in various industrial fields to support decision-making based on mathematical and statistical techniques, with deep learning at the forefront of this trend. This trend has been supported by improvements in the performance of computers and the expanding use of cloud computing, which has made it possible to access high-performance and sophisticated computers instantly and at a lower cost, without paying the initial costs to prepare data centres. In addition, this trend was also supported by the growing number or reallocation of engineering human resources that are now involved in building systems that utilise these technologies.

In recent years, epoch-making technological progress has been made in the area of natural language processing, which aims to enable machines to acquire abstract knowledge such as of contexts and concepts of human language and to solve problems written in the same, through the 'Attention' mechanism and its applications. The variety of tasks and the precision of machines in working with natural language have been greatly improved, and various applications are being intensively examined every day.

In the world of law, there is also a growing movement towards innovation through cutting-edge technology, including academic efforts such as the 'Legal Systems and Artificial Intelligence' project, to which I have the privilege to contribute. I see the same trend in the launch of several start-ups advocating legal technology.

## THE CHALLENGE TO CREATE A MATHEMATICAL MODEL OF THE LAW

**Ishihara:** The project mentioned before includes an advanced study of how the introduction of machine learning technology to the field of law can change the process of legal decision-making. Even those who have never been involved in disputes or majored in the academic discipline of law, if asked to imagine how AI might change the judiciary, would all focus on 'automated judging by AI'.

From the viewpoint of legal stability, it is desirable that legal conclusions are reproducible, so long as all the information related to the case is available without any gaps. In other words, we expect that in the legal system, if all the inputs are the same, the output must also be the same without any stochastic variety.

During the second AI boom in the 1980s, a judicial version of expert systems was considered, which would provide a clear logical description and automation of legal judgments by writing down every condition concerning legal decision-making. As typified by expert systems, there have been attempts to identify the factors that influence the outcomes in cases since the emergence of computers or the concept of AI, by expressing every information related to the judgment in mathematical terms. Currently, various attempts are being made to obtain the information used in judgments quickly and widely by applying natural language processing technology or to express causal relationships effectively using the directed graphs method.

However, there is a limitation insofar as legal systems are expected to exhibit reproducibility. The legal system has room to operate in order to adjust its behaviour to the individualities of different cases or to changes in society or culture that occur in the long term. The idea to leave sufficient room for legal interpretation conflicts with the former idea, i.e. the idea to create models to predict the result by expressing all information mathematically.

## SYSTEMS, AI AND HUMANS

**Ishihara:** Confronting these aspects of law, it is not enough to simply put the knowledge or concepts such as general common sense into mathematical symbolic expressions required for legal judgment. Instead, it is necessary to adaptively modify these expressions and models to the dynamics of society.

In this context, I would like to introduce the concept of Machine-Learning Operations (ML-Ops), especially the concept of Human-In-the-Loop (HITL), which has become an important topic in recent years concerning the building and operating practice of AI-based systems. ML-Ops is an idea that refers to all practices related to the operation of AI-based systems. HITL refers to designs that involve human judgement in processes such as system performance evaluation and continuous AI learning (refitting), to operate the entire system in a complementary and collaborative manner. For example, assessing the validity and accuracy of AI predictions and monitoring them with respect to the changes in the external environment are key points at which humans can complement AI-based systems.

Given the dynamic nature of law and the demands for its explainability, humans will continue to play an important role even if mathematical techniques such as AI are applied to the procedure of making legal judgments. From this perspective, the key issues are how far decisions are to be made by machines and the mutual feedback between humans and machines to improve the whole system.

The concepts of ML-Ops and HITL are ideas from industrial sectors where AI technology is leading the way. They will also be important when considering innovation in the legal system in the near future.

## INVITATIONS TO THE FRONTIER

**Ishihara:** Innovation through technology is the process of knowing what a new technology can achieve and using it to restructure the existing processes. New technology brings with it new operations, practices and ideas. While getting involved with the projects applying AI in the legal system, I found it exciting to see that the process of assessing the ability of this new technology is just getting underway.

For example, the automation of the trial process can be broken down into the process of fact-finding, inference and determination of conclusions. It is simple to determine the decisional boundary between the conclusions and the elements of fact-finding and inference. However, in this system, the accuracy of the elements becomes important.

Fact-finding is usually done manually, but there is a chance to build a model for making inferences. It may be possible to make an inference model such that the facts of a given case can lead to a concrete conclusion. This is the case when an expert system is used. But in some cases, it is difficult to provide concrete conclusions. These include the controversial issue of qualifying workers in the gig economy to be 'employees' of the concerned company and the long-standing issue concerning the definition of the concept of 'spouse'.

To create a mathematical model that can make reasonable inferences regarding these hard cases, we need a large number of inputs that cover different types of cases. Although affinity methods and technologies such as knowledge graphs have emerged and are being tested, gathering a large dataset still remains a necessary task.

It is essential to dream about what can be possible with advances in technology and to continue searching for a way to realise it. This requires not only the knowledge of the technology but also the unravelling of current practices and resources such as data. This is the essence of innovation and something I am enthusiastic about. For me, the field of AI and law is full of enthusiasm and innovation.

## QUESTIONS FOR FURTHER THOUGHT

- How do entrepreneurs facilitate innovation? In LawTech start-ups, how does the 'spark' happen that creates a new commercial idea?
- Are there particular ways to facilitate legal innovation in commercial settings?
- Where does technical legal innovation happen beyond start-ups?
- What are the barriers to using technology to create legal innovation?
- If technology makes justice cheaper, but in the first years perhaps less responsive to the specific issues of a case, what does that mean for society and is such progress desirable?
- How do the interests of those investing in LawTech start-ups shape the products that are developed?
- Does LawTech require new ways of regulation, or can we properly regulate LawTech with the regulatory tools used thus far?

# Conversation 4

## What Can We Learn from the Okawa Elementary School Tsunami Litigation?

ABSTRACT

This chapter focuses on the litigation that followed the tsunami, which hit the Okawa Elementary School. The tsunami resulted in the death of the children visiting the school. The following litigation concerned the question of whether appropriate safety measures had been put in place at the school before the tsunami occurred. The two lawyers leading the litigation for the parents of the children report on how they used innovative approaches in the litigation proceedings. The legal innovation employed concerns the composition of the litigation team, the involvement of the children's parents, the creation of witness statements addressing the emotional aspects of the disaster, the identification of the entity that should be liable, the doctrine determining liability, digitalisation of litigation and the distribution of risk in modern societies.

| | |
|---|---|
| *Speakers* | Kazuhiro Yoshioka and Masahiro Saito |
| *Moderator* | Mihoko Sumida |
| *Comment* | Mikiharu Noma |
| *Concluding Conversation* | Felix Steffek and Mihoko Sumida |
| *Questions for Further Thought* | Felix Steffek |

INTRODUCTION

**Sumida:** In October 2019, an innovative final judgment was handed down that would realise a legal remedy for victims who suffered damage that could have been avoided – the decision of the Sendai High Court awarding damages to bereaved families in a case seeking damages from the state in relation to the Okawa

Elementary School children tsunami incident. Today we have Mr Kazuhiro Yoshioka and Mr Masahiro Saito, the lawyers who won that landmark judgment, to talk about the nature of the legal innovation and what happened behind the scenes.

## STUDYING LAW TO SOLVE NOVEL EMERGING PROBLEMS

**Sumida:** Today we will have an interview-style class with Mr Kazuhiro Yoshioka and Mr Masahiro Saito as guest speakers. They won a landmark court decision as attorneys representing the bereaved families in a lawsuit seeking damages for the Okawa Elementary School children tsunami incident.

A few years ago, the then-prime minister Abe delivered the following message to the world: Japan is a forerunner facing a range of challenges. As you are aware, Japan faces various challenges including being a developed country simultaneously having the fastest ageing population in the world, resulting in an ongoing population decline, depopulation in rural areas and an excess concentration of its population in urban centres. As a result, Japan has no choice but to become a leader in solving these emerging problems ahead of the rest of the world.

I would like you to consider that, in the rapidly changing society we live in, the social framework must also change. The Civil Code, which is my area of expertise, establishes the basic framework for civil society, but it is totally unclear if we can solve our problems by merely following the precedent the Code sets.

We have planned a series of conversations to invite you to think about the following issues together: in this current era of rapid change, what should lawyers be? Who are the ideal lawyers needed to develop the future of our society?

Here is *my* tentative idea of what an ideal lawyer should be. In addition to merely knowing all sorts of laws, where they can be found, every single past court ruling, being able to extract this relevant knowledge when consulted and to clearly convey that knowledge to people in need, lawyers must be able to dynamically and boldly blaze the way with novel legal theory based on new ideas in anticipation that sticking to what has been done so far might not work in the future. In other words, my image of an ideal lawyer is a lawyer who makes innovation happen and attacks new frontiers in the world of the law. An excellent example of this are today's guests, the lawyers who won the landmark case we will discuss. By inviting them, I hope we can gain a better understanding on how to address novel legal issues.

## DEVELOPING NEGLIGENCE LIABILITY IN JAPAN, A NATURALLY DISASTER-PRONE COUNTRY

**Sumida:** Now we are moving on to today's topic, the lawsuit seeking damages for the Okawa Elementary School children tsunami incident. First, let me briefly introduce the challenges our guests faced in making their case. In this case, the directly contested issue was the existence of liability for negligence in the context of the 'principle of private autonomy', which is one of the three basic principles of the Civil Code.

The first issue was whether it is possible to hold someone legally liable for losses caused by a natural disaster. Mr Yoshioka has stated that since it was such a difficult case, he wanted the bereaved families to consult with another lawyer.[1] Based on the principle of private autonomy, I suppose that the starting point was that it would be difficult to hold someone legally liable for losses caused by a natural disaster. It is probably most people's gut feeling that a natural disaster is an act of God and cannot be remedied by the law.

That said, there was a case that might provide assistance – the Supreme Court's decision on a lightning strike during a football game.[2] In 1996, during a high school football competition, a game was not suspended by the coach during a thunderstorm. One of the players was hit by lightning and was seriously hurt. In 2006, the Supreme Court reversed the lower courts' decisions which denied possible liability for negligence on the part of the coach and rejected the case.

At this point, it is worth stopping to consider what 'negligence' is. The basic principle is that negligence is a failure to do what should have been done. From the aspect of the football case, 'what should have been done' means that 'the coach should have suspended the game at that time'. In that case, foreseeability and the duty to avoid risk were important elements. It was argued that it would have been possible for a person who led the team to foresee the immediate danger of the thunder, so he should have stopped the game and made the players evacuate the field.

Nonetheless, the decision in the Okawa Elementary School case adopted a new concept of 'organisational negligence', instead of adopting the logic that a specific person (i.e. the coach of the football team) should have been able to foresee the risk. This case is said to be groundbreaking because it did not adopt the logic of previous cases that a reasonable decision after a natural disaster occurred is sufficient to ward off liability for negligence.[3] Now, why did the lawyers in the Tsunami case go out of their way to try a new method instead of following the favourable precedent of the Football case? Mr Yoshioka and Mr Saito will be able to give us an answer.

## THE ESSENCE OF INNOVATION

**Sumida:** I apologise for the long introductory remarks, but I would like to ask Mr Yoshioka and Mr Saito to introduce each other rather than themselves to better approach them as innovators. According to Ikujiro Nonaka, Professor Emeritus at

1 Kazuhiro Terada, 'Two Lawyers Who Ventured into the "Okawa Elementary School" Lawsuit – Reason Why They Still Face the Bereaved Families after the Decision' (March 2021) <https://creators.yahoo.co.jp/teradakazuhiro/0200093049> accessed 1 November 2023.

2 Decision of the Supreme Court on 13 March 2006, *Hanrei Jiho* No. 1929, p. 41; *Hanrei Times* No. 1208, p. 85.

3 Shigeto Yonemura, 'Disasters and the Law of Damages' (2013) 6 Ronkyu Jurist 64; Takayuki Ii, 'Okawa Elementary School Tsunami Lawsuit and Its Significance', *The Newsletter of Senshu University Law Institute* No. 62 (February 2021), p. 65 et seq.

Hitotsubashi University and an authority on innovation research, the key to innovation is an interaction between non-conforming elements. In other words, he indicated that the key is for different people to work together. In that sense, I am interested in hearing how our guests introduce each other.

Professor Nonaka also says that innovation happens when the contradiction of binary opposition between analogue 'tacit knowledge' and digital 'explicit knowledge' is dialectically overcome. Given that legal theories can be considered 'explicit knowledge', how can innovation happen? Professor Nonaka also says that by grasping two extremes in terms of the big picture while keenly detecting comprehensive points and mutually expanding them, the two extremes will be united to sublate (*aufheben*, in German) them into something greater. Contradiction of binary opposition is a 'rational contradiction' and cannot be solved merely by a theory. What is needed is 'sensitivity'. Conflict of digital rationality, together with analogue sensitivity, will allow dynamic integration at a higher level. I would like to hear the story of the lawyers with this dynamism in mind.

Now, may I ask you, Mr Yoshioka, who actually created the scenario leading up to the winning of this landmark decision, to explain the scenario and the whole story about working with Mr Saito?

## THERE WERE ALSO VICTIMS OUTSIDE THE SCHOOL

**Yoshioka:** Hello everyone. When I heard from Professor Sumida about this planned conversation series, I envied the students at Hitotsubashi University. You hardly ever meet a professor who brings up a case such as the Okawa Elementary School tsunami case in a Civil Code class. The case does not fall in the typical framework of this type of class, and considering this, it is audacious but certainly an example to follow. So, my first impression was that you are so lucky to be in such an environment.

As requested by Professor Sumida, I would like to explain why I asked for Mr Saito's help. The tsunami that hit Okawa Elementary School affected not only the elementary school but also killed about 200 local residents living around the school. How can one assert that the death of 74 children at Okawa Elementary School alone was a human-made disaster when 200 adults were killed in the vicinity of the school? Many people said that this would be an extremely reckless way of pursuing the case and that it would be difficult to win. In order to take on such a case, I thought it was essential for me to get help from Mr Saito who specialises in the State Redress Act, so I asked him to be co-counsel in this case.

Also, we could not tell those who had everything washed away by the tsunami to pay legal fees for the lawsuit. Some of them were living in temporary housing with only the barest necessities. However, lawyers need money from their clients to maintain their practices, so there were not many people I could ask to be co-counsel when there would not be any compensation and we did not know whether we would win. At the same time, I believed that this was an extremely important issue that somebody had to take on, and I hoped Mr Saito would be willing to work with me.

I once worked with Mr Saito in a state compensation case involving Toyota Shoji. Throughout this case, I saw that Mr Saito is highly skilled when it comes to the topic of state compensation. However, filing the lawsuit in this case meant he would have to travel from Tokyo to the scene of the incident many times and that would be a heavy burden, but I still thought that Mr Saito would show spirit and accept my request. If he did not have tremendous enthusiasm, he would not have agreed to work with me.

I repeatedly asked Mr Saito to come to see the scene of the incident, but he was reluctant at first. However, he was in tears when he first heard the victims' testimony. He is such a warm-hearted lawyer. At the same time, he has a cool head. It is hard to find a lawyer who has a warm heart and cool head at the same time. There are many lawyers in the Sendai Bar Association, and I could have asked one of those lawyers to work with me. However, all things considered, I asked Mr Saito for help because I thought he would be the best partner, and he agreed to work on the case with me. That was the story of how Mr Saito became co-counsel on this case.

**Sumida:** Thank you. Next, Mr Saito, we would like to hear from you.

**Saito:** Mr Yoshioka, thank you for your compliments. You are far too kind. I was also educated at the Faculty of Law at Hitotsubashi University, but it has been almost 50 years since I started studying here. Looking back on the lectures at the Faculty of Law in those days, as Mr Yoshioka said, I am also envious of you all who can attend a conversation series like this one by Professor Sumida.

I would like to start by explaining how I became involved in the state compensation case involving Okawa Elementary School. I was asked to be part of this case by Mr Yoshioka many times for more than six months when I met him at meetings of committees of the Japan Federation of Bar Associations. He kept asking me to come to see the scene of the incident, but I thought it would be hard to go there from Tokyo and it took a while for me to make up my mind. I believe it is very important for lawyers to visit the scene of an incident, and I am sure Mr Yoshioka thinks the same. I believed that once I visited the scene and got a sense of what happened there and what the facts were, I would be compelled to think that I have to act and I could not sit by idly. I therefore hesitated, thinking that once I gave in to Mr Yoshioka's invitation and visited the scene, I would feel compelled to accept this case.

In the end, at the end of the year before we filed suit, I went to the scene with Mr Yoshioka, visited the bereaved families, heard their stories and carried out various associated investigations. In the course of those processes, I felt that this was not an issue that we could wrap up by advising that there is no recourse for the victims because it was a natural disaster. This was an unprecedented, human-made accident at a school that was caused by people who were charged with protecting the lives of the children of Okawa Elementary School but who failed to take appropriate measures. As Professor Sumida indicated, the complete lack of a remedy would be absurd and unjust. I felt that without our civil suit, the seventy-four children who lost their lives would not be able to rest in peace.

It was indeed an honour for me to be asked to work with Mr Yoshioka because he is an extremely talented lawyer who has a sense of artistry and at the same time is able to come up with and realise specific, dispassionate and reasonable strategies. I have not met many lawyers who are as capable as Mr Yoshioka in building legal scenarios. I had my eye on Mr Yoshioka since I first became a lawyer. I thought we could win this case, and I wanted to help, even if it would be only in a small way. That is how I became involved and worked with him on this case.

### THE BEREAVED FAMILIES SERVED AS 'DE FACTO COUNSEL'

**Sumida:** Mr Saito mentioned that Mr Yoshioka is an unrivalled scenario builder and strategist. Mr Yoshioka, when you were consulted and decided to accept this extremely challenging case, what scenario and strategy did you have in your mind?

**Yoshioka:** There have actually been around fifteen tsunami-related lawsuits filed other than the Okawa Elementary School case. Some cases were filed just after the earthquake, but none of them have been successful. It was believed that a natural disaster is an act of God and that it would be impossible to win a lawsuit claiming compensation for damage caused by the tsunami. At the same time, the bereaved families wanted to know about the final moments of their children's lives; however, the school would not give out any information. So, the only option left was filing a lawsuit. Although it would be a difficult case, the bereaved families wanted to uncover the truth. To fulfil their wishes, I instinctively thought that it would not be possible to approach this case as an ordinary case. If we went by the book, 30–50 lawyers would theoretically have had to work together on a case like this …

**Sumida:** Excuse me, can I just ask about this number? Do you mean 30–50 people would be needed to collect evidence in such a large case?

**Yoshioka:** That's right. The larger the case, the more lawyers are needed. Having multiple people examine the case can certainly be useful. However, in the Okawa Elementary School case, the evidence had been washed away by the tsunami. For example, if a lawyer were to appear out of the blue to speak with residents who were on the scene, the residents would be reluctant to talk because they would not want to get involved in a conflict. However, if those residents were approached by, for example, the father of a boy they knew in the neighbourhood instead of a lawyer, they would tell him what they know such as what the boy was doing at a specific time. Then the bereaved families could ask those residents to share the stories they heard in that way with the lawyers, and the residents would be comfortable telling the stories to the lawyers. In other words, it was necessary to have an arrangement allowing us to create an environment for interviews to be conducted in an order in which the bereaved families would first find relevant witnesses and then the lawyer would appear. The fewer lawyers there were, the easier it was to convince the bereaved families to use their connections and try to collect evidence from witnesses one by one. If there had been dozens of lawyers retained by the bereaved families in this case, the bereaved families would have left the case to the large counsel team and would not have been involved. I therefore offered the bereaved families to be 'de facto counsel' for the deceased children in place of additional professional lawyers in this case because, as I said earlier, much evidence had been washed away by the tsunami and many witnesses were difficult to find.

Also, viewed from another side, parents who have lost a child tend to blame themselves, asking themselves things like 'why did I not go to pick up my daughter?' or 'why did we send our child to that school?' They blame themselves thinking that the death of their child is entirely their fault. That is definitely not the case, but parents who have lost a child often feel stigmatised and at fault for the death of their child. I thought that the bereaved families could do something as parents for their deceased children by serving as counsel for the children, collecting evidence and voicing their feelings of resentment in court. This is another reason why I thought that the bereaved families should become 'de facto counsel'. I was able to build a case where, unlike a normal trial in which the lawyers stand in the front, in the Okawa Elementary School tsunami case, the lawyers stepped back and instead the bereaved families acted as 'de facto counsel' for the children by collecting evidence and facing the defendants in court.

This allowed the bereaved families, many of whom had not been able to even leave their beds out of grief, to stand up to fight for their children. The bereaved families started to get together and have discussions every night. They were able to collect a lot of good evidence by talking through the night about things like who would ask what kind of questions at a parents' explanatory meeting scheduled for the next day, or inconsistencies between the answers given at the last explanatory meeting and those given at the meeting before that. In that way, we were able to collect abundant evidence before trial. I think that the bereaved families' activities as 'de facto counsel' also improved the mental health of the families. In this sense as well, I think that appointing the bereaved families as 'de facto counsel' was one of the keys leading us to success in the case.

There is one more thing to add. When a lawyer visits a municipal office to ask questions, he or she is normally turned down, but if a family member of a deceased child asks questions at the information desk at a municipal office, the person working there would usually do his or her best to respond. That is only natural. There were ten explanatory meetings for the bereaved families, and each of them lasted for around four or five hours. It would not have been possible to have that many explanatory meetings if lawyers had taken the lead in the case. In fact, almost all of the evidence we relied on during the trial was revealed during questions and answers in those explanatory meetings for the bereaved families.

I think that our strategy of arranging to have the parents serve as 'de facto counsel' for the children was the key to success. Nonetheless, that is something normal lawyers would think is foolish; on reflection, it might have been far from a planned strategy and more of a gut feeling.

**Sumida:** Even though some believed that strategy was far-fetched, it succeeded. Mr Saito, would you like to comment on that?

**Saito:** As Mr Yoshioka said, I think that the bereaved families made a great effort. At first, shouts were exchanged during the questions-and-answers parts in those explanatory meetings. Ishinomaki City forcefully suspended the explanatory meetings of the bereaved families, and following that, the third session was held about six months later at the protest and strong request of the bereaved families. From the third explanatory meeting onwards, we started to see a change. The parents of the children who were victims were able to develop a list of questions by getting together in advance of each meeting, reviewing the records of exchanges at the previous explanatory meeting (minutes and videos), sharing their common understanding and discussing issues as well as asking questions. By sharing the roles and deciding who would ask questions and going through the explanatory meetings carefully and with patience, the bereaved families were able to elicit new evidence.

Further, there were witnesses at the scene and survivors who were near Okawa Elementary School when the tsunami hit, or who had gone to the school to pick up their children but had already left the school when the tsunami hit. Many of those people moved to different places following the earthquake. Nobody knew who had gone where, but the bereaved families searched for those people and spoke with them. As Mr Yoshioka mentioned earlier, if there were any people who were willing to talk to us, Mr Yoshioka and I visited them, listened to and recorded their stories and turned them into written statements. This is the process we have applied throughout this process.

## NO LARGE COUNSEL TEAM

**Saito:** We did not build a large counsel team. Having many lawyers is advantageous in many ways, but at the same time, opinions will be split, including opinions on how best to proceed, which legal theories offer the best prospects of success and how the evidence is to be interpreted. That is not a bad thing; it happens because each lawyer thinks that they must win somehow. However, confrontations can arise due to these different views. Of course, because each person is a lawyer and is headstrong, discussions can get heated, take time and become wasteful. To find the shortest way to a conclusion, it is necessary to start by fostering a shared understanding of the accident or incident; otherwise, it is not possible to have discussions on the basis of a common understanding. However, just building a basis for discussion requires a great deal of time, effort and money because someone in charge needs to prepare summaries, make reports for an hour or two and confirm the common understanding before starting discussions on how to approach the issue.

In contrast, this case had only two lawyers, who had been friends for forty years and knew each other and what the other thinks. So, although this was an extremely serious and difficult case, we could progress with the case without internal conflict. Even though this was such a major case, it only took six years from the first trial to the Supreme Court's final decision, which is incredibly speedy. All of this was done by the two of us. I think this can be attributed to Mr Yoshioka's strategy.

**Sumida:** Generally, a person who has gotten into trouble will consult with a lawyer and have the lawyer represent him or her. However, in the Okawa

Elementary School case, the bereaved families were assigned the role of counsel and the lawyers took a step back. This is ingenious, but how did you come up with that idea? Not to be a nag, but I still want to know the secret about that strategy.

## CREATING STATEMENTS WITH TYPOS THAT STIR THE EMOTIONS OF THE JUDGES

**Yoshioka:** Besides collecting evidence, another advantage of having the bereaved families serve as counsel was to move the judges in a hard-to-win case; it allowed us to appeal to the judges' emotions. The Okawa Elementary School case and the Football case mentioned earlier by Professor Sumida were both caused by a natural disaster, so the judges in charge of the Okawa Elementary School case had the Supreme Court decision on the Football case in mind. We assumed that the judges would have the mindset of comparing this case with the Football case as the trial proceeded, and we needed to appeal to the judges' emotions to think that they must give the bereaved families a win because the judges would not be moved by exclusively legal reasoning by the lawyers. Instead, the judges would be more touched if the parties concerned looked them in the eye and awkwardly spoke to them directly. For example, bereaved families usually express their feelings to judges through examinations of witnesses and the other party. However, if there are many victims, it is difficult to convey all of their voices to the judges. In those situations, one approach is to submit a 'written statement', or plainly put, writing a letter to the judges. However, it tends to be unusual for people to write written statements, and that is even more so these days when people send short messages by smartphone. So, when we asked the families to write statements to the judges, they were rather hesitant. In order to ease the bereaved families' minds about writing statements, I said to them, 'please write at ease whatever you feel because the judges like typos and omissions more than anyone – handwriting would be even better.'

**Sumida:** I see, so they did not use a word processor, right?

**Yoshioka:** To make them confident in writing a statement, I said, 'don't worry about any issues such as if your sentences are not connected. If you write the thoughts you want to communicate to the judges as a parent, they will take that seriously. Typos and omissions will make the judges think that the statements were written by the people involved and they have not been edited by lawyers, so please write whatever you want to tell the judges, including personal comments about your children.' They showed that they were parents full of love for their children. The statements were excellent, and Mr Saito and I could not read them without tears. I am sure that the judges were also moved by those statements.

**Sumida:** The credibility of the emotions was secured by typos and omissions …

**Yoshioka:** Yes. Rather than the coherent and dispassionate writing drafted by lawyers, these letters describing the emotions of the parents who lost their children needed to be written in the parents' own voices to appeal to the judges. We therefore worked out a strategy of having the bereaved families speak in court on each trial date about the pain and agony they were suffering from the loss of their children. The bereaved families' appeals in court made the courtroom audience sob each time, and I am sure that moved the judges' hearts as well.

## SUBSTANCE IS NOT NECESSARILY THE POINT AT ISSUE

**Yoshioka:** Another issue was identifying our core argument, or how to contest the case. The essential point of this case was that none of the evacuation manuals or crisis management manuals contained a clear indication of where to evacuate when a tsunami was approaching. Therefore, after the teachers evacuated the children to the schoolyard, they were confused and did not know where to go. As a result, they kept the children in the schoolyard for fifty minutes. The bereaved families at first asked us to focus on the point that the manuals were insufficient. However, we wondered whether we would really get a win from the judges with this argument if we sued for negligence based on wrongdoing that took place before the earthquake occurred. We thought that instead it might be better to make an accusation of negligence after the occurrence of the earthquake because the teachers did not evacuate the children even though a tsunami alert had sounded at a specific time after the earthquake. Some people warned the teachers that the tsunami was coming and told them to evacuate to the mountain behind the school. It was also possible to listen to the radio announcing that the tsunami was coming. Of course, we understood that the fact that there was no clear evacuation manual before the earthquake was also an essential point in the case, but we thought that the focus should be on the negligence after the earthquake occurred.

**Sumida:** You are talking about the first trial in the district court when you filed the first lawsuit, right?

**Yoshioka:** Yes. In the first trial, we made assertions about both the inadequate manuals before the earthquake and negligence after the earthquake, but we focused on asserting and establishing negligence after the earthquake. If we had started the first trial arguing the inadequate manual, we would probably have lost the case. I think that because we were able to win the first trial by asserting negligence after the earthquake, the High Court could expound with confidence the theory of organisational negligence in normal times before the earthquake.

**Sumida:** Was there any significant difference between the court of first instance and the High Court?

**Yoshioka:** Actually, a number of facts were revealed in hearings before the court of first instance, such as the fact that the school principal had previously said that the school would not withstand a 5-meter tsunami. While there had been no mention of 'tsunami' in the original evacuation manual, that term had been added about two years before the earthquake. Ishinomaki City also made a disaster plan in around 2002 envisaging a tsunami. Based on those facts, we came to think that they were prepared for a tsunami before the earthquake. So, why could they not implement those measures when the earthquake occurred? Backed by those facts, we decided to focus on negligence after the earthquake in the first trial. As a result, we won the first trial by using that strategy, but the judges in the High Court saw the record of the first trial and came to think that, rather than negligence after the earthquake, the blame might be on the school principal, head teacher, the board of education and the department at Ishinomaki City in charge of crisis management, who did not do their jobs properly before the earthquake. The point is that this was a dynamic trial. While we indicated in the written complaint the facts showing negligence both before and after the earthquake, we asserted, with varying intensity, negligence after the earthquake during hearings in the first trial and organisational negligence before the earthquake due to a lack of preparation in ordinary times in hearings before the High Court. We changed the emphasis and the point in dispute between the first trial and the High Court.

## WHO SHOULD BEAR LOSS RESULTING FROM A NATURAL DISASTER?

**Sumida:** The court of first instance held that there was negligence after the earthquake, and you won a landmark judgment. Then the High Court issued a ruling finding that what should have been done was not done before the earthquake, and the fault was not that of a specific person such as a supervisor or coach in the case of the Football case, but of an organisation based on the theory of organisational negligence. I will ask you to explain the process leading to that judgment later. First, Mr Saito, could you tell us a little about organisational negligence?

**Saito:** Sure. I think the concept of negligence is quite difficult to understand for the students who have recently enrolled. This might overlap with the explanation of negligence given by Professor Sumida at the beginning of the session, but liability for negligence is based on a failure to do what is expected to be done. However, there is a question at the very root of how to understand negligence: why does legal liability for damage arise where there is negligence? In the cases where someone is held to account for damage caused by a natural disaster, that fundamental problem is extremely important and difficult.

In our society, if someone incurs loss, does that person have to bear all the loss and is that person unable to hold anyone accountable? That is not the case, and the basic concept is that the person who caused the loss that has been incurred by another should provide compensation for that loss. As a basis for that concept, if someone was at fault (negligent) with respect to damage, it would be fair to hold that person legally liable to compensate the damage. This approach, the 'fault liability principle', is a basis of our society and is historically recognised as a basic concept in modern civil society.

In other words, in principle, the liability of a person who was at fault (negligent) is the starting point to consider the issue of damages. You will study the concept of tort under the Civil Code and that is structured according to individual-based liability.

**Sumida:** For example, if a patient dies due to a surgical error, the doctor who conducted that surgery will be liable for the death because the doctor failed to meet the relevant medical standards. Is that what you mean?

**Saito:** That's right. However, while the judgment of the High Court was based on the assumption that there were people who acted negligently in a certain incident, it did not conclude that the damage was caused due to the fault of specific individuals. Is it acceptable to treat the issue as an individual matter by saying that a person in a relevant position was required to or should have done some specific act, or that that person should have taken some specific measures – but failed? Should the organisation to which that person belongs have dealt with the issue systematically and across the entire organisation to ensure that things would be handled properly, in a way that ensured that no loss or harm would be caused? How about reframing the duties of specific people who are members of an organisation as the duties of a more abstract subject that is to be owed by people in proper positions or duties in the organisation, or reconstructing the liability for a breach of duties related to the entire organisation or system? I think that approach led to the High Court decision in this case.

The structure of modern society is extremely complicated. We have seen many events that cannot be prevented by individual power or responsibility and that cannot be simply attributed to individual persons, especially where there is immediate danger to our society – such as large-scale disasters like the Great East Japan Earthquake and the recent COVID-19 pandemic.

That does not mean that no one should be responsible no matter what happens. The greater or more serious the danger is, the more it is necessary to consider that as a responsibility for society as a whole, or specifically, the organisation to which the relevant people belong, or the people involved in building structures that are supposed to protect others.

Looking at this case from that perspective, we developed the idea that advance measures should have been taken to prevent the loss of human life due to a tsunami. Due to the absence of those measures, the children's lives could not be saved when the earthquake actually occurred and the tsunami hit. Therefore, the fault lies in the failure of exercising duties that should have been exercised. So, who should have taken those measures? It was not an individual, and in this case, it was the parties related to the school, of course the school principal and head teacher who were responsible for the operation of the school, the board of education and more broadly, the city department in charge of disaster prevention. They all must share the responsibility. The High Court decision did not clarify things in this regard, but it acknowledged organisational liability based on that perspective. My explanation might be a little complex, but I hope you understand.

## WAS THE UNPRECEDENTED DISASTER FORESEEABLE?

**Sumida:** The students might be concerned that no one could foresee what would happen, because the tsunami was an unprecedented disaster. How did you address that issue?

**Saito:** This relates to how we understand 'foreseeability' on which liability for damages is based. In the example mentioned earlier, for individual liability, the starting point would be that the individuals must have specifically recognised a risk of harm to the persons whose security must be protected – in this case, the children of Okawa Elementary School.

However, when viewed from the aspect of the fault of a system or an organisation instead of individuals, the issue becomes more abstract: what risk should have been dealt with by the organisation in advance? If we see the issue as 'what should have been done as an organisational response' in order to protect the lives of the children at schools in general, it is possible to think about the issue in broader terms.

The area around Okawa Elementary School in Ishinomaki City, Miyagi Prefecture, was also affected by the Miyagi offshore earthquake in 1978. Based on this experience, the prefecture and the city recognised that Miyagi offshore earthquakes are quite cyclic. In fact, historically, offshore earthquakes have occurred in the Miyagi Prefecture every 26–43 years. Given this background, it was necessary for the entire organisation to properly consider how to respond to the next offshore earthquake.

The question is not whether it was foreseeable that an earthquake would actually occur, a tsunami would hit Okawa Elementary School and the children would be engulfed by a tsunami and die. Rather, it was foreseeable with high probability that an earthquake of that size would occur in the future. However, the timing and epicentre of the earthquake were not specifically known. Nonetheless, if it was possible to foresee somewhat abstractly what the consequences of an earthquake would be if one occurred, then the harm caused by the tsunami was 'foreseeable' in relation to the duties to be exercised by the organisation. This may be a little difficult, but in the case of organisational fault, the event that needs to be foreseen is somewhat generalised.

However, for the court to acknowledge liability, it is necessary to find that (1) the incident was foreseeable, (2) there was a duty to act to protect the children's lives based on what could be foreseen, (3) this duty was not properly exercised, and (4) there is a reasonable causal relationship in legal terms between (1), (2) and (3) on the one hand and the loss of the children's lives on the other hand. (1) and (2) are elements of 'negligence' and (3) is an element of 'illegality' under the State Redress Act. The relationship in (4) is called 'reasonable causation'. In the case of organisational negligence specifically, organisational liability is not established unless reasonable causation is proved between the loss of lives and that the lives could have been saved if the organisation had exercised its duty. However, I think that the High Court took the approach I have explained earlier.

**Sumida:** This was a landmark decision. It was groundbreaking in that, while we are all at a loss at how to deal with unprecedented disasters or the COVID-19 pandemic, which is a crisis we faced for the first time in human history, it was pointed out in the decision that something needed to be done in order to protect people at the school from danger. Thank you, Mr Saito.

Mr Yoshioka explained earlier the general background of arguing in a trial based on the theory of organisational negligence. I would now like to focus on a decisive moment: there must have been a trigger for a breakthrough, so please share that episode with us. It seems to me that the approach you took was not a generally popular idea in Civil Code theory, so please tell us what encouraged you to argue this case based on that approach.

### INTERPRETATION OF 'LOWER COURT DECISION IS TO BE REVIEWED'

**Yoshioka:** When Mr Saito and I undertook this case, we both understood that it was important to work with the media. It is necessary in cases like this to have the media stir up public outrage, and thankfully, we received a lot of media coverage on each trial date. When an appeal was filed with the High Court after the first trial, the judges of the High Court probably read the record from the lower court. In addition to the record, if they watched the daily news, I think the judges at that time saw the true nature of this case.

In fact, the judges' first words on the first appeal hearing date were 'the lower court decision is to be reviewed.' Following that, they asked the following cryptic question:

> We ask both sides to submit documents about the following scenario: You receive a notification from the Board of Education before your child enters an elementary school saying, 'Send your child to Okawa Elementary School.' Under the current legal system, you cannot say 'I do not want my child to go to Okawa Elementary School' or 'I want to send my child to another school.' This is a problem of the so-called school district system and you would be subject to a penalty if you did not follow the Board of Education's decision. Accordingly, under circumstances in which you are told by the Board of Education to send your child to Okawa Elementary School and you are not allowed to say no, how would you interpret the provision of Article 29 of the School Health and Safety Act ('A school shall prepare a crisis management manual providing specific details and procedures to be taken by the school employees in the event of danger based on the situation of each school for the security of the school children'), namely, the provisions requiring the school to prepare a crisis management manual? How is that provision relevant to this case, or, to put it the other way around, how should Article 29 be interpreted? Please submit a statement on this question by the next hearing date.

I think that the words of the judge that they would 'review the lower court decision' made the counsel of the other side happy because they lost the first trial. However, we were also happy because our interpretation was that the question by the High Court asking about the interpretation of Article 29 of the School Health and Safety Act indicated that the High Court would consider not only negligence after the earthquake but also how a crisis management manual should have been prepared before the earthquake, and in the case of a failure to prepare a manual, whether Article 29 merely provides an obligation to make efforts or whether a violation of Article 29 would be the basis of a breach of a legal duty by the school.

**Sumida:** I see. So, both sides were happy.

**Saito:** As Mr Yoshioka mentioned earlier, I think the bereaved families strongly felt that their children would not have died if the school had taken appropriate measures in advance. For example, schools are obligated to build a system to properly transfer every single child to their parents if something happens, but the principal of Okawa Elementary School failed to do that.

In addition, the school should have had an emergency contact network, but it did not have one in place. After an earthquake occurs, it is necessary first to take cover under a desk until the tremors stop (primary evacuation), then evacuate to the school playground (secondary evacuation), followed by evacuation to higher ground if a tsunami alert is issued. However, Okawa Elementary School's crisis management manual did not specify the evacuation site or how an evacuation was supposed to be carried out, and, in addition to that, emergency drills had not been properly carried out. Considering all those factors, the bereaved families were convinced that the entire school was liable.

## THE COURT OF FIRST INSTANCE DID NOT ACKNOWLEDGE ORGANISATIONAL NEGLIGENCE

**Saito:** We therefore asserted in the written complaint filed at the beginning of the first trial that the school was liable for a failure to perform its duty to prepare a manual under the School Health and Safety Act. However, at the same time, we thought we could not win with this assertion. The approach taken by the judges on the court of first instance was not embracing this direction. We could see that as the trial proceeded.

In fact, the judges of the court of first instance also presided over a tsunami case for a driving school in Yamamoto Town in the same prefecture. The driving school was held liable in that case, but we found that this ruling was only based on negligence immediately before the incident, so we thought that in this case the issue of duties in advance of the incident would not become a point of contention. As a result, we had in-depth discussions and decided on a theory of organisational fault, but that happened only in the following High Court case. Mr Yoshioka and I had discussions and felt that, although we mentioned a breach of duties in advance of the incident in the court of first instance, this was not the main issue. Nonetheless, we asserted this point in the court of first instance.

Partly because of that, we specifically asserted this point in the final brief of the first trial. We asserted it as a legal theory as well, but ultimately the facts are most important. Okawa Elementary School, the scene of the incident, is about 4 km away from Oppa Bay, a bay on the Pacific Ocean, into which the Kitakami River flows. For a tsunami to hit Okawa Elementary School, it would have to go up the river for 4 km. In other cases, this would mean that a major tsunami would travel upstream for quite a long distance. However, it should be noted that the Kitakami River, which is a large river, passed right in front of the school.

One could argue that a tsunami going upstream would not be a problem if there was a proper riverbank and the school was, therefore, not liable. However, this was not an issue. Based on our in-depth investigations of tsunamis going upstream after an earthquake in the past, tsunamis travel upstream not by themselves but as a result of a preceding earthquake. Hence, it was necessary to discuss the risk of a tsunami going upstream based on the vulnerability of the riverbank. We made a lot of arguments based on these facts in the first trial.

The important thing is what the presiding judge of the High Court said on the first date for oral arguments. I took notes when I heard it:

> As to who owes what duty of care in the school as an organisation, the question in State Redress Act cases is whether individual teachers were at fault in an accident or injury suffered by a student in a swimming pool or on a school playground. However, this case is on a different level. It is not necessary to consider how to look at the fault of public officials in the school organisation, namely, a breach of duty of care. Responsibilities are divided in organisations, and it might be necessary to consider breaches of the duty of care of public officials based on this. This is beyond the scope of the responsibilities of each individual public official and is an issue of the responsibilities of the public school organisation and is, therefore, different from the case for the lower court judgment. Accordingly, the previous judgment does not serve as a useful reference. In that sense, the deliberations in the court of first instance were not sufficient and this decision is to be reviewed.

If you hear the word ‘review’ at the end, you may think that the higher court will come to a different conclusion, but this can be a big mistake.

**Sumida:** That is right.

**Saito:** The High Court judge was saying that the lower court’s deliberations on organisational negligence were insufficient. Therefore, after we received the cryptic question at the beginning of the trial, we had a lot of discussions and sought the opinion of a prominent authority on the Civil Code, Professor Yoshio Shiomi of Kyoto University, to complement our knowledge, and we decided that the High Court would probably agree with the points we had asserted since the first trial as the major point of judgment or point of issue. We, therefore, put greater effort into further studies and investigations to buttress our argument.

## A TSUNAMI GOING UP THE RIVER 27 YEARS AGO WAS THE KEY

**Saito:** As an aside, I would like to explain why the topic of the tsunami going up the river is important. The day on which the Middle Japan Sea Earthquake occurred in 1983 was the date for an examination of witnesses at the Niigata District Court Murakami Branch. The Joetsu Shinkansen had not been wholly opened yet, and I was scheduled to take an express train from Ueno Station early that morning to the Murakami Branch of the Niigata District Court. However, the train stopped at the station before Murakami Station because of the earthquake. I could not go back to Tokyo that day, and my client drove me to Niigata. When I turned on the TV at the hotel, I saw the image of a tsunami going up the Murakami River with white-crested waves, which made a strong impression on me. From that memory, I actually thought from the very start when I was invited by Mr Yoshioka that this is an important point. One cannot say that it was foreseeable that tsunami will come to Okawa Elementary School without mentioning that tsunamis can go up rivers. I conducted a lot of research and argued this point from the first trial. I believe that the High Court judges said that they would review the lower court decision partly because of that.

**Sumida:** When the judges asked the cryptic question Mr Yoshioka mentioned earlier with a straight face, the defendant side and plaintiff side interpreted this question in completely opposite ways. Both were delighted, but as Mr Saito said, if you listened carefully, the judges properly stated their understanding of the issues. What happened after that?

## CAN ADVISORY PROVISIONS BE LEGALLY BINDING?

**Saito:** At first, the High Court's cryptic question seemed extremely difficult. The court said that Okawa Elementary School is a public elementary school and the children at that school are required by law to go to that school. We were asked to examine the relationship between the requirement for the children to go to Okawa Elementary School and the School Health and Safety Act related to securing safety at schools in determining state compensation liability. One is an administrative law issue, but the State Redress Act, which also has an aspect of being a special law to the Civil Code, takes an approach that is similar to tort liability. Therefore, whether this legal starting point can form the basis of liability is a fairly difficult question.

We thought that measures to be taken by the school in advance could be a cause for liability and argued this point from the first trial, but there were no prior in-depth discussions as to the organisational negligence theory of liability mentioned by the Court. We, therefore, decided to ask for the opinion of a legal expert to cross-check our assertions and consulted with Professor Yoshio Shiomi of Kyoto University, who had assisted me previously. He said that he would make time to consult with us on what the High Court said, so we visited him at his office at Kyoto University and had a good talk with him. He prepared a written opinion for us in the end.

**Yoshioka:** Article 29 of the School Health and Safety Act provides that a school shall prepare a crisis management manual, but this is usually said to be a general advisory provision stipulating that schools must make an effort, so schools will not be held liable even if they fail to prepare a crisis manual.

**Sumida:** Are there any penal provisions, such as administrative punishment? Is this Act based on public law?

**Yoshioka:** We had to convince the judges that schools are legally liable to follow Article 29. In that regard, the written opinion of Professor Shiomi clearly indicated not only that Article 29 stipulates duties under public law but that it is also a provision providing for duties under private law to protect rights and interests.

The opinion proved compelling enough for the judges to follow this view in drafting their judgment, so we are very thankful to him.

### THE TRIANGLE ZONE THE CHILDREN HEADED TO AT THE END

**Saito:** To add one more thing, it is difficult to assert that organisational negligence should be recognised unless it can be clearly said that the incident was foreseeable well in advance, i.e. that it was possible to evacuate when the tsunami was actually approaching. From this perspective, I thought that the riverbank would be the key if a tsunami goes upstream because the riverbanks are, contrary to their general image, structurally quite fragile.

Mr Yoshioka is not only a great strategist, he is one of the top experts in Japan on defective housing and well-versed in engineering, geology, soil analysis and architecture. Using his connections, we had geotechnics experts prepare written opinions on the rivers and riverbanks. It was demonstrated that a riverbank can indeed be destroyed by an earthquake. Specifically, the opinions analysed the parts of the riverbanks that were destroyed by the Miyagi offshore earthquake in 1978, which occurred before the Great East Japan Earthquake, and how the parts and the way they were destroyed coincided roughly with the parts of the riverbanks of the Kitakami River that were destroyed by the Great East Japan Earthquake and how they were destroyed.

**Sumida:** I see.

**Saito:** In terms of establishing foreseeability, even without taking advance measures by clearly specifying the evacuation places, it could be argued that there was no breach of duty as long as the riverbank is not destroyed. However, that is Mr Yoshioka's area of expertise, so it was possible to analyse this aspect based on the expert witness reports on how it happened, and this led to the decision that it might have been possible, to a certain extent, to specifically foresee the risk of the destruction of the riverbank and the approach of the tsunami and so there was a duty to take advance measures. Mr Yoshioka, could you please explain this a bit more?

**Yoshioka:** When we considered how to demonstrate foreseeability, we made requests for access to official files to local development bureaus established throughout Japan by the Ministry of Land, Infrastructure, Transport and Tourism, such as the Tohoku Regional Development Bureau and the Kansai Regional Development Bureau, on what damage was caused to the Kitakami River at the time of each earthquake. We were able to obtain materials showing, surprisingly, that almost the same places had been destroyed by every earthquake.

The data revealed that the triangle zone, which was where the children at Okawa Elementary School were to evacuate at the very end, had been destroyed by every earthquake. According to experts of the geotechnical society, this is due to the characteristics of the riverbank. Unlike the foundations of houses, riverbanks are large, long structures that extend for tens of kilometres and that must be formed with materials of the same quality. However, it is difficult to collect soils of a uniform nature, and some parts necessarily become fragile. I think that we were lucky that we could devise ways of demonstrating, through expert evidence, that the riverbanks were in fact fragile even though they were made of concrete and looked robust.

## ANGRY EXPLANATORY MEETINGS TURNED INTO A VENUE FOR EXAMINING WITNESSES

**Sumida:** This is amazing. You first adopted a strategy to give the bereaved families the roles of representatives, normally played by lawyers, with yourself remaining in the background. And then you examined several moves by the court and collected evidence to remove obstacles in the way of your objective. That is exactly the story of what lawyers do – collecting evidence to build persuasive logic – and you used your legal skills to work out great ideas and using your connections. Although being armed with theoretical backing is necessary, how to develop a strategy comes first, and I appreciate your valuable story about this. Is there any other ingenuity you took advantage of in the course of activities such as collecting evidence? Please tell us if there was anything else you did.

**Yoshioka:** As I briefly mentioned earlier, the parents of the children, who are the bereaved families, did a really great job of gathering evidence. When it was decided that Ishinomaki City would hold explanatory meetings on why the school caused the deaths of the children immediately after the incident, the city intended to end the meeting series after one or two meetings. The first meeting was turbulent with the bereaved families yelling in sheer exasperation 'give our children back' and 'bloody idiot'. This was in fact welcomed by the city because it would give them an alibi that they got the meeting done while looking down, keeping still and enduring the shouting for two hours. But those meetings were not intended to be the place for the bereaved families to release their anger but the place to elicit answers from the other party, and they had to ask questions despite their anger. To that end, it was better if only a few people held the microphone and asked selected and well-thought questions. In most cases, the other party would not give an immediate answer saying that they did not know or that they had not yet investigated the issue. We reacted by asking them to investigate those matters by the next meeting and we got them to set a date for the next meeting. At the next meeting, following the explanations on what they had investigated, we would ask further questions about the explanations as to specific figures, and if they could not answer, we asked them to hold another meeting, and in that way, we would get them to set a date for the next meeting. In this way, although Ishinomaki City intended to only hold two meetings of one hour each, in the end, ten meetings were held and they were as long as four to five hours each time.

In a normal trial, an examination of a witness takes half an hour or an hour, or two hours at the longest. However, in the Okawa Elementary School case, plenty of time was spent by the bereaved families raising questions, and this enabled us to obtain the evidence equivalent to a lot of witness examinations in court. This was just a treasure trove. The judges ordered the City Board of Education to issue materials on the preparation of a crisis management manual, but this issue actually originated from the explanatory meetings for the bereaved families. The judges focused on this topic and asked the other party to submit such materials and found that the topic had been discussed a year before the incident. This led to the judges recognising that the lives of the children could have been saved if the people in charge had exercised their duties a year before the incident, if not sooner. In this way, the evidence collected by the bereaved families was the decisive factor in obtaining the favourable High Court decision in this case.

## THE SECRET TO OVERCOMING DIFFICULT OBSTACLES: BEING GOOD AT PRAISING PEOPLE AND DIGITISED DOCUMENTS

**Sumida:** Thank you. This story is really impressive, as the bereaved families worked together and built the case you developed.

**Saito:** In addition to his skills at building scenarios, Mr Yoshioka is also very good at letting each person play a role. I think that he has a gift for praising people. When the bereaved families did their homework properly, he said nice things such as ‘well done’ or ‘you did well’, making them happy and encouraging them to try to do their best again. In addition to the activities of the bereaved families mentioned by Mr Yoshioka, they did other helpful things, such as asking the city to disclose evidence in accordance with the Information Disclosure Ordinance. They got used to the process and became quite good at gathering evidence without needing instructions from us. For example, information on earthquakes and tsunamis was found in materials such as PR magazines issued by the city. When we asked the bereaved families to collect such information at the library by the following day, they complained a bit but they did their best to collect information and carry out research. We sometimes asked them to do a considerable amount of work, and they did it well. I think it was because of Mr Yoshioka praising them effectively.

There is one more thing to add, which is a technical matter. The files for the trial records for this case would physically fill three or four shelves of a large locker. I normally have to take all of those materials to meetings and trial dates. However, it was impossible for me because I went to the Court from Tokyo by Shinkansen, so I turned all of those records into electronic data at the beginning. Therefore, one USB memory stick was enough, and that was very useful.

Reading evidence thoroughly is important in a trial. The volume of evidence submitted just by us, the plaintiffs, was approximately 400 documents, and it was necessary to carefully read all of those in detail, as well as the records submitted by the other party. Nevertheless, there were occasions where the judges pointed out something we had not noticed and surprised us. Having digitised all the materials made it possible to retrieve the data and made things substantially easier, though that is a technical matter and it might not be essential.

**Sumida:** Well, I think that is quite important for future lawyers. I also think that Mr Yoshioka's gift of praising people is another important point, because building a case based on empathy is considered a key to effective management.[4] Hearing this, I begin to think that empathy is the starting point and driving force for innovation and that is true in law as well as in management.

**Saito:** I think we were able to get as far as we did because of a bit of ingenuity.

**Sumida:** Thank you. I think this covers almost the entire story up to the landmark decision that found organisational negligence. Now I would like to consider this case from a high-level perspective and ask if there are any issues you would like to raise with respect to the decision and what you think is the significance of the decision.

## HOLDING THE FIST THAT HITS LIABLE RATHER THAN THE BRAIN THAT GIVES ORDERS

**Yoshioka:** Previously, negligence was usually found at the point that arose closest to the accident. However, come to think of this, mistakes made by people at the scene may in fact be induced by instructions by or the fault of people who have given these instructions or made plans. Despite this, in past cases, courts have focused on the most recent point only and have not questioned the liability of those in charge of planning or giving instructions. To compare this to the human body, for example, if I hit Professor Sumida, in the past the fist I used to hit her would have been blamed. However, I hit her because my brain told my fist to do that, so the brain is to blame. I understand organisational negligence in this way.

It is not the people at the scene who are to blame, it is the instructing or planning departments or divisions that induced that fault – this perspective is not limited to school disaster prevention but will develop into various places such as disasters caused by corporations and other natural disasters, as well as medical and hospital errors. In the future, trials from the perspective of holding the entire organisation accountable, rather than each individual person, will become more commonplace. I also think that the approach will be changed from finding fault in actions taken after an earthquake occurs to questioning what measures should have been taken before the earthquake. In this highly complex society, placing blame on organisations rather than individuals will become a normal way of pursuing negligence claims.

**Sumida:** Thank you. You mentioned 'highly complex society' as a key word, and I had the impression that, in such a society, it is increasingly important to integrate and successfully manage the abilities of various experts. Mr Saito, what do you think?

4 Ikujiro Nonaka and Akira Katsumi, *Kyokan Keiei ('Empathy-Based Management')* (Nikkei Inc. 2020).

### WHAT DOES IT MEAN TO FILE A COMPLAINT ONE DAY BEFORE THE DEADLINE UNDER THE STATUTE OF LIMITATIONS?

**Saito:** We held a meeting in Sendai to report and examine the decision and at that meeting, Professor Shigeto Yonemura of Tokyo University commented at the end that 'without this Appeal Court decision, the Great East Japan Earthquake, with the loss of 17,000 people's lives due to the tsunami, would not have taught any lesson to Japanese society' and that 'this decision is the salvation of the children of Okawa Elementary School and the 17,000 people who died and also serves as an important step in changing Japanese society.' I could not agree more. Mr Hideaki Tadano, one of the bereaved family members, said that he only wanted to find out what happened. Why then did he have to file a lawsuit? I think the significance of the action and the resulting Appeal Court decision lies in those questions.

We have to take a real look at the consequences of the Appeal Court decision because it was obtained in exchange for many lives. However, regrettably, under the Japanese legal system, everything must be taken in terms of money in order to hold parties at fault accountable. Money is the only way to compensate for lives in the court system under the laws of Japan. Sadly, there are some people who think that those who want to find out who is responsible do so because they only want money. However, as Mr Tadano said, the bereaved families in no way decided to bring the action for that purpose. They wanted to clarify where responsibility lies for the fact that the children were left at the school for forty-five minutes. They also wanted to know how their children were at the end, even though knowing that would be hard for them. They had no choice but to file a lawsuit to know these things. You can also see the painful decision mentioned by Mr Tadano on the date on which the complaint was filed. In fact, the complaint in this case was filed one day before the deadline under the Statute of Limitations ran out, which was to expire three years after the incident.

**Sumida:** I will give an additional explanation here as our students have not studied the Statute of Limitations. The Statute of Limitations enshrines a legal principle that states that a claim may no longer be filed after three years from the time of the tortious act in question, the time the plaintiff became aware of the damage due to the tortious act, or the time the plaintiff became aware of the identity of the person who caused the damage. In other words, the bereaved families lost their children in the tsunami and were not satisfied with the explanations by the school or the city but were still reluctant to file a lawsuit – but they finally arrived at the decision that they had no choice but to file a lawsuit.

**Saito:** Yes, but there were people who took that the wrong way. This case received a lot of media attention, partly because of our strategy, but it also caused a strong public backlash, and that means that the bereaved families were victimised three times: the first time when they lost their children in the tsunami, the second time when they were harmed by the responses by the city and the prefecture and the third time when they brought this lawsuit. They were bashed, libelled and slandered – more than that: they even received a death threat. It is a serious problem that asserting legally protected rights can involve a heavy burden, including dealing with public backlash. We cannot allow libel, slander and intimidation. Such acts turn the foundation of society upside down. Therefore, when taking action or filing lawsuits, we should consider how to prevent those problems – and I think that this case as a whole and the Appeal Court decision were significant in that sense.

## THE PURPOSE OF LIABILITY FOR ORGANISATIONAL NEGLIGENCE IS TO SAVE HUMAN LIVES

**Saito:** Let me add one more thing at the end. The significance of arguing for organisational negligence in this case is that we can apply a lesson learned from this case in the future. If a large disaster, not just the Great East Japan Earthquake, occurs, is it possible for us to calmly and reasonably deal with that in the moment of the actual harm and danger? Under the current law, a person who was present at the scene and who was at fault would be held liable, but this might make it impossible to find out who is really liable. On the other hand, if organisational negligence is recognised, that would mean that no harm or danger would be caused or turned into reality, or even if it is caused, lives could be saved, as long as the rules established in advance are followed even if there is panic at the scene. This is not just an issue of liability for damages. If damage and harm do not occur when there is a disaster, the lives of more people can be saved. I think that the approach shown by the High Court is extremely significant in this regard.

**Sumida:** Thank you. The second topic covered by Mr Saito also connects to what Mr Yoshioka said. He said that if he hits me with his right fist, the focus used to be only on the fist but the focus should be on the brain, which ordered the fist. Mr Saito also brought up that the human nature of being inevitably filled with dismay after an earthquake should be taken into account. He said that focusing only on a specific fault at the scene after a disaster occurred or dealing with the issue from a micro-viewpoint was insufficient. That is something that looks easy once it has been done, like the egg of Columbus. The more brilliant and dynamic a new idea is, the simpler it is. Because it is extremely simple, people take it for granted once it is implemented.[5] Organisational negligence is such a new theory that captures the essence of reality, that is very convincing, and that can make a real difference in the world. In that sense as well, I am grateful for having these two innovators here today.

Also, I agree with Mr Saito that 'the bereaved families were victimised three times' is a deep-rooted problem in Japanese society. Having said that, I personally doubt

5 See Bruno Munari and Masayo Abe (tr), *Simpuru ni Matomaeru noha Yori Mutsukashi Koto* ('To Complicate Is Simple, to Simplify Is Complicated') *Munari no Kotoba* (originally published as *Verbale Scritto*) (Heibonsha 2009) 67.

whether we should only look at the negative side of Japanese society in this regard. As can be seen in the handling of COVID-19, while many countries took compulsory lockdown measures, Japan has managed to make society work on its own way without taking such measures. There are diverging views on this, but I think that the Japanese people are self-disciplined in their own way and that this discipline benefits society. While we have seen or heard about the turmoil caused by widespread looting in other countries during the confusion after the occurrence of a disaster, Japan rarely has had such a major panic and is admired throughout the world for this.

In that sense, there are both light and dark sides in Japanese society, and I think that Mr Saito raised an extremely important issue on the dark side. Basic social rules should continue to be set based on various legal rules and theories such as the Civil Code, and in the course of considering that, the issue raised by Mr Saito will be a very important theme.

## THERE IS A CRACK IN EVERYTHING, THAT IS HOW THE LIGHT GETS IN

**Sumida:** I am going to speak about one more thing in relation to today's theme, 'innovation'. This is from a book written by Taiwan's digital minister Audrey Tang.[6] I think she is quite famous among young people. She quoted a passage from a song by the Canadian singer Leonard Cohen, 'there is a crack in everything, that's how the lights get in'. She wrote:

> If you feel angry or impatient about some injustice or something that attracts no attention, try to change the anger or impatience into constructive energy. Then ask yourself questions like this. What can I do for society to prevent that injustice from ever happening? Keep asking those kinds of questions. In this way, you will be able to turn your anger into constructive energy. Then, you will be able to keep yourself on a path to create a prototype for a new positive future instead of attacking or criticising someone. By inviting others to the crack you found and let them join, the light will get in another way.

The world is not perfect as you all may agree. The world has flaws and challenges. I think lawyers are there to face them. 'To earnestly address those issues is the reason we all exist here.' This is what Audrey Tang wrote in that book, and I genuinely feel empathy for those words.

By the way, I am pursuing research with a particular interest in 'AI and law'. Technology such as AI is going to evolve considerably in the future and might be able to learn things such as court precedents much quicker than humans and give us advice such as 'according to the precedent of . . .' or 'how about this as an issue?' Something like this might even turn into a smartphone application. However, it

6 Audrey Tang, *The Future of Digital Innovation* (President Inc. 2020) 251 et seq.

might only be able to notice the cracks in the world rather than creating new lights in the future, as I mentioned earlier. From what we have heard from Mr Yoshioka and Mr Saito today, the key word 'sensitivity' is crucial. I think lawyers are expected to have the ability to come up with strategies that resonate and appeal to human sensitivity.

Now, I would like to conclude today's class by conveying a message to you, who are just starting to study law, from these two great lawyers and me: 'Do not be a poor-performance robot.' Thank you very much for taking time today out of your busy schedule.

## COMMENT

### *Human Resources for Legal Innovation*

**Noma:** A wave of disruptive technological innovation is creating new goods and services – significantly different from the existing ones. As a result, there are ever more cases where current laws and regulations cannot be applied directly to these new goods and services, requiring new laws. In addition to the need to formulate new laws and regulations, today's technological innovation is also impacting the world of law.

Artificial intelligence (AI) dispute resolution and online dispute resolution are illustrations of this development. In fact, some corporations have already implemented these services to handle disputes. However, today's innovative technologies are gradually encroaching on many aspects of the world of law and bringing about various changes in the legal landscape – this raises issues related to how the legal profession should operate, for example, and the business environment surrounding the judicial system.[7] Legal innovation is being driven by technology directly affecting the world of law.

The purpose of this column is to consider the human resources that create legal innovation. My awareness of this issue derives from the fact that the use of technology has not yet spread to Japan's legal world. When compared with Britain, Japan lags far behind in its use of technology in the legal world. Going forward, technology use in Japan's legal world is expected to increase significantly. At the same time, however, the encroachment of legal innovation, which has evolved through interaction with technology advancements, into Japan's legal world is, without question, a challenge to be addressed by Japan's legal community. I hope that those engaged in the legal profession today, including lawyers, judges, prosecutors and researchers, as well as students wishing to enter the legal profession, will consider not only legal innovation but also the human resources necessary to create such innovation.

7 See, e.g., Simon Deakin and Christopher Markou (eds), *Is Law Computable? Critical Perspectives on Law and Artificial Intelligence* (Hart Publishing 2020).

I will first look at some examples of technological innovation in the automotive industry and the relevant laws. I will then discuss the human resources required for legal innovation by applying the findings of innovation studies in new product development to legal innovation.

### *Technological Innovations in the Automotive Industry and the Relevant Laws*

**Noma:** The automotive industry is undergoing a once-in-a-hundred-year transformation brought about by technology called CASE, which refers to 'connected', 'autonomous', 'shared & services' and 'electric'. In Japan, legislative amendments have been recently made in response to new innovative technologies, particularly autonomous driving technology, and our policymakers are currently discussing how to regulate autonomous vehicles.[8]

The Road Traffic Amendment Act and the Road Vehicles Amendment Act took effect in 2020 to create a legal framework enabling regulators to expeditiously establish safety standards for Level 3 and Level 4 autonomous driving.[9] With regard to the concept of car accident liability involving autonomous vehicles, considered in the context of damage insurance, the General Insurance Association of Japan, a trade association representing licensed general insurance companies in Japan, published a report titled 'Legal Issues Concerning Autonomous Driving'.[10] This report provides an overview of the legal issues related to autonomous driving. Moreover, a government study group under the Ministry of Land, Infrastructure, Transport and Tourism's Road Transport Bureau has been discussing the issue of damage liability pertaining to accidents involving autonomous vehicles.[11]

Governments around the world are currently developing new laws and regulations that govern autonomous driving. This is not the first time that the world has experienced automotive technology innovation and that laws and regulations have been established in response to these innovations. An exploration of automotive history shows that when vehicle ownership began to increase around 150 years ago,

8 For discussion of the relationship between law and autonomous driving, see K Akita and others, 'Roundtable Discussion – Autonomous Driving: Current Status, Challenges and Prospects' (October 2020) 89 Law & Technology 1.

9 According to the guidelines issued by the Ministry of Land, Infrastructure, Transport and Tourism, the levels of autonomous driving are defined as follows: Level 0: No Driving Automation; Level 1: Driver Assistance; Level 2: Partial Driving Automation; Level 3: Conditional Driving Automation; Level 4: High Driving Automation; Level 5: Full Driving Automation. Levels 0 through 2 and Levels 3 through 5 differ in how driving safety is supervised and who takes control of the vehicle. With Level 0, Level 1 and Level 2, the driver is required to supervise safety and take control of the vehicle. With Level 3, Level 4 and Level 5, the autonomous driving system does both.

10 General Insurance Association of Japan, Legal Issues Concerning Autonomous Driving (2016).

11 Ministry of Land, Infrastructure, Transport and Tourism, Road Transport Bureau, 'Safety Technology Guidelines for Autonomous Vehicles' (September 2018).

governments moved to enact new laws and regulations governing vehicles that applied new technologies, very much like governments today.

After Henry Ford introduced the Ford Model T to the world in 1908, automobiles became ubiquitous in society, so much so that the twentieth century is called the 'Century of the Automobile'.[12] In the second half of the nineteenth century, about 40 years before Model T was first produced, the Locomotive Act, also known as the Red Flag Act, was enacted in Britain in 1865 requiring a crew of three – a driver, a stoker and a man with a red flag walking at least 60 yards ahead – to operate a self-propelled vehicle. The Act applied not only to steam-powered vehicles, which were emerging at this time in Britain, but also to gasoline-driven vehicles. The Act was repealed in 1896, but, until that point, hindered the growth of Britain's automotive industry.[13] The background to the Act's enactment shows a lobbying campaign by the stagecoach industry, afraid that the spread of cars would lead to job losses in the industry.

The Red Flag Act requiring a vehicle to be preceded by a person carrying a red flag is both odd and absurd when viewed today. Given the negative impact on Britain's automotive industry and its ultimate repeal, it is clear that the Act was a failure. The fundamental cause of its failure was the hidden agenda of the stagecoach industry that feared the loss of jobs with the rise of automobiles. In other words, policymakers prioritised the interests of the stagecoach industry and failed to recognise the common good for society.

### *Leaders Who Create Legal Innovation*

**Noma:** There are two abilities required of leaders who create legal innovation. In this section I will discuss the human resources necessary to create legal innovation by referring to two studies by Nonaka and Takeuchi that discuss the process of developing new products[14] and consider 'wise companies' and 'wise leaders'.[15]

First, legal innovation requires the ability to create new knowledge through interaction with people of different occupations, ways of thinking and behaviours, including businesspeople or entrepreneurs and engineers. Those who play leading roles in the legal sector are largely graduates from law school. By contrast, many entrepreneurs are MBA holders, and the engineering sector attracts people with

[12] See T Origuchi, *Jidosha no Seiki ('A Century of Cars')* (Iwanami Shoten 1997).

[13] *Dai 68 kai: Gekidou no Eikokusha Kouboushi: Chirijirininatta Eikou no Burando* (Issue 68: The Turbulent History of the Rise and Fall of British Cars: Scattered Glorious Brands) <www.webcg.net/articles/-/42365> accessed 1 November 2023.

[14] Hirotaka Takeuchi and Ikujiro Nonaka, 'The New New Product Development Game' *Harvard Business Review* (January 1986) 2.

[15] Hirotaka Takeuchi and Ikujiro Nonaka, *The Wise Company: How Companies Create Continuous Innovation* (Oxford University Press 2019).

computer science or mathematics degrees. Needless to say, many people also playing important roles in these fields have no such degrees.

Nonaka and Takeuchi's 1986 study examines a number of successful product development cases in the manufacturing industry in Japan and the United States. Using 'relay' and 'rugby' metaphors, the authors demonstrate that Japanese companies can develop new products flexibly and quickly. Developing new products involves various processes, including research and development, production and marketing. The 'relay race' approach, which is a linear approach, resembles a relay race where the runner passes on the baton to the next team member. Under this approach, each phase of product development is clearly segmented and the development project does not move from one phase to the next until all the requirements of the preceding phase are satisfied. On the other hand, under the 'rugby' approach, the phases are not clearly segmented and the baton is not passed on from one phase to the next. The 'rugby' approach is an overlapping approach under which each phase overlaps with the next, breaking down the barriers between the roles of the different teams involved and enabling them to work closely together in a product development project.

Focusing their attention on the manufacturing industry, Nonaka and Takeuchi argue that the 'rugby' approach is more effective. This argument can be applied to legal innovation as well. In essence, it is imperative for the legal profession to create new knowledge through interaction with people from other sectors who have different cultures, different ways of thinking and behave differently, including businesspeople and engineering professionals.

Second, legal innovation is based on the ability to make judgements from an ethical and moral standpoint while aiming to achieve high-order goals. Nonaka and Takeuchi's 2019 book calls leaders with practical wisdom 'wise leaders' and argues that 'every leader has to make judgments and take actions amid constant flux. Wise leaders, we believe, exercise judgment while taking a higher point of view and doing what's good for society.'[16]

At a time when disruptive technological innovation is gradually having a profound effect on the world of law, the ability to make sound judgements from an ethical and moral viewpoint in pursuit of higher goals is required. People who play important roles in the legal sector very likely already possess the ability to make judgments in pursuit of higher goals. I hope the leaders who create future legal innovation will also be 'wise leaders' in the sense that they take account of ethics and morality.

## CONCLUDING CONVERSATION

**Steffek:** After this session, Mihoko asked me to suggest a role model of a legal innovator. This is a very interesting question that requires us to define legal innovation, identify the types of legal innovation we value and look at the long list

[16] Ibid., 97.

of people who have contributed to the law over the centuries. As I enjoyed thinking about his question, I also asked some friends for their opinion. The first reaction of all of them was, 'this is a difficult question!' I think this first reaction is already part of the answer.

Yes, it is difficult to identify role models for legal innovation. I have come up with three reasons why. First, legal innovations have to be evaluated against the background of their times; second, legal innovators are operating within and benefiting from a network of other innovators; and, third, the definition of legal innovation plays a major role.

Taking this in turns, legal innovation happens at all times and against the background of the then-current state of the art. Some might point to Johannes Gutenberg introducing movable-type printing in 1439 to Europe, starting the printing revolution that transformed the way law was made and communicated. Today, almost 600 years later, the paper Gutenberg printed on is losing significance as law becomes more and more digitised. But it is difficult to compare the relevance of printing law and the impact of digitising law as their significance is rooted in time.

Second, legal innovators do not operate in a vacuum as interaction and communication are essential features of law. Legal innovators, perhaps even more than their contemporaries, learn from others. Aristotle, a strong candidate for the list of most impactful legal innovators, is a good example. While Aristotle's contribution to justice theory was a major step into uncharted territory, his ethics build on the thoughts of Plato, his teacher.

Third, the question arises what legal innovation is and what legal innovators contribute to it. Perhaps some readers were surprised to see Gutenberg and Aristotle included in a discussion of legal innovators in the first place. An argument not to include them might be that they are ultimately not lawyers, but a printer and a philosopher.

Instead, one could point to legal innovators who contributed to legal doctrine such as Nobushige Hozumi, a law professor co-drafting Japan's Civil Code at the end of the nineteenth century and developing legal doctrines covering technology such as the telephone. Or one could focus on the legal profession instead and point to the invention of law reports or the virtual law office. Lawmakers at the national, international and transnational levels are also strong candidates for a list of outstanding innovators.

A further consideration is whether legal innovation can be measured. Perhaps by counting the number of applications of an innovation or the value it generated. Measuring legal innovation raises the issue of what we value in legal innovation even more pressingly. Is it just change that matters or only change that made people's lives better? Against the background of the challenges of measuring legal innovation, I hope you forgive me that I refrain from giving you my definitive list of top legal innovators.

**Sumida:** Of course, as you say, I knew that this question would be difficult and challenging. I was waiting for your answer with excitement, but I am still surprised to see Gutenberg and Aristotle come up. By the way, let me confirm one point. I knew that printing technology played a role in the religious revolution, but what do you mean when you say that it changed the way laws were made and communicated?

**Steffek:** I think the context is similar to the Reformation. The printing press democratised the availability of legal information and sped up the dissemination of legal information in society. This was a breakthrough for the legal world.[17]

**Sumida:** I see, you meant to bring the idea of 'democratisation of information' to the world of law. Indeed, this is a ground-breaking innovation that changed the whole world.

Hozumi Shigenobu was a jurist who gave birth to the study of law in Japan at the end of the nineteenth century and is also known as one of the compilers of Japan's Civil Code. Recently, I rediscovered that Professor Hozumi had written a very exciting paper entitled 'The Telephone and the Problem of Law', in which he had investigated the effect of a new communication tool that appeared in the nineteenth century, the telephone, on the principles of contract law. Thus far, the law distinguished the conclusion of contracts in the parties' presence from the conclusion of contracts where parties were in different places (for example, by letter). The question was whether a new category was needed for the conclusion of contracts by telephone or whether the existing legal principles could capture this.[18] After examining the debate that was dividing European academia at the time, he concluded that only two categories – in presence and in absence – were needed. This division, which is truly timeless, was also confirmed in legal reform in Germany at the beginning of the twenty-first century.

Thanks to this interpretive theory, civil jurisprudence has been liberated from the drudgery of having to enact new laws every time a new communication tool is introduced. It is difficult to know whether we should enact a new law or amend the Civil Code, which is the basic law of society, and whether we should change the interpretation of existing laws.

By the way, I asked for 'role models of legal innovators' because I think that the readers who will pick up this book are those who are currently in the legal profession, those who aspire to become legal professionals and those who are involved in

17 See James Wilkinson, 'The Most Significant Innovation in Legal History?' (*Lexis Nexis Future of Law*, 27 April 2018) <www.lexisnexis.co.uk/blog/future-of-law/the-most-significant-innovation-in-legal-history> accessed 1 November 2023.

18 For more detail, see Mihoko Sumida, '*Ishihyoji no Koryoku Hasseijiki Kitei no Gendaika – Riigaru Inobeshon Josetsu*' ('Modernization of Determination of Effective Time of Manifestation – Introduction to Legal Innovation') in Hiroki Okamoto, Masami Okino, Yasushi Toriyama and Akio Yamanome (eds), *Minpogaku no Keisho to Hatten – Nakata Hiroyasu Sensei Koki Kinen* (Succession and Development of Civil Code Study – In Celebration of the 70th Birthday of Hiroyasu Nakata) (Yuhikaku 2021) 211 et seq.

legislation. I thought it would be a good idea to create a more concrete model to guide their actions and thinking.

I completely agree that it is a Herculean task to rigorously define legal innovation and to rank it. But even if we cannot define it, we wanted to at least identify the direction we are aiming for and share it with our readers. What would you say, for example, if a law student asked you how they could become a law professor like you, doing cutting-edge research and contributing to society at the same time? Or, for example, how to tackle the challenge recently advertised in the *Financial Times*, i.e. to identify role models for solving legal problems together?[19]

**Steffek:** What is the road to legal innovation? This is another difficult question. I think there is more than one path. Some people may innovate on a whim, while others plan their research and use a rigorous methodology. Some people might innovate by having a conversation to clarify or summarise their ideas. Others may find inspiration alone, in an office or during a walk in nature.

But it is the willingness to be open, to have a passion for improving legal practice, to be able to transfer concepts from other disciplines into law, to find pleasure in new approaches, to learn from others, to try out ideas in practice and, last but not least, to try, fail and try again! This list is by no means exhaustive, but if you would like to know more about innovators, I would recommend taking a look at the empirical literature on the characteristics of innovators. Alternatively, you can take the initiative to innovate yourself.

## QUESTIONS FOR FURTHER THOUGHT

- Who contributes to innovating the legal system?
- Which role do lawyers play as regards legal innovation?
- What is the role of the courts and litigation as regards legal innovation?
- What role do external shocks such as natural disasters and economic crises play in legal innovation?
- Is it possible to anticipate legal innovation such that new legal rules and reformed legal institutions are in place when they are needed?

19 'Wanted: Role Models for Solving Legal Problems Together' (*Financial Times* 13 May 2021) <www.ft.com/content/2024c7c4-e302-4d08-9ad2-958cd1027927> accessed 1 November 2023.

# Conversation 5

## Corporate Governance in the Age of Artificial Intelligence

ABSTRACT

This conversation addresses the impact of artificial intelligence and sustainability aspects on corporate governance. The speakers explore how technological innovation and sustainability concerns will change the way companies and financial institutions are managed, controlled and regulated. By way of background, the discussion considers the past and recent history of crises, including financial crises and the more recent COVID-19 pandemic. Particular attention is given to the field of auditing, investigating the changing role of internal and external audits. This includes a discussion of the role of regulatory authorities and how their practices will be affected by technological change. Further attention is given to artificial intelligence in the context of businesses and company law. As regards digital transformation, five issues are reflected, namely data, decentralisation, diversification, democratisation and disruption.

| | |
|---|---|
| *Speakers* | Kiyotaka Sasaki, Souichirou Kozuka and Takuya Izumi |
| *Moderators* | Felix Steffek and Mihoko Sumida |
| *Concluding Conversation* | Felix Steffek and Mihoko Sumida |
| *Questions for Further Thought* | Felix Steffek |

### A FINANCIAL CRISIS UNLIKE ANY OTHER

**Sumida:** We are about to begin the fifth conversation of the 'Legal Innovation' series. Today's topic is 'Corporate Governance in the Age of Artificial Intelligence' and we have three guests. The first speaker is Professor Kiyotaka Sasaki, Visiting

Professor at Hitotsubashi University, Graduate School of Business Administration. He joined the Ministry of Finance and worked abroad for nearly ten years in total, including twice with the OECD at its Paris headquarters and three years at the IMF in Washington, DC. In 2010, he joined the Japanese Financial Services Agency's Inspection Bureau. He then served as Deputy Director-General of the General Affairs Bureau of the FSA's Inspection Bureau in 2010, Director-General of the FSA's Certified Public Accountants Audit and Review Board in 2011, Director-General of the FSA's Securities and Exchange Surveillance Commission in 2015 and Director-General of the FSA's General Policy Bureau in 2018.

After retiring in 2019, he has been a Visiting Professor at the University's Graduate School of Business Administration and head of the Global Financial Regulation Research Forum. He is also involved in educational and research activities in collaboration with the FinTech Research Forum led by Professor Mikiharu Noma, who is also contributing to the Hitotsubashi University–Cambridge University research project on legal systems and artificial intelligence.

Professor Sasaki, we are very much looking forward to hearing your thoughts.

**Sasaki:** Thank you for your kind introduction. The topic of my talk is 'Corporate Governance Challenges in the Era of COVID-19'. If you look at this title alone, you may wonder what it has to do with innovation. One of the things that became clear during the COVID-19 pandemic was the acceleration of digitalisation and innovation. So, although I say, 'in the Era of COVID-19', there is a deep connection with technology and innovation.

My original background is in finance, particularly in supervision, inspection and regulation as well as in global cooperation in these areas of finance. Today, I would like to talk about the relationship between innovation and corporate governance from the perspective of financial and securities market supervision and audit firm supervision. These are the areas I worked in as a regulator.

I will first briefly speak on the COVID-19 pandemic and the many insights I have gained from it. Second, I will talk about how corporate governance is changing in terms of digital transformation (DX). Third, I will talk about changes in corporate governance from a sustainability perspective.

When I was at the Japanese Financial Services Agency, I faced the global financial crisis triggered by the failure of Lehman Brothers in 2008, the so-called Lehman Shock, and, going further back, the Japanese financial crisis in 1998 when major banks and securities companies failed. Whereas the past two financial crises were caused by financial products, in particular the non-performing loans of Japanese banks and, in the case of the Lehman Shock, by investment banks trading derivatives products, the most recent crisis was caused by COVID-19. Here the risk is directly related to human life and health. To reduce this risk, quarantine and a reduction of human contact have been implemented. Some countries have locked down cities and, in Japan, a state of emergency has been declared.

The measures to reduce the risk to human life and health have resulted in a contraction of the real economy, which has been spilling over into the financial markets.

In other words, the COVID-19 pandemic differs from the last two financial crises in both cause and risk-spillover pathways. Since the cause is a virus, the best solution is the development of medicines and vaccines, or a new way of life known as the 'new normal'.

## WHAT PROBLEMS HAVE EMERGED AS A RESULT OF THE COVID-19 PANDEMIC?

**Sasaki:** The pandemic has highlighted a number of problems, which can be divided into two main categories. One is the manifestation of existing problems, particularly in the case of Japan, where digitalisation has been lagging behind. The other is new challenges associated with the pandemic, which have made the issue of inequality more apparent. More to the point, I have the acceleration of DX in mind. DX is expected to accelerate in order to cope with the new normal of infection control. I call this COVIDX, which is a combination of COVID and DX.

In terms of disparities, infection and mortality rates vary from country to country, region to region and between age groups. In addition, there are economic disparities where the shrinking real economy has a significant impact on vulnerable groups and small and medium-sized enterprises. In the case of the Lehman Shock, large global companies were particularly affected, whereas in the case of the COVID-19 pandemic rather small and medium-sized companies such as restaurants and hotels were affected. Education is also a big issue as regards inequality. Even prior to the pandemic, there were large disparities in education between schools and regions. Since the pandemic, much teaching moved online and big differences in learning opportunities have been noted depending on the economic and IT situation among families. These are just some examples, but the disparities that have existed in the past have become clearer and wider with the pandemic.

From that point of view, there are two relevant aspects of corporate governance. One is the acceleration of DX, and the other is the impact of environmental, social and governance (ESG) issues, in particular the issue of sustainability.

## THE FIVE DS OF ADVANCING DX

**Sasaki:** Next, I would like to talk about changes in corporate governance, particularly changes due to the acceleration of DX, or, in the case of the COVID-19 pandemic, the acceleration of COVIDX. The need for DX has been much discussed, even before the pandemic. When I was at the FSA, I inspected and supervised virtual currency, i.e. cryptoassets and service providers and was also in charge of various issues associated with the digitalisation of the financial sector. In promoting DX, especially in the field of finance, I would like to discuss the five Ds, representing major aspects of digitalisation.

The first D is 'Data'. The point of DX is that the data itself will have value. The use of data will become so important that it will determine the future of a company.

The second D is 'Decentralisation'. As the name suggests, the central bank is the centre of finance, issuing money and controlling monetary policy. In addition, stock exchanges have traditionally been centralised mechanisms. However, virtual currencies such as blockchain are intentionally built on decentralised systems with no central controller in place. They pose challenges to the traditionally centralised mechanisms. Looking at this from the perspective of a traditional central bank, take, for example, the Facebook-led Libra digital currency announced in June 2019, there is strong opposition to financial systems without a central administrator. In any case, the second D reminds us that the movement to 'decentralise' traditional centralised mechanisms will accelerate.

The third D, 'Diversification', refers to new players in finance. Traditional financial players have been banks and brokerage firms, but the traditional financial players are being challenged by GAFA – the collective name for the four major US IT companies Google, Amazon, Facebook and Apple – FinTech and other players.

The fourth D is 'Democratisation'. Conventionally, the supply side or the providers of financial services have had more power than the customers of the services and consumers. However, with DX, as with the internet, customers, clients and users will have more power than the providers. Customer satisfaction and touch points with customers will be crucial.

The last D is 'Disruption'. The first four Ds of the DX have disruptive effects on the existing financial players as well as on the authorities that are still mostly stuck within the traditional legal system and supervision.

## HOW GOVERNANCE WILL CHANGE WITH DX

**Sasaki:** Along with the DX represented by the five Ds, there will be a change in the concept of the 'Three Lines of Defence', particularly in the area of governance. I am not sure how familiar you are with the term 'three lines of defence'. At least in the world of financial supervision, since the Lehman Brothers collapse in 2008, supervisors around the world have adopted this as a common concept. Financial institutions are thought to need three lines of defence in terms of governance, risk management and internal control. The first line is the frontline sales department, i.e. the traders and dealers who generate revenue. The second line is risk management and compliance. The third line is internal audit. The key point is that the first line of the three lines of defence, in particular traders and dealers generating revenue, also has a defensive role. In any case, it is the board of directors or the governance of the company or financial institution that is responsible for building these three lines of defence. The authorities and regulators review whether the three lines of defence have been built and are functioning effectively. This concept is not only applicable to financial institutions but also to public companies, for example. I believe that this concept of the 'Three Lines of Defence' will change as DX progresses. I expect the entire three lines of defence to become digitalised.

If all three lines of defence, including the first line, which is mainly responsible for generating revenue, are digitalised, then the basis of the business will be system-managed. Businesses will no longer function without the system. This will make it impossible to take undesired risks. In other words, if risk controls are embedded in the system, then a trader or dealer in the first line trying to trade illegally or take a risk that is too high will be stopped by the system. This will lead to more sophisticated control and defence capabilities in the first line.

Now let us look at risk management – also referred to as compliance – in the second line. It is also expected to become more sophisticated thanks to digitalisation. Risk management will be carried out based on 100 per cent of the data and 100 per cent of the population of transactions as opposed to a sample basis. This will enable risk management in real time. This is already happening and will accelerate in the future. What used to take a lot of time and effort in the second line will be reduced and may even be done in the first line. If this happens, then the question arises as to what the difference between the first and second lines will be.

Furthermore, if digitalisation progresses, the role of internal audits in the third line may also change. As each of the three lines of defence becomes more sophisticated through digitalisation, it becomes possible for companies to produce perfect financial statements internally. Until now, when a company prepared its financial statements, there was an incredibly labour-intensive, multi-layered checking process. Data was collected from the business units, checked by risk management and compliance, checked by internal audit, checked by the CFO and board of directors and then checked by the external audit. Even then, accounting irregularities occurred and errors were made. If the three lines of defence become digital and the control functions become more sophisticated, there is a possibility that companies will be able to produce error-free financial statements themselves – 100 per cent perfect financial statements.

## CHANGING PROCESSES AND POSITIONS

**Sasaki:** This raises the question of what will happen to the role of accounting audits and external audits. For example, will the financial institutions be able to control 100 per cent of the bad loans that erupted during the Lehman Shock or the Japanese banking crisis without having to be checked by the authorities? This also raises the question of what will happen to the role of inspection and supervision by the authorities.

The concept of the Three Lines of Defence changing in terms of the activities of the first line of business and the second line of risk management is almost the same for financial institutions. If the accuracy is considerably improved, then why not use two lines instead of three lines? It is important for the third line, internal audits, to be independent. So, it is unlikely that the entire third line will disappear. However, when the first and second lines are merged, what will the role of the third line be? What will be the role of the board of directors, and what will be the role of the audit committee, which is mandated by the Companies Act? What will be the role of the external audit? What will be the role of inspection and supervision by the authorities in the case of financial institutions?

I expect that the concept of the three lines of defence and the role of management and supervision, including external audit and regulatory audit by the authorities, will change in the financial industry. If this happens, it may be necessary to review existing governance frameworks, such as the Companies Act, the Financial Instruments and Exchange Act and the Corporate Governance Code in the case of Japan, among many others. Of these, I am particularly concerned about auditing. Traditionally, audits are compliance audits, looking at whether standards have been met or not. I think there is a possibility that these conventional audits could be disrupted by DX.

## WILL AUDITING SURVIVE?

**Sasaki:** I used to be in charge of reforming financial inspections and supervision when I was at the FSA, and I used to face similar questions. Conventional financial inspections and supervision were basically ex-post checks, with a focus on superficial compliance with laws and regulations. DX will disrupt the traditional inspection and supervision carried out by the authorities.

What is the role of auditing that will not be disrupted by DX? My response to this question is that audits should be forward-looking to prevent misconduct and other risk factors, analyse the root causes in a holistic manner and ultimately add value to the management of the company. Overall, the impact of DX on governance will appear largely in terms of changes in the three lines of defence, particularly with the possibility of consolidating the first and second lines of defence as well as the role of audits.

## ESG PRIORITIES CHANGING AS A RESULT OF THE COVID-19 PANDEMIC

**Sasaki:** Another thing I would like to talk about is the 'Three Ss of the COVID-19 pandemic' from a sustainability perspective. The first of the three 'Ss' is 'Social' or 'Society'. The second is 'Sustainability', as the sustainable development goals (SDGs) have been increasingly discussed and promoted around the world including in Japan. 'Solidarity' is the third S, which means unity and cohesion instead of division within societies and between people. In any case, the concept of the three Ss has become more important throughout the pandemic.

As an extension of this, the concept of ESG is attracting attention and making progress internationally, both in the financial sector and in the field of governance. Before the pandemic, governance was the most advanced area of ESG in Japan. Governance was the first to progress, including the development of a corporate governance code, followed by environmental matters, particularly climate change and the growing awareness of greenhouse gas issues.

Compared to these two areas, Japan is lagging behind in the 'Social' area. There are various issues in the social area, such as human rights, gender equality and diversity. In Japan, ESG has progressed in the order of governance, environment and social in terms of priorities. However, the pandemic, which posed risks to human life and health, has highlighted the importance of people-oriented thinking. Thus, the area of 'Social', which includes health and safety of life, employment, community and education, is now the priority among the ESG issues. Environmental matters have long been actively discussed in Europe, particularly climate change and decarbonisation. The COVID pandemic cannot be considered unrelated to public health and climate change.

Governance is undergoing change as well. Even before the start of the pandemic in 2019, the US Business Roundtable, an organisation similar to Keidanren Japan, emphasised that a broader, multi-stakeholder perspective is important, rather than the traditional shareholder-centred approach. The 2020 World Economic Forum also stressed the importance of governance from a multi-stakeholder perspective.

To sum up, through the pandemic, the importance of 'Social' has been significantly raised as well as the increasing importance of environmental issues and change of governance structures with a multi-stakeholder perspective and focus on sustainability.

**Steffek:** Thank you very much. I tremendously enjoyed this presentation. There was a lot of information in it and you touched many different things. If you allow me to, I would like to raise an idea.

## DX ENABLES PREDICTION

**Steffek:** You mentioned the five Ds, namely data, decentralisation, diversification, democratisation and disruption. I wondered whether there could be a sixth D, 'Design'. I am talking about design since technology supports actors in anticipating consequences rather than being surprised by certain events after they have made their decisions. Technology can be used to predict economic events. It can also be used to design and plan legal and economic relationships. I would be interested in your opinion on whether technology in this area could also lead to people designing, i.e. pre-planning, rather than being surprised afterwards.

**Sasaki:** Thank you very much for your insights. I think you are right that these five Ds, or DXs, will raise expectations and make it possible and important to be more proactive and involved in planning and design. In my mind, this was included in the fourth D, 'Democratisation'. I think that would be a relevant part of the supply-side focus. Each and every individual who owns data, each and every data user, should be proactive in protecting and using it.

The traditional governance of financial markets or financial supervision is no longer viable. From my perspective as a former regulator in charge of the rapidly changing securities market sector, I can say that market self-regulation and what is known as soft law are becoming more important than laws and government rules to respond to the changes and innovations in the markets. As DX advances, such self-regulation, self-rulemaking among the market participants and the design of self-regulations and soft law will become even more important. In this respect, I think the points you have just raised are exactly right.

However, I have a tendency to group five Ds, three Ss and so on into odd numbers. I think that odd numbers are a bit cooler than even numbers (laughs). Adding a sixth one is also possible, of course.

**Steffek:** So, how about considering a seventh one?

**Sasaki**: That's fine too, but generally people can't remember more than three. I think five is the maximum (laughs).

**Sumida:** Thank you (laughs). Now, let us move on to the next presentation.

## ACHIEVING THE SAME AS BEFORE WITH DX?

**Sumida:** I would like to ask the second speaker, Professor Kozuka from the Faculty of Law of Gakushuin University, to give a presentation. He graduated from the Faculty of Law of the University of Tokyo and has been teaching at the Faculty of Law of Gakushuin University after serving as an Assistant Professor at the Faculty of Law and Economics of Chiba University and as a professor at the Sophia University Law School. Many students attending this conversation series said that they became interested in legal innovation after reading his new book, *The Age of AI and the Law*.

We have asked Professor Kozuka to give a presentation on the 'Implementation of Artificial Intelligence in Corporate Governance'.

**Kozuka:** Thank you. When Prof Sumida suggested the subject for my talk today, I thought that I could talk about how to make sure that Japan's Principles on AI, which Mr Izumi is going to talk about next, are actually being implemented and how to place them within the context of corporate governance. However, while drafting a new paper[1] on AI during the New Year holidays, I came up with a new topic, which I cannot help but talk about. Therefore, I will talk about the relationship between innovation and technology in business organisations.

As Professor Sasaki mentioned, when technology is developed, the organisation must adapt to it. Regardless of how many Ds there may be in the DX of corporate governance, the organisation of a company must also change. In the field of law, particularly with regard to digital technology, it is claimed that the equivalent function that had been achieved before digitalisation shall now be realised digitally. It means that people can do the same thing digitally that they used to do with papers and physical objects. This is what lawyers often say.

In the international scene, such functional equivalence is often required under international rules on digital commerce by UNCITRAL, the United Nations Commission on International Trade Law. Under such an approach, people do the same thing as before by using digital technology. This makes me doubt that innovative technology contributes to social change. Maybe lawyers tend to stand by the *ancien régime*.

1 Souichirou Kozuka, 'ＡＩとデジタルで変わる『法』', (2021) 119 *Kaiho THINK Shihôshoshikai Ronsô* 10, available online <www.shiho-shoshi.or.jp/gallery/think/52657/> (in Japanese) accessed 1 November 2023.

One of the issues in the context of COVIDX, as Professor Sasaki named it, is the practice of Japanese companies using seals (*hanko*) too often when signing documents. It was claimed that there were people who could not work remotely and had to come to the office to stamp the seal during the COVID-19 pandemic. I do not know how many such people there actually were. Still, it was decided that this Japanese business practice should move to the digital realm.

## WHY DIGITISING STAMPS AND SEALS IS NOT EASY

**Kozuka:** In the digital era, we have the technology of digital signatures. As the Japanese seal is equivalent to a signature in the West, it is no surprise that the idea of replacing the seal with a digital signature comes up. The problem is that the Japanese law on electronic signatures is outdated. For example, the Japanese Electronic Signature Act was enacted in 2001 when there was no cloud technology. Article 3 of the Act provides that electronic signatures are to be made using a code and a device. It is presumed that a smart card is used as the 'device'. To be specific, a person is identified as 'Ms A' by the smart card, and then she produces a digital signature by using the code of Ms A. Arguably, the Act does not allow electronic signatures using the cloud and that is just one reason why the Act needs to be reformed. That being said, there is a risk of destroying a sound established practice if the reform is made without examining why Japanese companies have relied on seals and not electronic signatures, i.e. why they have resisted the move to electronic signatures.

The students in this conversation series will be familiar with a personal seal, but a corporate seal is a little different from a personal seal. To begin with, there are two types of corporate seal. One type is the 'round seal' and the other is the 'square seal'. Both are shown in Figure 5.1. If you look closely at the round seal, there is an inner circle inside the outer circle, with the company name written between the two circles. In the centre, there are six Chinese characters reading 'CEO's seal'. This means that this seal is used by the CEO of the company when the company concludes a contract.

Round seal (used for contracts) Square seal (used for receipts and invoices)

FIGURE 5.1 Two types of corporate seals

Another type of seal, the square seal, is used for receipts and invoices, not contracts. Thus, companies use these two types of stamps depending on the nature of the document to be signed.

Every company has rules on who is allowed to stamp these seals and when they are allowed to do so. These rules prevent the unauthorised use of a seal. The basic rule is that the company's CEO is required to stamp the seal when entering into a contract. However, the CEO may not have the time to stamp all the contracts. If they really did so, they will have pains in their arm. Therefore, there is often a rule that senior employees other than the CEO may get a seal from the head of the organisation and then seal the contract for their department. After the seal is stamped onto the document, the employee returns the seal to the original place of storage, thus ensuring security.

With electronic signatures by smart cards, the same thing can be done: the smart card can be stored away and only brought out when necessary. An employee can use it to make an electronic signature with the smart card under a regulated procedure. However, such a procedure cannot be replicated when the digital signature is made using the cloud. In that case, there is only a password but no device. Once you know the password to conclude a certain contract, you cannot delete the knowledge from your memory. As a result, control over the power of concluding a contract is looser than before. Against this background, I anticipate that Japanese companies will not be able to move easily to electronic signatures, especially cloud-based electronic signatures, as long as they wish to seek a functional equivalent of the current control over the use of a seal.

However, there is a solution to this: you can give authority to senior employees to conclude certain contracts subject to specific limitations. There is a provision in the Companies Act that can be used for that purpose. It says that an employee such as a division manager or a general manager if given authority over a certain matter, can conclude a contract within the scope of that authority. This can be found in Article 14 of the Companies Act. Unfortunately, there are only a few court decisions on this provision. Those who have studied the Companies Act will be aware of this article, but Japanese companies do not resort to it. The reason why they do not use it is the employment system in Japanese companies. It is known as a 'membership system', in which the responsibilities and authority of individual jobs are not clearly defined. As a result, there are no clear authorisations as regards contracting. The assumption underlying the provision in the Companies Act is a 'job-based' employment system as seen in Western companies.

## THE JAPANESE EMPLOYMENT SYSTEM AND THE USE OF SEALS

**Kozuka:** The abovementioned provision of the Companies Act was originally transplanted from German law. European companies have an employment system in which the scope of authority of each employee is clearly defined. A rule stating that 'a contract can be concluded within the scope of the employee's authority' raises no problem in Germany. But in Japanese companies, despite the provision in the Companies Act, the actual employment system is membership-based. The employment contract in Japan does not say 'Ms A's authority extends to the subjects as described below.' Therefore, a division manager in Japan typically cannot conclude a contract by using a seal. Instead, with the premise that the person who stamps a seal is usually the CEO, the company keeps the practice of letting a senior employee stamp the seal as a temporary alternative to the CEO, saying, 'just for today, please stamp the seal instead of her'.

Unless we change the system of employment in Japan itself, we will not be able to move from seals to digital signatures. Furthermore, if Japanese companies start delegating powers to senior employees without changing the membership-based employment system, some employees, whose scope of power is not explicitly determined, may end up exercising more power than they should. Hence, the abuse of power by employees will become an issue. Allowing the company to discipline an employee for exceeding their power, even to dismiss them, requires a reform of labour laws such as the rules on dismissal. Thus, the issue surrounding seals is not simply that of the substitution of a seal with a digital signature. Functional equivalence of a seal and a digital signature is only achieved after adapting corporate governance, labour law and the employment system. When focusing on individual issues, the pursuit of functional equivalence might appear to be a conservative approach. The truth is, however, that we have to place them in the broader context of the evolution of organisations adapting to the development of technology. Otherwise, DX may never take place in the true sense.

## WHO IS RESPONSIBLE FOR MISORA HIBARI BEING REVIVED BY AI?

**Kozuka:** The next topic I would like to address is the control of AI through the corporate governance of Japanese companies. Here, too, we focus on how organisations change. In Japan, the basic principles are stated in the 'Social Principles of Human-centric AI'. Under these principles, the AI Research and Development Principles and the AI Utilisation Principles were developed. It is meaningless to produce such principles unless they are actually used. They must serve as the standard reference when a Japanese company develops AI and provides AI-based products or services. The approach is the same in Europe, where the term 'AI ecosystem' is often talked about.[2]

To think about this point, let us consider the anecdote of 'Misora Hibari revived by AI'. In 2019, NHK, Japan's public broadcasting entity, aired a programme titled 'Reviving Misora Hibari by AI'. 'AI Misora Hibari' also appeared in that year's *Kohaku Uta Gassen*, the annual TV music show on New Year's Eve. Misora Hibari was a pop singer, a great star of the post-war era. Making her debut as a girl

[2] See Souichirou Kozuka, 'A Governance Framework for the Development and Use of Artificial Intelligence: Lessons from the Comparison of Japanese and European Initiatives' [2019] Uniform Law Review 315.

prodigy a few years after the devastating defeat of Japan in World War II, she was an extremely popular singer from the 1950s to the 1980s. She passed away in 1989, the same year as the Showa era ended. To mark the 30th anniversary of her death, a project was organised to use AI to create music that Misora Hibari would have sung if she were alive in 2019.

The project itself is remarkably interesting. But when the music was aired on the New Year Eve's show, a famous artist said, 'It is blasphemy against Misora Hibari to air something like that. It is just unacceptable.'

While there may be pros and cons, I am interested in how the governance worked that led to 'Misora Hibari revived by AI'. I am curious about who had the final decision-making power, who was responsible and whether the governance was properly organised at all. The NHK reported that they had consulted various people and made decisions together. It is reported that the members of Misora Hibari's fan club, who visit her tomb every year, Misora Hibari's son and Yasushi Akimoto, who wrote lyrics for Misora Hibari and also wrote lyrics for this project were consulted. At several points in the process, they said, 'This still does not sound like Misora Hibari' or 'Now it sounds very close to Misora Hibari.' It is claimed that each of them listened to the final version of the song produced by AI and gave their consent. I would argue, however, that if everyone decides together, then no one really took responsibility and no proper governance was in place.

## GIVING THE AI PRINCIPLES THEIR APPROPRIATE PLACE

**Kozuka:** Defective governance such as in 'Misora Hibari revived by AI' should not happen. The AI Principles need to be properly placed in the context of corporate governance. The sociologist Albert Hirschman[3] argued that there are three ways of making decisions in a group: exit, voice and loyalty. Loyalty means following the decision taken elsewhere without complaining, while exit means that those who disagree leave the group. In between, there is voice, under which one expresses one's opinion, effectively saying 'no, that's not right'.

If people conclude that a certain AI product is not appropriate, it will not sell and will eventually disappear from the market. This is the mechanism referred to as 'exit'. Under the 'loyalty' approach, a law is enacted and compliance with a certain set of rules is required. The AI Principles developed for Japan rely on this approach. The AI Principles as a whole, however, are not based on law. The idea is rather to uphold the ideal of human-centred AI[4] and collaborate with countries that share the

[3] Albert O Hirschman, *Exit, Voice, and Loyalty: Responses to Decline in Forms, Organizations, and States* (Harvard University Press 1970).

[4] The terms 'human-centred' or 'human-centric' in the AI Principles mean that AI must be used as a tool to enrich human society, rather than AI controlling humans. There was the same concern a century ago about modern machines ending up controlling human life, as depicted in the famous movie '*Modern Times*' directed by Charles Chaplin. This idea is widely

same ideal, such as the UK and Germany. In this way, we pursue the 'human-centred' ideal in a way that is different from prescribing legal rules. If this is the case, then companies should decide to implement these principles as a matter of corporate governance, and then appeal to consumers to use products that respect the AI Principles – rather than those that do not. This means that companies can claim that their product is based on the idea of a human-centred society in the expectation that customers will buy it even though it is a little more expensive than competing products.[5]

Where shall such AI governance be located in the context of the corporate governance issues discussed by Professor Sasaki? If the rules are determined by law, then the issue is compliance. Currently, we do not know how those parts of the AI Principles that do more than just restate the law are treated in corporate governance. Japanese companies tend to lump together all unfamiliar issues and label them as corporate social responsibility (CSR), meaning that they are socially demanded, but not legally. Every listed company has a CSR page on its website, where many of these unfamiliar issues are addressed. However, as Professor Sasaki mentioned earlier, the term 'ESG' has become increasingly important in the last few years.

Simply put, the basis of the ESG argument is that it is not enough to pursue only the interests of shareholders. However, the situation in Japan is a little different from that in other countries. Japanese companies have not always been dominated by shareholder interests. The corporate governance reforms in Japan that began around 2010 were rather the opposite of those in Western countries. The reforms required companies to think about the interests of their shareholders. Since ESG emerged in this context, some corporate managers said that the traditional Japanese way of considering stakeholders' interests was right and that the primacy of shareholders' interests was not the way to go.

As argued in the UK and other countries, companies pursue the interests of shareholders. But the shareholders' interests should be enlightened ones, i.e. interests that the insightful shareholder pursues, not just the greed-driven shareholder interest in making money. In the UK and France, directors have responsibilities to take into account social issues, such as not buying materials from suppliers whose employees are working under conditions equivalent to slavery and to consider the effects of their activities on the environment.

accepted, as seen in the Second Law of Robotics in Isaac Asimov's *I, Robot* prescribing: 'A robot must obey the orders given to it by human beings . . .'. By the way, in the context of ecology, anthropocentrism is criticised as subjecting the natural environment to the benefits of human beings and affirming the remodelling of nature. The relationship of being human-centred and anthropocentric has not been fully explored. Issues such as whether a 'strong AI' (humanoid) should be considered human and whether the conservation of nature shall ultimately be for the sake of enriching human society or for its own sake are yet to be fully examined.

5 Souichirou Kozuka, 'Corporate Governance for the Responsible Use of AI' (2022) *ECGI Blog*, <https://ecgi.global/blog/corporate-governance-responsible-use-ai>, accessed 1 November 2023.

I would argue that the same is true for the principle that AI must be used to create a human-centred society and that an AI's decision must be based on proper data, with consideration for privacy and security and not be discriminatory. This approach fits neatly with general corporate governance principles.

## TO WHAT EXTENT ARE COMPANIES BEING HELD RESPONSIBLE?

**Kozuka:** Besides discussing technological innovation in the context of corporate governance, we need to look beyond it. As already discussed, in Europe (and elsewhere) it is not enough to address social problems only in your company. Subcontractors of your company should not be tainted, either. Suppliers in the so-called supply chain, those who provide raw materials and components, must also be examined. As far as AI is concerned, business partners who develop datasets and programmes must also adhere to the AI Principles. Suppose that a large, well-known company intends to create an AI product and contracts with a small AI company to write an algorithm. The former company must stipulate in the contract that the AI Principles must be adhered to. This will probably lead to a significant change in the way contracts are drafted in Japan. The contracts will come to include the rules to make the counterparty adhere to the AI Principles, threatening termination for non-compliance and on-site inspections for supervision. Therefore, the discussions of corporate governance in the age of AI extend to discussions of the governance of contractual relationships, including the supply chain. In fact, there is the idea that the company itself is actually a nexus of contracts. If that is the case, it is no surprise that the governance of contractual relationships can be considered as an extension of corporate governance.

Ultimately, both the issues of seals and digital signatures and of the AI Principles share the same theme: organisations go through transformation when technology develops. For organisations, which includes companies as organisations in a narrow sense and contractual relationships as organisations in a broad sense, issues that fall under the 'S' of ESG emerge. It is important to understand the AI Principles as a manifestation of sustainability. Doing so enables us to continue to build and develop the same kind of society we have maintained before the era of AI. I believe this is the ultimate functional equivalence to be pursued in the AI era. Thank you for your attention.

**Steffek:** Thank you very much. I very much enjoyed this presentation. You raised the very interesting question of functional equivalence. You looked at how technology may be a functional equivalent of the things that we have done before in another way. You talked about e-signatures and seals, but then you moved on to consider how technology may change goods and services. As regards goods and services, it may not be a functional equivalent, but it may be something new that technology brings. Based on your analysis, I wondered whether technology will also change the organisation of firms and companies. Nobel Prize winner Ronald Coase, already many decades ago, taught us that companies are a reaction to transaction costs and the problems that we face in organising businesses by way of contract. So, if technology changes the way we cooperate and provides new ways of cooperation, then I think it could be quite interesting to think about how the original analysis of Ronald Coase in the 1930s will be transformed today. This is related to Professor Sasaki's idea that there will be more democratisation. Perhaps companies and businesses will become less hierarchical because technology allows more decentralised decision-making processes. Ronald Coase has explained the existence of companies based on the idea that the hierarchical form of organising business is a solution to the transaction costs burdening contracts. So, people, instead of organising their business based on contracts, form companies in order to use hierarchical structures to organise the production of goods and services. But if technology facilitates better cooperation, then maybe these hierarchical structures will not be necessary anymore and decentralised structures may be more efficient. That was just one thought I had, and I would be interested in your opinion.

Just to add a second thought: I very much agree with your emphasis on the human-centricity of AI because it helps us to use AI for the benefit of individuals and ensures that AI does not become more important than humans. Ethical guidelines for the use of AI are often, in practice, implemented by computer experts, programmers and coders. However, these addressees are not used to reading and engaging with such ethical guidelines. It is rather the lawyers who are used to working with such guidelines, while the coders are not. Coding and programming, however, are key for the creation of AI services. Hence, we need to think about the design of ethical guidelines for coders and programmers. They are doing the real work. Thank you very much again for your excellent presentation.

## AI PRINCIPLES IN JAPAN

**Sumida:** Thank you. Regarding the first point, Professor Steffek has co-convened a conference on 'The Future of the Firm'. I am wondering if he was inspired by this work to consider the issue of business organisation. As to your second point, I think it was a message of encouragement for Mr Izumi from the Ministry of Economy, Trade and Industry, who will be speaking now. Mr Takuya Izumi, Director for Information Policy Planning, Commerce and Information at the Policy Bureau of the Ministry of Economy, Trade and Industry will give a presentation on 'The State of AI Governance in Japan'. Thank you very much for your contribution.

**Izumi:** Thank you for the introduction, Professor Sumida. My name is Takuya Izumi from the Ministry of Economy, Trade and Industry. I would like to invite you to join me today for a short time to consider 'AI Governance in Japan'. AI governance is an issue for which we are still searching for the right answers, and I hope to think about these answers together with you. The content I am going to talk about has been analysed by the Ministry of Economy, Trade and Industry for a long time. Professor Sumida is also participating as an expert in this area.

● Towards the implementation of the **AI Principles**, study ideal **AI governance** in our country, including regulations, standardisation, guidelines and audits, which will contribute to enhancing our country's industrial competitiveness and social acceptance, while also taking into account domestic and international trends. CSTI, MIC and METI

(The Integrated Innovation Strategy 2020 & the AI Strategy 2019, revised based on follow-ups last year)

**AI Principles** = Social Principles of Human-centric AI (March 2019)

- Basic Philosophy
  Dignity: A society that has respect for human dignity
  Diversity & Inclusion: A society where people with diverse backgrounds can pursue their well-being
  Sustainability: A sustainable society
- Social Principles of Human-Centric AI
  1. Human-Centric, 2. Education/Literacy, 3. Privacy Protection, 4. Ensuring Security,
  5. Fair Competition, 6. Fairness, Accountability and Transparency, 7. Innovation

**AI Governance** (definition in the discussion of Expert Group)

- Design and operation of technological, organisational and social systems by stakeholders for the purpose of managing risks posed by the use of AI at levels acceptable to stakeholders and maximizing their positive impact.

FIGURE 5.2 Ideal approaches to AI governance

The government sets various targets every year. For example, the Integrated Innovation Strategy 2020 and the AI Strategy 2019 Follow-up set the following targets shown in Figure 5.2.

**Izumi:** Note specifically the overall goal: 'Towards the implementation of the AI Principles, we will study ideal AI governance in our country, including regulations, standardisation, guidelines and audits, which will contribute to enhancing our country's industrial competitiveness and social acceptance, while also taking into account domestic and international trends.'

After the sentence of the goal, CSTI, MIC and METI are listed – METI is the abbreviation for Ministry of Economy, Trade and Industry. This means that METI should work towards the goal. I think that the goal has two key elements: the AI Social Principles, which Professor Kozuka touched on somewhat earlier, and AI governance. I would like to invite you all to think about these two areas together.

## LAWS FAIL TO CATCH UP WITH REALITY

**Izumi:** Japan's AI Social Principles are contained in the document 'Social Principles of Human-Centric AI', which was published in March 2019. The document sets out three basic principles and seven social principles. The three basic principles are: (i) a society where human dignity is respected; (ii) a society where people from diverse backgrounds can pursue diverse happiness; and (iii) a sustainable society. The seven social principles are human-centricity; education and literacy; privacy; security; fair competition; fairness, accountability and transparency; and innovation. It is important to put these into practice.

Why is AI governance raised as a separate issue? There are problems that cannot be solved by the AI Social Principles alone. The AI Social Principles were developed because AI, while a very useful technology, can also have a negative impact on society. The goal of the AI Social Principles is to control such negative effects and to use AI beneficially. How to put this into practice is the challenge of AI governance. The METI study group defines 'AI governance' as 'the design and operation of technical, organisational and social systems by stakeholders with the aim of maximising the positive impact of the use of AI while managing risks arising from its use at a level acceptable to stakeholders'. Simply put, the government's stated goal is to consider the design and operation of such systems in order to put the AI Social Principles into practice.

What is difficult is the design of AI governance itself. The challenge is that the law cannot keep up with the speed of technological development and the complexity of society. The standard of AI technology is evolving day by day. Depending on the design of AI systems, there are many possible applications. Depending on each specific application, the characteristics and magnitude of the risks will vary. How to control and govern all of this is a difficult challenge.

## COMPLEXITY OF AI BIAS ISSUES

**Izumi:** Let us take the application of AI in the job selection process as an example that you may be familiar with and interested in. Amazon in the United States developed a system that uses machine learning to screen CVs and rank them on a five-point scale. When Amazon tried using it for selection, they discovered that it disadvantaged women for certain jobs. If you have been reading articles on AI governance, you may be familiar with this case study. The news spread quickly and the mistake was widely recognised as a bias issue. Job hunting is an especially important process for young people, so it is absolutely essential to avoid situations where they are disadvantaged by bias.

On the other hand, it has been suggested that the use of AI in the selection process may have eliminated unconscious bias. For example, in the book *Freakonomics*, which became a topic of conversation about ten years ago, a case study was reported in which the content of a CV was the same, only the name was changed to indicate a white applicant and a black applicant. These CVs were then sent to a number of companies. The case study found that white applicants were more likely to be called for an interview. This suggests that unconscious bias may be present on the human side and that AI could be used in the selection process to eliminate unconscious bias in people.

Just considering the bias issues shows that AI governance is not an easy issue to solve. There are other relevant insights to digest. I found an interesting article in the Harvard Business Review, stating that AI holds the greatest promise for eliminating bias in hiring for two reasons. It can eliminate unconscious human bias, and it can assess the entire pipeline of candidates.[6] An IEEE paper states that in recent years, computer scientists have constructed fair clustering algorithms to counteract bias. A novel approach described in a paper handles multiple factors simultaneously.[7] We are required to address the issue of bias. And we believe this is part of the AI governance challenge.

### GOVERNANCE INNOVATION: FROM RULE-BASED TO GOAL-BASED

**Izumi:** How, then, should the problem of laws not being able to keep up with the speed of technology and the complexity of social change be solved? A suggestion is made in the METI's report 'Government Innovation: Redesigning Law and Architecture for Society 5.0', which Professor Sasaki referred to earlier.[8] The report points out that it is preferable for laws and regulations to be goal-based, indicating the values ultimately to be achieved, rather than rule-based, i.e. including detailed behavioural regulations. It also points out that when goal-based regulations are introduced, a gap arises between the regulations and the company's operations, and therefore it is necessary to develop non-binding guidelines to help the operators achieve the goals. The same problem of a gap between regulation and operations exists in AI governance, so we believe that providing some guidelines may be a solution.

Those attending Professor Sumida's class may feel that perhaps goal-based regulation sounds similar to the Corporate Governance Code. The goal-based approach is similar to the principle-based approach of corporate governance codes. We believe that AI governance should be well integrated into corporate governance, guided by the implications of governance innovation, as Professor Kozuka mentioned earlier. For example, the reference material for the Corporate Governance Code states that 'the Code does not adopt a rule-based approach, in which the actions to be taken by companies are specified in detail. Rather, it adopts a principle-based approach so as to achieve effective corporate governance in accordance with each company's particular situation.' In his book *Preventing Corporate Scandals*, Mr Tadashi Kunihiro states that in today's rapidly changing world, rules cannot keep up with changes in society and that, in short, what stakeholders are looking at is not rule-based, but rather the principle-based question of is this company honest?[9] The book is not directed at the AI issue, but the analysis that in today's rapidly changing society, rules cannot keep up with society might have been said with AI in mind.

6 See <https://hbr.org/2019/10/using-ai-to-eliminate-bias-from-hiring>, accessed 1 November 2023.

7 See <https://spectrum.ieee.org/algorithm-groups-people-more-fairly-reduce-ai-bias>, accessed 1 November 2023.

8 See <https://www.japan.go.jp/publications/news/2020-08-08_401.html>, accessed 1 November 2023.

9 Tadashi Kunihiro, *Preventing Corporate Scandals* (Nikkei Publishing Inc. 2019).

## LEARNING FROM THE WISDOM OF PREDECESSORS

**Izumi:** This is a little off-topic, but Emeritus Professor Iwao Nakatani of Hitotsubashi University cited a book entitled 'Physics and Beyond' written by Werner Heisenberg, the father of quantum mechanics and winner of the Nobel Prize in Physics, in a 2001 Nikkei newspaper column entitled 'The Art of Reading Half a Step Behind'. The relevant part reads:

> [O]nly those revolutions in science will prove fruitful and beneficial whose instigators try to change as little as possible and limit themselves to the solution of a particular and clearly defined problem. Any attempt to make a clean sweep of everything or to change things quite arbitrarily leads to utter confusion. In science only a crazed fanatic – for instance, the kind of man who maintains that he can invent a perpetual-motion machine – would try to overthrow everything, and, needless to say, all such attempts are completely useless.[10]

As I have a science background, I like this passage.

When we talk about AI, there is inevitably a special atmosphere and an air of needing to do something new. Just as Heisenberg's achievements in quantum mechanics rewrote only the physics of the micro-world, but not the Newtonian mechanics of everyday life, it seems to me that the emergence of AI does not negate most of the arguments on governance that have been made, but that we need to make good use of the wisdom of our predecessors, including corporate governance knowledge, to develop AI governance principles. Not only corporate governance but also, for example, privacy issues have been considered previously. I think the right direction is to manage AI to align with such existing knowledge. More to the point, the AI Principles are being shared globally. The elements of the AI Principles, such as fairness, transparency and accountability, are generally shared by all developed countries. Hence, it makes good sense to refer to insights and examples from other countries.

## WHAT IS A FUSION APPROACH THAT FITS OPERATIONAL REALITY?

**Izumi:** The Ministry of Economy, Trade and Industry defines two approaches to AI governance: one is the explanatory approach. The Ethics Guidelines for Trustworthy AI, compiled by European experts, have an accompanying checklist, which provides explanations, for example, on what transparency means and how to meet transparency requirements. However, no integration with corporate governance is considered.

The other approach is referred to as the fusion approach. METI believes that this is preferable. For example, the UK guideline 'Explaining Decisions Made with AI'

[10] Werner Heisenberg and Arnold J Pomerans (tr), *Physics and Beyond: Encounters and Conversations* (George Allen & Unwin 1971) p. 148.

provides guidance on what data protection officers, compliance officers, technology departments, senior management departments, etc. should be doing. This is easier to integrate into corporate governance. Another example is Singapore's 'Model AI Governance Framework'. For some reason, this one is better known in Japan. Instead of focusing on explaining the AI Principles, it is presented in such a way that it can be integrated into practice giving practical examples, such as internal governance structures and measures, determining the level of human involvement in AI-augmented decision-making, operations management as well as stakeholder interaction and communication. I believe that this direction is helpful.

Let us return to the government's objectives, which I mentioned at the beginning. The Ministry of Economy, Trade and Industry was asked to think about ideal AI governance in our country. We are in the process of putting it together right now, with the help of Professor Sumida and other experts. If you would like to know more, please see the report that will be published in due course. We plan to publish it in English at the same time, so we hope that people from overseas will read it too.[11]

## WHY WE CREATE A UNIQUE GOVERNANCE SYSTEM IN JAPAN

**Izumi:** To overcome the problem of laws failing to keep up with the speed and complexity of society, we should aim for goal-based AI governance. Fortunately, we already have those goals in the Social Principles of Human-Centric AI. The question then becomes how we can achieve the goal of human-centric AI. This concerns the gap between regulation and operations, which I have mentioned earlier. To solve this problem, we should create non-binding governance guidelines for companies. We should be aware of the interactions with corporate governance and integrate AI guidelines well into corporate practice.

You might think that we should just take examples from the UK or Singapore, but it is not that simple, as each country has its own strengths and weaknesses. For reference, let's look at the example of Singapore. At the end of Singapore's Model AI Governance Framework, the names of cooperating companies are listed: Apple, Facebook, Google, Microsoft, IBM, Salesforce, AIG, Mastercard, etc. There are no names of Japanese companies. The names of so-called GAFA tech giants dominate the list, which leads us to speculate that the guidelines may be specific to such businesses and may have been designed to successfully absorb the risks of a particular industry.

[11] The Ministry of Economy, Trade and Industry held meetings with the Expert Group on Architecture for AI Principles to be Practiced and published 'AI Governance in Japan Ver. 1.0' on 15 January 2021, inviting public comments. The Ministry of Economy, Trade and Industry, taking the public comments into account, continued the discussion with the Expert Group and published 'AI Governance in Japan Ver. 1.1' and 'Governance Guidelines for Implementation of AI Principles Ver. 1.0' on 9 July 2021, inviting public comments on the guidelines. Finally, 'Governance Guidelines for Implementation of AI Principles Ver. 1.1' was published on 28 January 2022. All reports and guidelines are available in English at <www.meti.go.jp/shingikai/mono_info_service/ai_shakai_jisso/index.html>, accessed 1 November 2023.

It has been pointed out that in Japan, the strength lies in OT, Operational Technology, rather than IT, Information Technology. The areas of application of AI may be different and the risks we face may be different. We hope to support companies by creating governance guidelines that carefully delve into these areas and can be successfully integrated into corporate governance.

After providing governance guidelines, there are still issues to be considered. The guidelines are non-binding, so after the guidelines are created, it is important to encourage companies to use them. Various ideas have been proposed on incentives to encourage use, such as a slight increase in points for complying with these guidelines in government procurement. As Japanese AI technologies and products go out into the world, we would like to continue our discussions so that we can lead the world in a direction that maximises social benefits while minimising risks. We hope that today's talk has provided you with an opportunity to consider AI governance. Thank you very much.

**Sumida:** Thank you very much, Mr Izumi, for your invaluable presentation. Let me start with the panellist, Professor Kozuka, who is an expert on the subject matter. Professor Kozuka, would you like to comment?

**Kozuka:** Many thanks. I would like to connect this with the issues Professor Steffek has raised earlier. Ronald Coase, who Professor Steffek mentioned, was an economist well-known already before World War II. He posed a question about why corporations exist and why they do not procure all products and services on the market through contracts. He suggested that a corporation exists when it is less costly to trade in the form of an organisation rather than trade in the market, a phenomenon which people later called transaction costs. In the 1980s, it was suggested that transaction costs are in fact largely caused by information problems, such as having only insufficient information to make decisions for the transaction or an information gap between the parties. This has been developed in the field of information economics. I think this is very relevant in the age of AI. It is almost impossible for people to get all the information they need, and at some stage, they have to decide what action to take. When making that decision, if AI analyses more data than a person can and shows some suggestions, it may be useful in overcoming the information problem. Conversely, the AI may draw a person into an inappropriate decision and adversely affect human behaviour. In the latter case, how to correct errors so that the benefits of overcoming information problems prevail becomes the issue. This is where the topic of AI governance comes in.

Mr Izumi emphasised 'goal-based' policymaking, which is also very suitable for AI. We cannot identify each factor behind a decision, pointing to the data that was determinative in a certain decision, because the process of AI reaching a conclusion is a black box. On the other hand, we cannot accept that data causes discrimination and prejudice as a result of AI decision-making. So, what we need to do is to create a system, the governance structure, which does not allow this to happen. Thus, the whole story is important, from the great economist before the War to the most recent report that will be published tomorrow.

**Sumida:** Thank you. Professor Sasaki, would you like to comment?

**Sasaki:** Yes, thank you. Firstly, when talking about governance, my presentation was more about the state of governance in organisations, companies and financial institutions. However, both Mr Izumi and Professor Kozuka talked about the state of rules and norms in the world as a whole, including AI, and what the governance of individual companies, organisations and financial institutions should be. This perspective focuses on the way society as a whole should be governed and the goal-based approach of Society 5.0. Therefore, my first point is that the discussion has gone beyond conventional corporate governance and is now about the governance of society as a whole, not just in Japan but in the world as a whole.

## WHAT WILL YOU DO WITH AI?

**Sasaki:** My second point is that whether we talk about innovation or DX, they are only the tools or means, and what you ultimately do and realise with them is important. What is the purpose of what we do? AI is ultimately a tool, so the people who use it, how they use it to improve the world and one of the Ss, 'Social', are becoming increasingly important.

Law is ultimately a tool, too. As Professor Kozuka said, we must use the law as a tool to change and improve society. People should not be used by the law. People should use the law to make the world a better place. That is the basic premise. For students who, in particular, study law, it is important to be well aware of the technical details, such as what statutory rules say or what the past precedents are, but it is also important to be well aware of the purpose of the law. The discussion today has made this truly clear.

**Sumida:** Thank you. Are there any students who would like to ask a question?

**Student A:** I would like to ask Professor Kozuka. This is a bit of a departure from the topic, but I saw in a presentation by the Ministry of Internal Affairs and Communications that you wrote about AI developments that ignore social values, and I would be very interested to know what exactly you mean by that.

**Kozuka:** For example, if there is a country where there is a severe ethnic conflict, it is conceivable that a facial recognition AI that identifies one of the ethnic groups is used by the dictator who supports the other ethnic group. There is a possibility that some of the managers of the companies who are approached to develop such a recognition system might think that this is an effective way to make money. We have to prevent such decisions.

Another current problem is AI weapons. It is already a reality that drones equipped with AI are used for an attack with the command 'eliminate this terrorist stronghold'. Still, the weapons currently used are 'semi-autonomous', i.e. weapons that are subject to human supervision. Lethal weapons fully operated by AI – so-called lethal autonomous weapon systems (LAWS) – have not yet been developed. It is argued that the development and use of fully autonomous AI weapons should be banned.[12]

At the very least, Japanese companies should not be engaged in the development of AI involving such conflicts. I also believe that we must expand the coalition around the world to prevent such production from happening.

**Sumida:** Thank you – we have time for one more question.

## BEATING AI BY ANTICIPATING ESSENTIAL ISSUES

**Student B:** I have a question for Professor Sasaki. You mentioned that companies will be able to carry out audits on their own, but in that case, what kind of mechanisms can be considered to ensure that the audits are appropriate?

**Sasaki:** Thank you for your question. This is slightly different from the current discussion on AI. In the first place, there are accounting audits and inspections by the authorities to ensure that a company's financial statements are correct. At that time, there are standards for determining whether they are correct, which may be laws or auditing standards. The problem is that simply determining whether they are correct in accordance with those standards is no longer sufficient.

As Mr Izumi explained, the rules are not keeping up with the changes in the world. It is no longer possible to audit in the conventional compliance way, where the audit is to check whether the rules and standards are being met.

What are we going to do in the future? One idea is, as I told you today, to think about governance without rules. If we wait for rules, we will not be able to catch up. Of course, it is not right to have no rules, but as Mr Izumi explained earlier, instead of the government regulating in the form of laws, as has been the case in the past, it is better to provide a goal-based, principle-based direction and leave it to proactive initiatives to decide how to put it into practice. However, principles alone will not be enough to determine whether they are being followed or not. How can this be ensured? This is an exceedingly difficult question.

One thing I have in mind is that auditing is a job that requires looking at many different things. I used the term 'forward-looking' earlier. We look at many things, not just one company or one department. In this way, we can see issues that are common to many things that cannot be seen by looking at specific things individually. I refer to this as, 'from micro to macro'. It is possible to abstract from the individual stories and to understand common implications. This kind of capability is a feature that AI cannot have. AI is good at analysing past data and predicting the future. Human judgement in this area is extremely important.

Therefore, in legal education, after memorising past precedents and statutory rules, we need to think about future issues, about the common issues in the legal system that

[12] 新保史生「自律型致死兵器システム(LAWS)に関するロボット法からの考察」IEICE ESS Fundamentals Review１３巻３号〔２０２０〕２１７頁。

emerge and what issues exist in fields other than law. It is about predicting these issues, abstracting from the micro to the macro and finding common implications, and then connecting that to the next agenda setting. These are the kinds of capabilities that AI cannot replace. Even in an age without rules, this will be something that can assert the *raison d'être* of auditing. It is a difficult problem to solve.

**Sumida:** Thank you very much. Finally, Felix, is there anything else?

**Steffek:** Thank you – very briefly. I agree with what Professor Sasaki, Counsellor Izumi and Professor Kozuka have said. I would like to make an attempt at bringing it together. What is the goal? I would say it all starts with the people and their interests. Technology and law should aim at helping people to fulfil their interests, but also to help people to find solutions where their interests collide. So, that would be my answer. I would like to leave it there, but of course, we could discuss this for a full day. I found your comments and presentations very inspirational. Thank you.

**Sumida:** We have indeed had a very productive session today. With that, I would like to close today's fifth session.

## CONCLUDING CONVERSATION

**Sumida:** Professor Kiyotaka Sasaki, Visiting Professor at Hitotsubashi University's Graduate School of Business Administration, spoke about the nature of corporate governance reform and how it is being transformed through the evolution of technology and the COVID crisis. He based his comments on his experience of leading inspection and supervisory reform at the FSA. Without using the technical terms of the many laws and regulations, he explained what many corporate governance reforms have tried to achieve and what he considers to be the keys to achieving reform in the future. It was as if we had a compass and a chart in our hands. For example, given that the COVID crisis is different from previous financial crises, the vectors of change are also different. Given the severity of the crisis, including the fragmentation of society, he emphasised the importance of ESG in creating corporate value and the need to revise our understanding of ESG.

The discussion went well beyond the topic of technology enabling real-time audits and improving corporate governance. We heard that there is a possibility for the first and second of the Three Lines of Defence to merge. It could even become a service provided by a platform. We also discussed that forward-looking auditing is necessary for the third to keep its relevance. In this context, we have also heard about the significant role of human thinking to be involved. This is a very concrete way of looking at the world. At the same time, this is an argument that has the potential to revolutionise the way we think about compliance, auditing and corporate governance. I was overwhelmed by its persuasiveness.

**Steffek:** I found Professor Sasaki's approach very interesting. He distinguished between internal corporate governance and external corporate governance and discussed the impact of technology on both sides. He predicted major changes in both areas and linked them to the 'Five Ds': data, decentralisation, diversification, democratisation and disruption. I very much agree that these five aspects will drive innovation in corporate governance. In the discussion, I had raised the question of whether we needed to add another 'D' for 'design'. I had in mind the question of whether corporations and their counterparties will more and more use technology to design their relationships on the basis of live information and predictions based on AI. This would lead to better-informed contracts and to fewer surprises later. In other words, corporate governance would suffer less from informational constraints and would become less conflict-prone.

**Sumida:** The question from the students at the end of the session sounded like the voice of a person in the field who is confused about how to take charge of governance in the age of AI (laughs). Professor Sasaki talked about forward-looking decisions, a particularly critical issue for legal innovators. He also advised us not to form silos and to zoom out from time to time. We had planned this conversation series so that the students would be encouraged to become legal innovators. I am happy that this has worked out.

**Steffek:** Then Souichiro Kozuka, professor at Gakushuin University, spoke on the implementation of advanced technology in businesses and the effects on corporate governance. I found his approach especially useful under which he concentrated on 'functional equivalence'. With functional equivalence, he had in mind whether modern technologies replaced the function of an older approach to doing something. As an example, he mentioned the replacement of physical seals (stamps) by e-signatures, which had been allowed by statute in Japan from about two decades ago. Against this background, he asked what tasks advanced technologies will replace in businesses and what this means for corporate governance.

**Sumida:** I took Professor Kozuka's analysis as shedding light from a different angle on the structural problems faced by Japan's large companies, which Hiroto Koda had clearly and unambiguously highlighted in the first session. However, for me, the reason why Professor Kozuka introduced the concept of 'functional equivalence' and summed up his talk with this concept, including his vision for the future, was not quite clear. It seems to me that it is a concept for a rather static comparison. I was wondering if it is a concept that should be used when discussing dynamic processes where creative destruction occurs, which is what Professor Sasaki refers to in the last D, disruption. This is a topic I would love to discuss if I have the chance.

The topic of 'de-stamping' was indeed a symbolic topic of digitalisation in our country. Electronic signatures were legislated about twenty years ago, but the practice of physical stamping persisted. During the pandemic, the problem of having to come to work just to stamp a document was exposed and became a social problem. De-stamping society has been an important topic in Japan since the start of the pandemic. This example shows why digitalisation in Japan has been delayed. What was your impression of the differences in stance between the guests on this point?

**Steffek:** I think both approaches, i.e. an approach where one tries to understand what functions technology has and an approach where one tries to understand the changes and disruption caused by technology, can be useful. The first – functional – approach helps to understand what technology does at a task level. The second – dynamic – approach helps to see changes over time. Against this background, I would like to ask whether technology will only replace existing functions or whether technology will also transform businesses more fundamentally? A further question I would like to raise is what effect the changing environment will have on corporate governance. It is not only businesses themselves that are affected by modern technology. Technology also transforms societies, the ways people live and the ways they do business. Will this also affect corporate governance?

**Sumida:** We discussed the 'AI Misora Hibari' case. Japan is home to some of the world's leading android researchers and robot theatre directors. They have created androids of famous Japanese writers and actors to perform in robot plays. This has raised provocative questions such as: who has the right to bring great people back to life? Are there any limits to what can be shown in an android theatre? Is there a need for 'Fundamental Android Principles'.[13]

Data remains beyond life, and rights over data are still an unexplored area for the law. In the discussion, it seemed to me that the only viable option for norms is to be principle-based because reality overtakes the rules.

**Steffek:** The final speaker of this session was Takuya Izumi, Director of the Information, Policy Planning and Coordination Division at the METI. He presented the White Paper on AI Governance. In the meantime, METI has published the final report on 'AI Governance in Japan'.[14] A core principle of the AI governance approach presented by Director Izumi is a human-centric approach. He emphasised that good AI governance contributes to businesses solving people's problems. I could not agree more. Business models that are based on solving real problems that people have will be sustainable. And vice versa, pushing products and services into the market even though people ultimately do not need them will not be sustainable in the long run. Another perspective on this is to ask what the interests of people are. The interests of people are the flip side of their problems. In this sense, the principle that is at the core of METI's approach to regulating AI is in good company. The OECD, for example, takes a remarkably similar design approach when recommending, for example, that laws and dispute resolution should follow a people-centric design.

[13] Natsume Soseki (ed), Basic Principles of Androids: Who Has the Right to Bring Soseki Back to Life? (Nikkan Kogyo Shinbunsya 2019, in Japanese); see also <https://robotstart.info/2019/02/26/suseki-android-symposium.html>, accessed 1 November 2023.

[14] All reports and guidelines are available in English at <www.meti.go.jp/shingikai/mono_info_service/ai_shakai_jisso/index.html>, accessed 1 November 2023.

## QUESTIONS FOR FURTHER THOUGHT

- Will corporate governance become instantaneous in the sense that both internal and external governance can relate to data that is comprehensively up-to-date at the time decisions are taken?
- How will external corporate governance institutions, such as financial services authorities, have to change their practices if they can base their interventions on live data as opposed to historical data?
- Which role will AI play in corporate governance? Will we see self-driving corporations that are managed by AI only?
- How will technology change the internal organisation of businesses? Will they become less hierarchical?
- What will the effects of technology be on the size of corporations? Will corporations become bigger because technology enables them to minimise the cost of internal organisation? Or will they become smaller because technology facilitates cooperation with others by way of contract?
- How can lawmakers ensure that their regulatory principles are not only followed by the legal profession but also by the computing profession, which might be less used to reading laws and regulations?

# Conversation 6

## Innovation in Financial Services and Supervision

ABSTRACT

This conversation centres around innovation in the financial services sector and the related regulatory supervision. Three 'Techs' are especially relevant: FinTech, RegTech and SupTech. 'FinTech' combines the words 'financial' and 'technology' and refers to technological innovation in the delivery of financial services and products. 'RegTech' joins 'regulatory' and 'technology' and describes the use of technology by businesses to manage and comply with regulatory requirements. 'SupTech', finally, unites the words 'supervisory' and 'technology' to refer to the use of technology by supervisory authorities such as financial services authorities to perform their functions. Particular approaches presented in this session include regulatory sandboxes to promote innovative technology in the financial sector, automated data analysis, the collection and analysis of granular data, digital forensics and internet monitoring systems. The speakers also address collaboration between financial institutions and supervisory authorities, for example, in the creation of data collection formats and data sharing.

| | |
|---|---|
| *Speaker* | Norichika Ikeda |
| *Comments* | Kiyotaka Sasaki and Akira Nozaki |
| *Moderators* | Felix Steffek and Mihoko Sumida |
| *Concluding Conversation* | Felix Steffek and Mihoko Sumida |
| *Questions for Further Thought* | Felix Steffek |

### WHY THE FSA ENGAGES WITH INFORMATION TECHNOLOGY

**Sumida:** Today, we again have splendid guests and experts allowing us to hear from the cutting edge in financial services. Our first guest is Professor Ikeda, Project Professor at the University of Tokyo's School of Public Policy. After serving as an expert for the Japan International Cooperation Agency (JICA) dispatched to the State Bank of Vietnam he took the position of Director for Financial Markets Planning in the Financial Markets Division of the Planning and Coordination Bureau of the Financial Services Agency (FSA). Professor Ikeda joined the Financial Supervisory Agency – now the FSA – in 1999. In 2019, he became Director of the Asset Management Business Office in the Securities Business Division of the FSA Supervisory Bureau and assumed his current position in 2020. Now, without further ado, please welcome Professor Ikeda.

**Ikeda:** Thank you. Today, I would like to talk about the following three issues: (i) RegTech and SupTech, (ii) the FinTech Support Desk and FinTech Demonstration Hub and (iii) digital forensics and internet monitoring systems. I would like to start by talking about RegTech and SupTech, followed by an additional explanation of the other two issues, including my own personal experience.

You may have heard of FinTech, but you may not exactly know what RegTech and SupTech are. RegTech stands for Regulatory Technology, which allows private financial institutions to use information technology to efficiently comply with financial regulations imposed by the FSA. SupTech stands for Supervisory Technology, which is the opposite of RegTech on the private sector side and refers to information technology used by authorities such as the FSA and the Bank of Japan (BoJ) to make inspections and supervision more sophisticated and efficient. In short, RegTech is used by those who are regulated, while SupTech is used by those who supervise.

The FSA is now emphasising the need for RegTech and SupTech as a result of the Agency reviewing its inspections and supervision procedures. In the past, the FSA faced the 'bad loan problem'. After the loan bubble burst in the 1990s, it was not possible to recover loan monies in their entirety due to the insolvency of the borrower and the collapse of the price of real estate used as collateral. Since then, the monitoring of financial institutions has been centred on periodic inspections, such as once a year, once every two years, etc.

In the popular drama *Hanzawa Naoki*, Inspector Kurosaki walks into the bank saying something like 'it's been a while'. This is the very image of traditional monitoring. Recently, however, ensuring the banks' profitability has become more of an issue than detecting non-performing loans. It is no longer enough just to check for non-performing loans or to see if there are any suspicious borrowers, as has been the case in the past. In a nutshell, the banks are not making much money anymore. They have to do more to ensure their profitability. As a result, it is not enough to just look at where they are giving excessively risky loans. It is now necessary to understand and discuss whether the bank has a sustainable business model and whether it can remain profitable. If we want to have a substantive dialogue, we can no longer simply go to a bank every once in a while, have a look at some documents, and say, 'this company that you lent to is not doing very well' as Inspector Kurosaki does. It has become essential to collect and analyse more data on the operations of financial institutions.

Traditional monitoring is mainly operationalised by periodic inspections which come with the receipt of a lot of detailed data when on-site. Outside of the off-site monitoring period, the supervisory office regularly obtained basic data from the banks. We had a system in place to make sure that banks were submitting such basic data regularly, similar to periodic preventative health check-ups.

## HOW TO COLLECT DATA ON FINANCIAL INSTITUTIONS

**Ikeda:** To accurately ascertain the substance of the situation in the bank, information must be collected off-site on an ongoing basis, and, when necessary, more detailed and accurate data must be gathered on-site. There is continuous monitoring, on- and off-site, where those who work in the bank and those who work in the supervisory authority work together. The concept of continuous monitoring that we are talking about here does not only apply when the inspector is on-site. It also applies during the rest of the time, in cooperation with the off-site people in the authority. This approach requires a system that is suitable. For example, we have recently developed the ability to analyse Big Data. This enables us to process detailed information. We also need to build an 'ecosystem' of cooperation between the public and private sectors, so that the authorities and banks can work together on various aspects of supervision.

As digitalisation progresses and technology that can process detailed data is developed, there is a need to develop a system we call RPA – Robotic Process Automation. With this system, operations, tasks and responses that previously had to be carried out by humans can be carried out automatically using robots, AI and cloud computing. In particular cloud computing has led to digitalisation in the field of financial institutions and FSAs. At present, complex tasks cannot be automated yet, but simple laborious manual tasks in particular can be.

Yet another thing is the introduction of APIs – Application Programming Interfaces. This refers to the connection specifications and mechanisms for calling up and using the functions and data of one application via another application. By opening up APIs to other companies – open APIs – FinTech companies can access the bank's data from outside. This allows them to securely utilise the bank's data and provide services that would otherwise be unavailable.

In light of the introduction of information technology and digitalisation in the field of financial institutions and supervisory authorities coupled with the need for more sophisticated monitoring, this is the right time for the FSA to promote RegTech and SupTech. In order to make monitoring more sophisticated and efficient, it is essential to upgrade and improve the efficiency of data collection, storage and analysis. The introduction of SupTech is indispensable since SupTech and RegTech are practically inseparable.

In 2017, the FSA set out three initiatives highlighting its own digitalisation efforts: (i) centralisation of data requirements and system links with the Bank of Japan; (ii) utilisation of granular data; and (iii) automation of data analysis using RPA. The digitalisation of information from financial institutions and the evolution of the collection, storage and analysis of information received from financial institutions by the FSA means that, instead of authorities and financial institutions developing their own technology, both need to join hands and work together. The reasons for this will be explained later. The public and private sectors will cooperate in these three areas, starting with those that seem easiest to tackle. We aim to work towards practical implementation through experimentation.

## UNIFY FSA AND BOJ DATA

**Ikeda:** I will now explain the current status of the three initiatives, starting with the centralisation of data requirements and system links with the BoJ. In addition to the data collected by the FSA from financial institutions, there is also data collected by the BoJ from financial institutions. Some of the data collected by the BoJ overlaps with or is similar to data collected by the FSA from financial institutions. This similarity is a tricky thing. If there are duplicates, only one request for information is needed. However, similar means similar but slightly different, so financial institutions have to produce two sets of documents, one for the FSA and one for the BoJ, with similar but not identical content. It is costly to produce two similar but slightly different documents for two different destinations. In order to keep costs down, we should review the 'similar but slightly different' parts to see why they are different and unify them as much as possible. If we can make things consistent in this way, there is no duplication of efforts on the side of the regulators either. This means that we have to centralise such data collection as much as possible.

Once we have one set of data, the next step is to create a secure data-sharing mechanism between the FSA and the BoJ, so that we have a single point of reporting. That way, the reports that used to be sent to each of the FSA and the BOJ would only need to be sent to one of them. For example, if there is a mechanism whereby reports are sent to the BoJ and then automatically sent to the FSA as well, companies need not send them to two different places. We would expect this to be more efficient.

First, we started coordinating between the FSA and the BoJ to centralise similar data, and at this point, we have centralised two types of data. Of course, there is a mountain of 'similar data' and two is not enough at all, but it got us started with what we could do with regards to the centralisation of similar data. In fact, the FSA and the BoJ are continuing to discuss this kind of 'data sharing'. We have formed a task force including both parties and we are continuing to study the centralisation process. Currently, financial institutions still submit their reports to both the BoJ and the FSA, but we are considering merging this process.

## SHARING DETAILED DATA ON BORROWERS WITH THE FSA

**Ikeda:** The second initiative, 'utilisation of granular data', is developed against the background of monitoring extending to more detailed business models. It is no longer enough to use one-size-fits-all data. It will also be necessary to collect detailed background data, for example, not only on the number of loans but also on the type of people to whom loans are provided. When we received large amounts of such information in the past, the FSA was not able to digest it. So, we would say, 'we can't collect that kind of data'. Now digitalisation is in progress and the capacity of data processing has improved. Now there is room to analyse more detailed data. We have also started working with regional banks, in particular, to collect such detailed data.

Specifically, when the FSA and regional financial institutions engage in dialogue, we gain a detailed understanding of individual financial institutions' portfolios and their regional characteristics. Now, we do not only obtain figures on the number of loans but also solid data to understand the background, such as where the borrower is located, what type of business the borrower has, how big it is, what kind of creditors it has, etc. It is necessary to have detailed information about the borrowers.

In addition, together with the FSA collecting information from various financial institutions, the FSA sometimes gives feedback to the financial institutions, such as 'this is how your financial institution is doing'. If we provide high-quality feedback, the financial institution can realise that they are, perhaps, lacking in an area and that they need to strengthen this area. We want to get good quality information in order to give the financial institutions feedback of high value.

## 'NORMALISING DATA' TO REDUCE THE BURDEN ON BANKS

**Ikeda:** In order to make efficient use of data we also provide data to others who need the kind of data we have. Creditworthiness, for example, is the kind of data that we give to other organisations, such as credit bureaus. If there is a difference between the credit management datasets sent to the FSA and the datasets sent to credit bureaus, then companies will have to create two types of datasets, one for the FSA and one for credit bureaus. This creates unnecessary work and should be improved.

Some of the data includes 'unscheduled ad-hoc data'. The FSA receives such data when it asks financial institutions to 'give us as much information as they can by tomorrow'. This happens when there is a need for urgent information on something that has caught the agency's attention. Such urgent matters are irregular and different from normal business, so the burden on the financial institution to submit the information is quite high. In such a context, we need to ask: 'Can you submit the information in the first place? How long does it take to find out?' When I was supervising at the FSA, I used to ask my contacts at the financial institutions these questions. Reducing the burden on banks to submit their documents will be an issue that we need to consider intensely in the future.

Against this background, we selected a few regional banks and asked them, 'how much detailed ad-hoc data can you provide?' and 'how much effort will be required to create this data?' We have been considering measures to minimise the burden on the banks as much as possible so that they can provide the data as they have it in their system. Based on the results of such fact-finding, we will discuss how to obtain more detailed data in the future. When we obtain information on the competitive environment, e.g. supply chains and the state of financial intermediation, we need to conduct regional analyses reflecting regional differences. We need to understand the region, whether we are in a rural or urban area, or whether we are in a depopulated mountainous area with fewer branches than in an urban area. In rural areas deep in the mountains, the number of bank branches may be reduced, for example. If we manage to collect detailed data on industries and time series, we will be able to analyse the situation from various angles, such as how it is now and how it was in the past.

Until now, the FSA would regularly ask to submit data in a predefined format. Having the data in a format that suits the FSA's system is essential for system management on the FSA side. It is also useful in terms of comparing data of other banks. Obviously, the FSA data format is not convenient for everyone. In particular, the regional banks do not store the information in the format that the FSA prescribes. So, we decided to just ask the regional banks to submit the information in their own format. We call the associated process 'normalisation of data', which is the process of putting the data into a format that can be processed by the FSA's systems. Essentially, we ask the regional banks to submit the data saying, 'The FSA will normalise the data, so please just submit it as it is. If you don't, you will have to put every single piece of detailed information into the FSA format, which will require a mountain of work, so we ask you to just submit the information as you have it.'

In the process of verifying such granular data, we will need to know how much data can be collected and processed in the first place, what kind of feedback can be given based on the analysis, and how the data will actually be used.

## EFFECTIVE USE OF THE CORPORATE NUMBER

**Ikeda:** In addition, in the area of 'data utilisation', there is the utilisation of companies' 'My Number'. The corporate My Number – or simply, corporate number – is a 13-digit number. If you look it up on the internet, you can find out how many corporate numbers a company has. The Commercial Code stipulates that the same trade name cannot be used more than once in the same area. However, there is no problem if the company has the same name but a different type of business. This is why financial institutions are also required to check the corporate number.

The corporate number is also useful for financial institutions. When the FSA receives the data, it also includes such corporate numbers. This allows the FSA to link credit information to the corporate numbers. As a result, the FSA's information on the creditworthiness of the borrowers becomes more robust. The FSA can also use the corporate number to make various comparisons, such as Bank A lending at this rate but Bank B lending at a better rate. It is hoped that this will ultimately lead to more sophisticated credit management. If we can link corporate numbers, we can compare and contrast the credit systems of financial institutions and their systems for exercising their financial intermediary function.

Furthermore, in cases where lending information is provided by banks to different authorities, we will also start matching it with the data from such authorities, e.g. tax authorities. The aim is to have a single set of data that can be used to respond to requests from all sorts of authorities. We are now in the process of conducting experiments to enable more detailed information to be used in a variety of places.

## DETAILED DATA COLLECTED IS ORGANISED BY ALGORITHMS

**Ikeda:** The more granular and detailed the data collected this way, the more work is required on the part of the FSA to digest it. Furthermore, if each bank is allowed to use its own format in order to reduce the amount of work required on the submission side, the work involved in collecting and analysing this data on the FSA side becomes even more complicated. Hence, we are trying to reduce the workload of the people handling the data at the FSA. This is where the third of the three pillars, 'automation of data analysis' and the promotion of Robotic Process Automation (RPA), comes into play.

In the beginning, we spent less than 200 hours on RPA. As the years went by, the amount of time spent has increased rapidly. By having various tasks automated, the time spent requiring human input is reduced and the people who used to do that work can now focus on tasks that only a human can do. Unlike in the past, government offices are gradually becoming stricter as regards long hours of overtime work, a trend that RPA supports.

Until now, the person in charge had to download data from the government system by pressing a button, find the location of the folder and click again in order to save the data in the designated folder. Now, the system itself can download and store the data. There are about 100 Regional Banks and about 400 Credit Associations and Credit Cooperatives. So, downloading and so on for each item is a routine task, but a very laborious one.

Tasks such as emailing financial institutions, preparing documents and organising documents submitted by local financial bureaus and financial institutions are now automated at a rate of 96 per cent. In the past, all of these documents were manually stored in folders by young officials who worked very hard. Often, half a day would pass just taking care of these tasks. Thanks to automation, officials can now focus on analysing the documents created by RPA. Many of the automated tasks are still rather rudimentary. As more complex tasks can be taken over by computers, more time can be spent on human thinking and analysis. So, I think, it is necessary to continue to promote this approach in the future.

## FINANCIAL INSTITUTIONS AND AUTHORITIES WORK TOGETHER TO DEVELOP DATA SYSTEMS

**Ikeda:** If RegTech and SupTech are progressively promoted and digitalisation progresses, financial institutions will be able to utilise digitalised information and become data-driven in their management. Of course, the authorities must also become data-driven supervisors. At present, financial institutions have not progressed that far and are only collecting and accumulating digitised information or utilising it on a departmental basis. Financial institutions as a whole still have a long way to go. Some financial institutions are, for example, not using the corporate number.

Nevertheless, the FSA will continue to monitor the use of information by financial institutions, while making good use of digitalisation. As the level of digitalisation of financial institutions increases, the level of digitalisation of the FSA will also need to increase. However, if we follow the financial institutions' progress in using information and say, 'the financial institutions have made a lot of progress, so we will develop a data system too', then we need to be aware that it will take around three years to develop such a system. In the meantime, the systems of financial institutions will evolve. So, when the system we commissioned three years ago is finally completed, it may happen that the financial institutions are no longer using the systems we were working towards.

As Professor Sasaki will explain later, in order for financial institutions and the FSA to solve their respective problems in collecting, storing and utilising information, they need to work together to create an ecosystem in which they can simultaneously raise the level of RegTech and SupTech to a more advanced level. Without this, it is difficult to make progress. In short, the idea of a RegTech/SupTech ecosystem is for the financial institutions and the FSA to work together.

**Ikeda:** What kind of things must be in place for the ecosystem to work? First, effectiveness, which refers to improving the accuracy of monitoring. Secondly, efficiency, which, as mentioned many times, refers to the need to centralise data and correct discrepancies between similar datasets. Third, flexibility, such as the ability to respond properly to new technologies and the flexibility to deal with non-financial players. Fourth, timeliness, i.e. new information is immediately communicated to everyone concerned. Fifth, interactivity, means that it is not a one-way report from the financial institution to the authorities or from the authorities to the financial institution, but a conversation. Sixth, simplicity: a system that is simple and can be developed quickly in an agile way is better because a heavy system takes a long time to develop and when it is ready, it is already outdated and useless.

Even if the system is easy and flexible, it should not be vulnerable to information leaks. If the system is to include the BoJ, the Financial Services Agency and the financial institutions, it needs to be secure and confidential such that shared information is not leaked to anyone not involved. Based on this concept, and with clear goals in place, this public-private collaboration should be carried out.

## WHERE TO START IMPROVING EFFICIENCY

**Ikeda:** At the start of such changes, it is not possible to suddenly change everything at once. It is better to focus on a limited number of issues. Our policy is to start with small target areas and business categories and gradually expand the target areas and business categories where it is deemed appropriate. In the construction of this public-private ecosystem, we proceed from small to large areas in order to realise this concept in a responsible and sustainable way.

A specific area we are considering is 'data sharing through API collaboration'. This is often discussed in FinTech, where FinTech companies use bank data for their business. A similar mechanism could be used to submit bank data to government authorities. Connecting municipal offices and financial institutions via APIs, allows the municipal office to see new data as soon as a financial institution changes the data it has registered. This means that financial institutions no longer have to report every time they make a change in their own systems. They would automatically be able to complete the registration of the change. This would be very efficient, as the authorities would always be able to see the most recent and up-to-date data.

The reporting burden could also be reduced if questionnaires, etc., were conducted on platforms, or if Know Your Customer (KYC) and customer verification data could be used to improve credit decisions, for example. If customer data is used properly, it can add value to the risk management of financial institutions. If it can be shown that 'because the customer has this kind of characteristics, we can provide this kind of loan', then it would be good to experiment in this direction. This is what the FSA has in mind in the RegTech/SupTech area.

## TOWARDS INNOVATION WITH FINTECH

**Ikeda:** There are two more topics that I want to address. One is the FinTech Support Desk, and the other is the FinTech PoC (Proof of Concept) Hub. First, the FinTech Support Desk was established by the FSA in December 2015 as a central consultation and information exchange telephone point for FinTech. FinTech-related businesses sometimes offer new services that are very difficult to understand. Sometimes it is very difficult to understand what the business is in the first place, legally speaking. It may be difficult to determine which rules the service falls under in terms of current law, for example, whether it is related to the Banking Act, the Financial Instruments and Exchange Act or the Payment Services Act.

One-way consultations by email are usually not very clear, so we often have a direct hearing over the phone, where we can exchange views and give advice after a thorough dialogue. The FSA website also publishes FAQs on the most frequently asked questions since its launch. These FAQs are useful if you are thinking of engaging in related business and want to know more about the FSA's views, but are not active enough to make a phone call.

The FAQs include: 'How to register as a business', 'Relevant rules for transactions', 'I want to engage with cryptoassets', 'Open API and electronic payment agency businesses' and other areas closely related to FinTech companies, such as robo-advisors, electronic money and loyalty points as well as fund transfer business. The items related to crowdfunding – a method of fundraising in which the purpose of fundraising is set out and small investments are solicited from an unspecified number of people to achieve the goal – which is often seen on TV, and insurance products using technology such as InsurTech were among those for which many enquiries were received.

The second topic is the PoC Hub. In the governmental Growth Strategy 2017, which was approved by the Cabinet in June 2017, it was stated that steps should be taken to promote innovation in FinTech and that the FSA would take measures 'to facilitate demonstration experiments in the area of FinTech'. As part of the facilitation measures, the FinTech PoC Hub was established in September 2017 as a contact point for FinTech companies and financial institutions to dispel any hesitation they may have when conducting unprecedented experiments.

The PoC Hub provides ongoing support to FinTech firms and financial institutions in their experiments, particularly with regard to issues they wish to sort out, such as compliance and supervisory risks as well as practical issues relating to the interpretation of laws and regulations that may arise when providing services to the general public. The policy is to form teams within the Agency for each individual experiment and to provide ongoing support. We are currently dealing with some of these issues. In fact, I was in charge of one of these teams this month, just as I was in my previous position as an asset management business supervisor.

## IS THE PDF VERSION OF THE PROSPECTUS A PROBLEM ON A SMARTPHONE?

**Ikeda:** PDFs are optimised for paper, but nowadays, people are viewing them on their smartphones. However, unlike PCs, smartphone screens are small, so the paper version is very small and difficult to read. If you use HTML format instead of PDF, it is displayed at the optimum size and is easy to read when viewed on a smartphone. However, the screen is a little different from the paper version, and as you know, when you zoom in, the position of the line breaks in the text can be misaligned. If you ask me whether I prefer PDF or HTML, I would normally say that the one that is easier to read is better, so why not use HTML format. From the point of view of financial institutions, this can also be a problem. However, at the end of the day, it is better to have a large, easy-to-read format, so when we encourage them to switch to HTML, they are willing to carry out this kind of experiment.

In addition to the FSA, the BoJ has also established a FinTech Centre. It was set up within the Payment and Settlement Systems Department in April 2016. Governor Kuroda, in his speech on the opening of the FinTech Centre, said: 'To foster FinTech, communication among a wide range of players, including those affiliated with traditional finance industry and academic community, is required. [...] The Bank will also endeavour to play an active role as a catalyst for promoting interaction among financial practice and innovative technologies, research and study as well as the needs of the commercial society."[1] The FinTech Center has been very active overseas and in the academic world, organising FinTech forums, conducting joint research with the European Central Bank and contributing to and giving lectures on a wide range of topics.[2]

## DATA ERASURE AND POLICING

**Ikeda:** This brings us to the last topic, which is a little different from those discussed thus far, and that is policing. Digital forensics concerns the preservation of electromagnetic records stored on PCs and smartphones and their use as evidence. The FSA has a department called the Securities and Exchange Surveillance Commission (SESC), which investigates violations of the Financial Instruments and Exchange Law. This includes violations of disclosure rules such as insider trading, market manipulation and securities reports and requires specialised equipment and personnel. Specific systems are also put in place for financial inspections, in line with the efforts of the SESC. There was a scene in the *Naoki Hanzawa* drama in which the data on the internal network of a securities company was erased, and I thought while watching TV that if there was a real digital forensics team, they would have easily solved the case.

One typical activity that digital forensics teams engage in is copying electromagnetic records from electronic devices that have been secured in an investigation. In some cases, they can do things like restoring records that have been erased. The records are then viewed and searched by the investigator. In some cases, work is also carried out to secure the data in a suitable form so that it can be used as evidence in litigation or for other purposes in court or elsewhere.

Electronic devices are evolving. Smartphones are being used more and more, and equipment and software need to be constantly updated as various data technology innovations and forensic methods themselves are updated. As equipment and software are upgraded, the personnel who handle them also need to update their knowledge. It is necessary to train people internally or acquire them externally such that they know or can learn the latest technology. Having our people participate in training courses where they can learn cutting-edge technology can build up our knowledge as an organisation so that we are always able to use the most up-to-date equipment. I am not sure if this falls into the FSA's SupTech category, but this is what we do in terms of law enforcement using technology.

Another example is the Internet Patrol Monitoring System. The internet is full of all sorts of information about financial instruments, including so-called rumour spreading. This is spreading false information for the purpose of impacting the price of securities. Attempts are made to manipulate markets with stories such as 'there is a

1 Bank of Japan, Message from Governor Kuroda on the Occasion of the Establishment of the FinTech Center (1 April 2016) <www.boj.or.jp/en/paym/fintech/message.htm/>, accessed 1 November 2023.

2 For more information on the Centre's activities, see Bank of Japan, FinTech Center <www.boj.or.jp/en/paym/fintech/index.htm/>, accessed 1 November 2023.

person who is raising the price of certain shares'. The SESC constantly monitors the internet. The challenge is that such posts can easily be updated and deleted. As a result, the SESC has to flag social networking sites where such posts are made, storing the data and conducting searches to ensure that they are not missed or deleted. Even if you make a small post and then immediately delete it, there is a record of it, so we know who did it. We are looking at even small instances of false information to provide effective deterrence.

I could go on and on, but I think that's enough explanation, so I'll hand over to the moderators. Thank you very much.

**Sumida:** Thank you very much for explaining a wide range of very advanced topics from an insider's point of view in a way that was easy to understand. We will now have comments on Professor Ikeda's presentation. The first commentator is Professor Sasaki, who also appeared in the previous session. He graduated from the Faculty of Law at the University of Tokyo, joined the Ministry of Finance and was seconded to the OECD and the IMF before becoming Director General of the Strategy Development and Management Bureau of the FSA in 2018 and retiring in 2019.

## WHERE IS THE BLOCKCHAIN?

**Sasaki:** Thank you very much. Professor Ikeda mentioned SupTech and RegTech. I would like to talk about three things in this regard. One is that the way enforcement must change with the advancement of innovation, including digitalisation and DX – digital transformation. The enforcement that I am referring to here is not limited to the financial sector. It also includes, for example, the police and other authorities, which will have to change their way of enforcement. As I explained in my last lecture, the key to innovation is the digitalisation of information. Everything becomes electronic data, and such data can be used as evidence. The challenge for authorities then becomes how to obtain that data, how to analyse the data obtained and what actions to take based on the results of that analysis.

In the past, there was a lot of information that had not been converted into data. In order to obtain it, the authorities had to talk to various people and analyse paper documents. From now on, everything will be converted into electronic data, and analysis will be possible using Big Data approaches. Accordingly, the way we get data and the way we analyse it is changing.

To give you some specifics, about two years before I left the FSA, I was investigating virtual currencies and cryptoassets. As you may know, cryptoassets and records of transactions using those cryptoassets are located on the blockchain. When I started this job three years ago, I was a complete novice when it came to cryptoassets, and I asked questions like 'where is the blockchain?' For data from ordinary bank transactions, the recording data is stored on a server in the bank's computer and the FSA authorities can obtain it from there. In contrast, the blockchain, where the records of virtual currency transactions are kept, is virtual. It doesn't physically exist somewhere. If the cryptoasset is on the blockchain, you wonder how you can access the relevant data. The authorities have the power to access this data through inspection and supervision. They can ask virtual currency exchanges to submit data. But how do they get the data on the blockchain: by email, via files or through other tools? And even if they can obtain it, can the data obtained be analysed by the FSA's IT systems? In other words, when I asked, 'where is the blockchain?', I was essentially asking 'how do you access the blockchain, how do you get the data, how do you analyse it, and can it be done on the FSA's computers?' As it turned out, the answer is no.

## CONTRADICTIONS WHERE AUTHORITY EXISTS BUT CANNOT BE ENFORCED

**Sasaki:** Legally, there are powers to supervise, inspect and obtain data. The powers are there, but the infrastructure is not in place to effectively exercise those powers and fulfil the associated responsibilities. This is a typical enforcement challenge. Therefore, and this is true not only in Japan, but in all countries, even if the authorities have the authority under statutes and regulations, the mere fact that they are empowered to enforce the law does not guarantee the effectiveness of enforcement. This is a problem that cannot be solved by law alone. The law is effective only in so far as it is enforced. The challenge I am addressing is becoming greater in the context of digitalisation. Specifically, we not only need to create new laws, but we also need new systems to enforce them. This is what we mean by SupTech, the technology used by regulators and law enforcement.

Here, too, it is not enough to just use new technology. The people who use the technology, analyse information and make decisions based on the results are crucial to the success of law enforcement. Even if the authorities were to use artificial intelligence (AI) to obtain information, analyse it and find that certain conduct is illegal, the court would not be able to make a decision based only on the AI's conclusions. I believe that AI-only decisions would not stand up in court. Therefore, while it is necessary to make enforcement more sophisticated by using SupTech and AI, at the end of the day, enforcement is a question of judgement. Authorities need to be able to explain their methods of data analysis and their basis for taking action to the parties concerned, society and Parliament.

With the increasing sophistication of technology, the question of how to ensure accountability becomes more important. Especially when using technologies such as AI, where there is a risk of a 'black box', we need to question how we can ensure accountability to Parliament and the public in our use of technology. This presents a substantial challenge. As a result, the very nature of enforcement itself has to change considerably. This is my first point.

## WHAT IS THE GPS FUNCTION IN A SMARTPHONE FOR?

**Sasaki:** Second, as mentioned by Professor Ikeda, ecosystems are becoming more important. Traditionally, when a financial institution developed a system, the authorities would develop a system to supervise and inspect it based on a thorough understanding of the purpose of the system. In essence, the regulatory model was that the authorities developed the systems after the private sector. This is no longer viable. We need to think in terms of an ecosystem, where the development of systems by the private sector and the development of systems by the authorities are carried out in unison and in parallel.

A concrete example concerns the GPS in smartphones. The GPS function is essential for smartphones, to the point that there is no current smartphone without GPS functionality. When a crime occurs, the police and other investigative agencies may seize the suspect's smartphone and check its location at the time of the crime. While the police authorities are legally empowered to obtain and analyse GPS data from smartphones, manufacturers are not required by law to include GPS functionality in their smartphones.

Smartphones are developed by the private sector, but their GPS function is very beneficial to the police and investigative authorities, which is part of the ecosystem. GPS is a plus for us as individual smartphone users, and investigators can use it, which of course requires authorisation. The private sector takes the lead in the development of this technology, and this also creates advantages for the authorities. If, for example, GPS were made mandatory by law, it would be difficult to call this an ecosystem since it did not evolve naturally. In short, it is necessary to create a win-win-win situation for users, market participants and the authorities, so that everyone benefits. This is my second point.

## DIGITALISATION ISSUES BLOCKED BY THE COURTS

**Sasaki:** Now to my third point. I have already mentioned that the way investigative authorities engage in enforcement must change, not only in terms of their legal powers but also in terms of their systems, human resources and work methods. The enforcement side, especially the financial authorities and the police, will introduce certain technologies, obtain and analyse data and finally impose penalties or prosecute financial institutions based on human judgement. These developments will have a significant impact on the way the courts work.

The enforcement side, specifically the financial authorities, police and prosecutors, is trying to respond to the RegTech movement, but I think that in the courts, these discussions have not yet progressed far. In my experience, the courts are still paper-based instead of taking advantage of digitalisation. Now that the world as a whole is going digital, and enforcement is also going digital, I think we need to urgently consider how the courts will respond to digitalisation.

I believe that technology is a tool. Therefore, the question is not whether it is important to adopt technology, but what we do with the tools of technology. In short, there is a possibility that the very nature of court proceedings and the very nature of the courts themselves will change. If this happens, the fundamental nature of the law, including the way trials are conducted, and the qualities required of judges, may also change.

I do not think this issue has been discussed in Japan yet. As a result of the COVID-19 pandemic, the courts have finally started to have a system where parties can engage with the court and each other online and remotely. However, this does not mean that the traditional court procedure itself has been digitalised. Rather, only parts of the trial, such as the collection and management of evidence, have been subject to digitalisation. However, if the way enforcement agencies do things before trials is changing, what should be the way trials related to enforcement should be conducted? In short, my third point is that we need to think about not just the positive law, but also about technology and human resources, including the role of judges, in the future.

**Sumida:** Thank you very much for your very valuable comments. I would now like to invite Mr Akira Nozaki, Director of the FinTech Office in the FSA's Policy Division, to make further comments.

Mr Nozaki joined the Financial Supervisory Agency (now the Financial Services Agency) in 2000 and has worked as an Assistant to the Prime Minister, Deputy Director of the Corporate Disclosure Division of the Coordination and Planning Bureau of the FSA and as a Senior Policy Analyst at the OECD, before taking up his current position as Director for Organisational Strategy and Human Resources Policy and Head of the FinTech Office at the Strategy Development and Management Bureau of the FSA in 2020. He is a science graduate who majored in physics at the University of Tokyo.

## BANKS MAY DISAPPEAR, BUT FINANCIAL SERVICES REMAIN

**Nozaki:** Thank you very much for giving me this opportunity today. The most important points have been covered in the earlier talks by Professor Ikeda and Professor Sasaki, in particular the advancement of financial supervision and the regulatory response through digitalisation in the form of RegTech and SupTech. We are now in a phase where we are re-examining the fundamentals of what financial regulation and supervision are needed for in the first place. The term 'FinTech' has been heard more and more frequently since around 2015. The trend to solve social issues, such as improving customer experience, through the fusion of finance and technology, is spreading in the private sector. Some people say they do not need a bank, they just need Banking as a Service (BaaS). In this light, the role of the financial supervisory authority also needs to be reconsidered.

There are many ways to define the role of financial supervisors, such as dealing with financial system stability, customer protection and cross-border supervision. In terms of financial system stability, we are talking, for example, about how to deal with new risks, such as the moral hazard and adverse selection problems that can be caused by platform providers on P2P lending platforms. Other issues range from user protection and the issue of accountability, as mentioned by Professor Sasaki, to providing tailor-made services by analysing customers' personal data using Big Data and AI, rather than conventional uniform services, and dealing with the issues of data ethics. We believe that the financial authorities need to be aware of these issues and work on them. In relation to today's theme, 'Innovation in Financial Services and Supervision', the blockchain issue that Professor Sasaki mentioned earlier, particularly in relation to decentralised finance, is a major challenge for the authorities.

The blockchain itself has tremendous potential. When you think of blockchain, many people think of cryptoassets such as Bitcoin. But it can also be used to create reliable transaction records that ensure traceability, for example, for the purposes of food safety. The significance of being able to ensure traceability, whereby the entire history of past transactions can be viewed, is enormous. There are advantages to combining this with financial services, which can lead to significant improvements in convenience. On the other hand, there are also risks such as money laundering, reduced consumer protection and legal ambiguity. The legal ambiguity of decentralised finance may render it difficult to ensure the effectiveness of financial regulation in this space.

## FREE AND OPEN BLOCKCHAIN BRINGS MANY CHALLENGES

**Nozaki:** I want to make six points on the challenges of blockchain. First, in terms of specific examples of risk, in a decentralised financial system, there is no intermediary that fulfils something like a traditional financial intermediary function. In the case of blockchain, such as Bitcoin, all people have the same data. If you search 'bitcoin.com' on the internet, all people can see the same data. In such a situation, while there is no intermediary and a free market is maintained, there is a concern that the targets of regulation will be too vague and numerous for enforcement. It is not possible to regulate everyone who is trading on the blockchain. It is also not possible to limit the scope of who is subject to regulation any further.

My second point concerns autonomy. Bitcoin will continue to be traded incessantly, as it cannot be stopped by third-party intervention. The FSA may publicly state that trading bitcoin is a violation of the law and that trading should be stopped immediately, but this is ineffective. The autonomy of Bitcoin from traditional financial institutions and regulation means that Bitcoin is something that cannot be stopped – even if the FSA tried to ban it, or even if all the financial authorities in the world tried to ban it.

The third and crucial issue is anonymity. The blockchain has the advantage of making transactions transparent but, on the other hand, the technology allows transactions to be conducted highly anonymously. This means that there often is no possibility of tracking the identities of those who transact on the blockchain.

The fourth point is resistance to tampering. As network participants cannot amend or delete data on the blockchain, it is not possible for the authorities to go beyond issuing a cease-and-desist order by ordering the correction of records on the blockchain or the rescission of transactions. This means that ex-post corrections to the blockchain cannot be made.

The fifth point is internationality. In the digital world, global transactions can be realised without any restrictions, so borders are being crossed more and more. Even if the Japanese FSA, Germany's BaFin and the British FCA work together on regulation, they may find themselves out of control since they lack jurisdiction in other countries.

Sixth is openness, meaning you do not need to get permission to engage in decentralised finance. Anyone with a PC can develop and build such a decentralised financial system. Since there is no need to obtain permission from the FSA, the risk is that it will be unclear who takes responsibility for damages arising from such a system.

While these issues have already been recognised, there is still no effective solution and, as Professor Sasaki said, it is a very difficult problem to solve. Instead of trying to address all the issues by the authorities alone or by legislation alone, discussions started in February 2020 on how the various stakeholders around the world, including authorities and private sector technicians, can work together to address the issues. That is the Blockchain Governance Initiative Network, and we have set up such a network also for Japan.

## HOW DIGITAL INNOVATION WILL CHANGE JOB QUALIFICATIONS IN THE FINANCIAL MARKETS

**Sumida:** Thank you very much indeed. You have provided valuable information from a variety of perspectives and raised some fascinating issues. There is one point I would like to know more about. As the FSA is an authority with a strong history of dealing with digitalisation issues, I would like to ask you to share your experience of what the FSA in particular has done in this regard.

**Nozaki:** Thank you for your question. Perhaps it would be better for you to ask Professor Sasaki about this, as he had a very strong influence on the issue when he was at the FSA. He was one of the first to tackle the blockchain issue when he was at the FSA, and he was a strong proponent of improving the technological literacy and mindset of staff to allow them to understand the situation.

The FSA also employs a number of professionals from the private sector, such as cybersecurity experts. This has been a feature of the FSA since its inception, with around 30 per cent of its staff being professionals from the private sector, including lawyers and accountants. In terms of improving the skills of the FSA's own staff, we consider the strengthening of the data science field in particular to be a medium- to long-term challenge. It is necessary to face digitalisation from the perspective of both the immediate import of skills from the private sector and the medium- to long-term skill development of career staff. Professor Sasaki will be able to talk more about this.

## CREATING A CULTURE WHERE FAILURE CAN BE POSITIVE

**Sasaki:** I agree with most of what Mr Nozaki has said. I have studied law at university, and I am a complete amateur when it comes to technology. I do not know how to use a smartphone or a computer that well. But the field of finance, which I have had experience in over the last twenty years, is virtual and global in nature. The major factors today are technology, innovation and digitalisation. As a supervisor of financial businesses, you have to understand the law, you have to understand the economy, and at the same time, you have to understand technology. I do not know about the technical aspects of blockchain and AI, about what is in the black box. I understand that AI, blockchain and innovation can be quite transformative for finance, but at the same time it can be quite a big risk, and it can be a risk for the authorities.

Even though I understand the risks and that these issues are important, it remains an area that I do not understand. So, I have to bring in people who do understand. If those people are not in the FSA, I have to bring them in from the outside. So, I recruited more and more people from the science sector and the private sector, including Mr Nozaki.

Many of you are experts in law. I am sorry to say this, but the legal approach is basically to analyse what has happened in the past – ex post facto – and how to apply it to the next issue. In the field of innovation, I think there are areas where we do not know what will happen and the past is not very helpful. In that sense, we have to change the way we think about studying the law.

In reforming the FSA, it is important to be agile and start from where you can. In the traditional way of working, you work hard for a long time to understand the details and only then move on to action. This is no longer the case. We just have to start. This is still a minority approach in the Japanese bureaucracy, but this kind of approach is becoming more and more necessary. Speaking of mindset, we are also trying to change the personnel evaluation system. Even if you fail to take an agile approach, you can be evaluated as a 'good failure'. If you take on a challenge, you are evaluated for taking on the challenge itself. We are not 100 per cent there yet, but the FSA is changing a lot, at least compared to traditional government offices.

**Sumida:** Thank you very much. That was a very informative and encouraging talk for the young people in the audience. Felix, do you have any questions or issues you would like to raise?

## IS A DATA COLLECTION FORMAT NEEDED?

**Steffek:** First, a great thank you to all three speakers. I very much enjoyed the presentation and comments. I have, in fact, many comments and questions. I will first concentrate on two issues if that is okay. My first area of questions concerns data because all three of you mentioned data. One question I had while you were speaking was whether we need new processes for establishing data collection and formatting data because all three of you emphasised how important data is. I found it very interesting that you also went into the practical aspects of collecting data. Then I started thinking about how we determine which data is collected. You showed, for example, that different banks have their own data collection systems and then there is the FSA data collection and there is the BoJ gathering data, and the collected data needs to be adjusted. So, one question is whether we can make things easier by somehow unifying the data collection format and the data collection processes. While we want unified data and standardised data, on the other hand, we need to be flexible and allow private actors to collect new data. Are there ways to innovate and have better data collection processes?

One idea I had is this: Would it make sense to form collaborative bodies where you have public bodies and private representatives of, perhaps, the financial institutions to think about data collection standards? However, I do see the trade-off between the advantages of unification and standardisation versus the problem of allowing flexibility for financial institutions to collect new data. The data collection process is, perhaps, something that we can delve further into.

**Ikeda:** If there is a crisis in a certain region, at first, we try to collect data that we have to collect and require to make an assessment immediately, on an ad hoc basis. Then, when it becomes an ongoing need, we format it and keep collecting it. Eventually, people start saying things like 'don't keep that kind of data forever', and recently, they have started saying things like 'why are you collecting this data?' and 'please remove data that you do not use or do not need from the data collection list'. I think that is quite common. In many cases, new data is collected because something has happened, and that is the trigger for collecting it. I would appreciate it if Professor Sasaki and Mr Nozaki could follow up on this as necessary.

**Nozaki:** Thank you. First, I would like to answer Felix's question about data collection. The general answer is that the BoJ and the FSA are becoming more efficient as they work with each other to collect the data required for monitoring financial institutions. Other than that, I think we need to analyse more Big Data as well, rather than just taking traditional financial data. For example, we are considering whether combining data from credit card usage histories, individual company data from the Teikoku Databank and other data held by financial institutions might provide some insights. We think that we need to move forward with Big Data analysis. I think there is still room for ingenuity in this area, which is evolving on a daily basis.

**Sumida:** Felix, if you have any further questions, could you ask them now, please?

## FINANCIAL SERVICES WILL BECOME TAILOR-MADE TO PUT THE CUSTOMER FIRST

**Steffek:** Yes, I have many questions, but I will only ask one. How will the changes that you talked about in terms of data collection and data analysis change the business of the financial institutions? We have discussed how it changes the business of the regulators, how it changes the FSA and how the FSA works, but ultimately, we are interested in creating a good ecosystem for the financial institutions and the actors. In the future, how do you think the framework for financial institutions will change? How will the practice change for, not just the regulators, but for those who are being regulated?

**Nozaki:** I think your question is about how financial institutions and financial services will change as data analysis and other technologies evolve. Until now, core financial functions, such as loans, fund settlement and deposit taking, have been performed by financial institutions that have built heavy, grand and stable systems and provide services within that framework. For example, if you look at an ATM terminal, you still see an old-fashioned screen with only five buttons, which you press, enter your PIN and take out money. On the other hand, the smartphones you have are becoming more and more functionally advanced. As a result, the way of providing financial services, where the customer has to adapt to the system created by the financial institution, has to change, and this is exactly what is going on now. Smartphones can now be used to make deposits and transfer funds. Household account bookkeeping software is also very advanced, allowing users to check their assets with their smartphones. Systems have been developed using AI to make recommendations on what investments to favour. This will probably lead to a shift from financial institution-centred services to customer-centred, tailor-made services for each and every customer.

In other words, banks will no longer need to offer deposits and loans as a combined set. Customers will be able to use providers of deposits and loans in any combination they wish. The very nature of finance itself will change. As a result, the supervisory authorities will not be able to ensure that financial services run smoothly if they only keep a close watch on financial institutions at the institution level. They will also have to monitor platforms, where they will be able to check what functions and services are provided as a whole, since various services are provided by various institutions.

## WHAT IS YOUR SELF-ASSESSMENT OF THE FSA'S APPROACH?

**Student A:** Thank you very much. I have two quick questions. First, with regard to the three initiatives of the FSA that you introduced today, I am sorry to say this, but to the untrained eye, rather than doing something that is technically very difficult, it seems to me that the FSA is now doing things that should have been done earlier but were not done because they were considered too complicated then. How do you perceive this? My second question concerns the term digital transformation. Can simple digitalisation such as RPA and centralising data be called digital transformation?

**Sumida:** These are some edgy questions. Thank you very much.

**Sasaki:** I would like to answer your question by saying that you are 100 per cent right. I have been involved in the digitalisation of the FSA for twenty years now and, as you said, whether we are talking about RPA or digital forensics, which I started fifteen years ago, or data exchange with the BoJ, we are talking about pre-digital transformation. Since I was at the FSA, around 2015/2016, I am saying that these activities are about digitisation, not DX. Digitisation refers to digitising the paper base, it is about not using paper. This should have been done a long time ago. You are right, this is digitisation, and the problem is that we did not do it when we should have done it.

The story of virtual currencies is somewhat different because the subject is digital in the first place. As you mentioned in your second question, digital transformation is not just about eliminating paper. Digital transformation is about changing the way work is done. Digitalisation is a tool. It is not clear enough what we are going to do with digitalisation or what we are going to do with DX. When I reformed the FSA, the ultimate goal was to strengthen the financial function. By going through the DX of financial institutions and the corresponding DX of the work of the FSA, we can see how financial innovation can benefit society and how finance can contribute to solving social issues. For the FSA, this means that supervising is more than just supervising financial institutions. Benefiting society is the ultimate goal, but we have not reached it yet.

What we are doing now is digitisation before DX and we are also trying to do something slightly closer to DX but, as you say, we are very far behind. I have been acutely aware of this since I was at the FSA. Professor Ikeda, Mr Nozaki and others are now working on it, but I still feel that we are lagging behind.

There are problems that cannot be solved by the authorities alone. This issue will not change unless we change the business model of the authorities, especially in terms of system development and supervision. So, first of all, we need to digitalise the conventional type of supervision and get information into digital form. You are right that this is still a work in progress. In the end, the whole way of supervision has to be changed.

**Ikeda:** What Professor Sasaki has said is true. Personally, I see that technology is catching up with the timing of the FSA's upgrading to live monitoring. The technological conditions are just right, so we are trying to do it right this time. The centralisation of data with the BoJ is not something that is new, but something that has been requested for a long time, since Professor Sasaki was at the FSA. Due to various restrictions and other priorities, it has been difficult to achieve thus far. However, in this day and age, it is no longer acceptable to leave it unattended. The current situation is that the FSA is finally getting to grips with the heavy lifting.

In terms of highly granular information, the FSA is now trying to use it in order to strengthen the oversight of the financial intermediary function, for example, to improve the flow of finance to the private sector. Also, technological advances have enabled both financial institutions and the authorities to analyse very detailed data. The timing of this has coincided with the introduction of the new data analysis system. Until now, valuable detailed data was contained in the large amount of data we received, but it was buried without being utilised at all even though it was digitised.

## ABOUT THE FINANCIAL SURVEILLANCE SYSTEM

**Student B:** This may be a little bit off the subject of finance, but you mentioned in your talk that digital forensics and ways to constantly monitor and store social networking sites and other information when cracking down on finance-related crimes will also be necessary. If that entails private citizens being monitored all the time, it would be scary. I feel like my right to free speech is not guaranteed if I am being monitored. I am curious about the kind of legal guarantees in place in this regard.

**Ikeda:** The current practice is a little different from strictly monitoring the internet. It is a system that automatically patrols and saves. It does not involve monitoring or manually storing anything that is not allowed on the internet. From the perspective of lawyers who support victims of malicious posts on the web or leaked images, it is very common that once something is written or uploaded on the web, no matter how many requests are made to delete it, it is difficult to erase it completely and it remains forever. In that sense, I understand that the authorities are not the only ones engaging in data storage. The general public can also save data if they want to. What the FSA does is a somewhat systematic collection of such data.

**Sumida:** I guess the question expressed a concern from a privacy point of view. The student seemed to worry that we are becoming a surveillance society.

**Ikeda:** We do not have the resources to store everything that you write. We have narrowed down our monitoring to the websites that are about stock prices. We are keeping an eye on inappropriate things that might be written. We do not have surveillance cameras everywhere. Unless you have been marked, you do not have to worry about it that much.

**Sumida:** Thank you all very much for your very valuable contributions today. It was a really precious opportunity to hear your frank comments and to raise important issues. I would like to now close today's session.

## CONCLUDING CONVERSATION

**Steffek:** Norichika Ikeda, based at the FSA and also a professor at the University of Tokyo, spoke on the impact of technology on the financial sector and those who are regulating the financial sector. The focus of his presentation was on enforcement, i.e. on making sure that laws and regulations are not only in the books but that they become reality.

**Sumida:** What really struck me, in terms of highlighting the essence of this issue, was the comment by Professor Sasaki, who has led the financial services industry that the biggest challenge for law enforcement is dealing with technology. Even if the authorities have the 'legal' authority to obtain data, they cannot obtain it, analyse it, make decisions and take action without the necessary technology and skills. When the issue of virtual currencies was discussed, we heard that the first questions were: 'Where is the blockchain?' and 'Can the FSA get the data and analyse it?' This part of the discussion was very revealing. I think it is fair to say, however, that the financial sector itself has been one of the first to go digital and it's important to note that law enforcement has been a front-runner in terms of digitalisation.

**Steffek:** I agree. We are confronted with a new reality and, therefore, need to think about it. Law enforcement is an area where technology has the potential to make things better. However, we have also discussed the associated risks in this regard. I also found the part that explored the future direction of regulatory bodies like the FSA very interesting. Professor Ikeda emphasised that the mission of the FSA itself is undergoing a major change. He said that whereas in the past the FSA had aimed to identify problematic situations, such as banks that did not have enough assets to meet all of their claims, in the future the FSA's objective will be to ensure the success of financial institutions' business models. In other words, instead of detecting insolvency, the FSA is aiming to ensure profitability.

**Sumida:** Yes, he said that the mission of the FSA's inspection and supervision authority has shifted significantly from dealing with the bad loan problem to achieving a deeper dialogue that goes back to the business model in order to strengthen financial functions. He said that it is now necessary to collect and analyse a lot of data, including continuous on- and off-line monitoring and a detailed understanding of the actual situation.

**Steffek:** Indeed, it is data that is the key to success. Professor Ikeda's presentation also explored some of the challenges and possible solutions for data collection and analysis. One issue that I thought was particularly important was the issue of data protocols. For example, it is not enough that the FSA's data protocols and the BoJ's protocols are similar; rather, the data must be compatible. We will also need to take into account that data collection and analysis will need to be automated. In other words, there is too much data for comprehensive human involvement. Should we invest valuable human effort in reconciling the data? Professor Ikeda's presentation made it clear that those who deal with data and technological innovation need to solve granular data problems. This leads, I think, to the interesting question of whether lawmakers can support the generation of compatible data.

**Sumida:** That raises an extremely interesting question! By the way, in the meantime, a new administrative body called the Digital Agency has been established in Japan.[3] Not only the financial sector but also the entire Japanese government has taken a major step towards digitalisation and is now considering the issues we have discussed.

The hidden hero of the session may have been the student who dared to challenge the guest speakers (laughs). Although the project 'centralisation of data collection and system integration with the Bank of Japan' may indeed give the impression of 'simple digitisation that should have been done a long time ago', it needs to be seen in the larger context of a 'reporting dashboard'. The development

[3] For more information on the Japan Digital Agency, see <www.digital.go.jp/en/>, accessed 1 November 2023.

of a 'reporting dashboard' system is now underway. It will enable all applications, filings and reports to the FSA to be made online.[4]

**Steffek:** Kiyotaka Sasaki, Visiting Professor at Hitotsubashi University and former Director General at the FSA, pointed out further challenges regarding data collection. For example, it is not only the public institutions that have different data protocols. Also, individual financial institutions have all developed their own data formats over time. He therefore raised the interesting question of the need for a data ecosystem. He added that this ecosystem, ideally, should also include courts and other public bodies beyond the regulatory authorities. He also pointed out that ultimately everything can be turned into data. The next step is then to think about whether there is information that would be useful but that is currently not available as data.

**Sumida:** It is also important to add the keyword 'public-private collaboration' to this ecosystem. The background to this idea of a public-private ecosystem is the awareness of the problem that government-led system development is not enough. GPS on smartphones is a private-sector initiative, but as readers know, it is very important for investigations because it gives the authorities access to the data when a crime is committed. This public-private collaboration is also taking place in the area of data improvement, which caught my attention as well. As a practical example, Professor Ikeda has introduced us to the uses of the corporate number. As there are no restrictions on the use of this number, the FSA has added the corporate number to the loan details received from regional banks and returned the data to them. The FSA is examining whether this will contribute to a better understanding of the actual situation of customers and to more sophisticated and efficient credit management. This may seem like a modest step, but I thought it was an important step in terms of data improvement.

**Steffek:** Akira Nozaki, Director of the FSA's FinTech Office, introduced new perspectives in his comments. I found particularly interesting the risks he identified in the decentralised approaches facilitated by advances such as blockchain. Mr Nozaki pointed out that decentralised services, e.g. those based on blockchain, have no mediators. This makes them difficult to regulate as the target of regulation is unclear. Regulators such as the FSA do not have full control over decentralised systems. This means that the FSA has problems, for example, to stop trading in a decentralised system. I learned from this that decentralised systems raise particular problems for regulatory bodies.

**Sumida:** The discussion's shift in perspective towards 'How will digitalisation change the supervisor and the market?' has revealed the nature of the changes brought about by technology.

4 鬼頭武嗣・水井大「金融分野における昨今のRegTech/SupTechの動向」金法2015o号24頁以下。

This reminded me of a question asked by Professor Koda in one of the other sessions: 'What should we think about the significance of the judicial system reforms of the 1990s in Japan?' How will the world of the twenty-first century face the challenge of integrating the unbanked into financial networks? This is not about building more financial institutions or reforming the education system to increase the number of people working in financial institutions. Today, looking at smartphones with payment applications installed, we are in a different world already. I will continue to think about this question and hope that regulators, legislators and the judiciary continue to think about it as well.

## QUESTIONS FOR FURTHER THOUGHT

- Do we need to develop new approaches for the formatting and collection of data in regulatory environments?
- How can legislatures contribute to solving data challenges of regulatory bodies?
- Do we need new institutions concerned with data protocols mediating data requirements between different institutions?
- Which new data confidentiality issues arise if the regulators are not only collecting data identifying problems but also if data defines the core business models of companies?
- Is there scope to make some data collected by regulatory bodies public? Perhaps data that all businesses could benefit from, thereby increasing social welfare overall?
- Will data and technology change the power balance between market actors and public regulators in the future?
- How can regulators such as financial services authorities be put in a position to effectively control decentralised systems?

# Conversation 7

## Artificial Intelligence and Legal Services

ABSTRACT

This chapter investigates the impact of artificial intelligence on legal services. The questions addressed include: How will artificial intelligence change and improve the legal services offered by lawyers? How will the legal profession change as a result of the increased use of artificial intelligence? How will artificial intelligence change the way lawyers work and the way they organise, charge for and finance their work? A key insight discussed concerns the focus when thinking about the impact of artificial intelligence on the work of lawyers: concentrating on the 'tasks' that lawyers perform reveals more insights than asking whether artificial intelligence will destroy 'jobs'. Exploring the impact on 'tasks' of lawyers shows that they are both consumers and producers of services augmented by artificial intelligence. Focusing on 'tasks' also helps in understanding what kinds of activities are affected by artificial intelligence and which activities will be performed, at least for the foreseeable future, by human lawyers. The discussion also deals with the emergence of multidisciplinary teams and the success indicators for LawTech start-ups.

| | |
|---|---|
| *Speaker* | Mari Sako |
| *Comments* | Masakazu Iwakura |
| *Moderators* | Felix Steffek and Mihoko Sumida |
| *Concluding Conversation* | Felix Steffek and Mihoko Sumida |
| *Questions for Further Thought* | Felix Steffek |

## THE IMPACT OF AI ON LEGAL SERVICES FROM AN ECONOMIST'S PERSPECTIVE

**Steffek:** Good evening in Tokyo and good morning in the United Kingdom. It is a great pleasure to introduce Professor Mari Sako, who speaks both English and Japanese. Since I do not speak Japanese, I am afraid, I must do my introduction in English. You will benefit from our excellent translation. I would like to use this opportunity to thank our fantastic translators, who have been with us during these sessions.

Professor Sako is Professor of Management Studies at Saïd Business School, the University of Oxford. She is an economist, not a lawyer, but very much interested in what LawTech people do. Her main areas of expertise include global strategy, comparative institutional analysis, which I think we will benefit from today, outsourcing, offshoring and professional services. That is another topic we are looking at today. Her most recent work has focused on business and professional services and on outsourcing. Her work has attracted the interest of policymakers, and she has, thus, been active in the field of policymaking. For example, her research on the globalisation of legal services and its impact on the profession has led to her becoming a member of the UK Legal Services Board Research Strategy Group. So, when Mari told me earlier that she did not know much about the law, it was not the truth (laughs). Mari, you have been engaging a lot with lawyers and you wrote excellent articles with lawyers, so at least you are friendly with lawyers. We can probably say that much. Mari, it is a great pleasure having you here – over to you.

**Sako:** Thank you very much for the kind introduction, Felix, and thank you so much, Professor Sumida, for giving me this opportunity to address a Japanese audience, which will be my first time for this particular topic. In the next hour, I will engage you in a conversation around several topics related to the adoption of artificial intelligence (AI), which are as follows. First, the impact of AI on what lawyers do. Second, the impact of AI on new business models that are being created in legal services. Third, opportunities for LawTech start-ups using some new business models to capture value in this field. And last, implications of AI adoption for the future of what lawyers and law firms do in the face of competition. I am very interested in your reactions, either as a law student or as a practising lawyer or even as a LawTech start-up entrepreneur. This is a global field and what is happening primarily in the United Kingdom and the United States, I think, surely will have implications on what is going to happen in Japan as well.

My interest in looking at the technology, AI, is very much predicated on understanding its impact on the legal profession, what lawyers do. I will focus on the combination or the alignment of new business models and organisational design to see what the exact impact on the legal profession is. As an academic trained in economics, I do empirical work, so much of what I am going to say is based on seventy-plus interviews that we have conducted with respondents not just in law firms, but also in in-house legal departments, alternative providers of legal services and LawTech start-ups. We conducted a survey, about a year ago, of solicitors in

England and Wales and we also interviewed start-up founders and investors comparing LawTech and FinTech as well in different locations, London, New York and San Francisco. This is joint work with some of my Oxford-based colleagues, some of whom are in the law school. Others are in the economics department, in the business school like me or computer scientists who are researching at the forefront of applying things like deep learning and natural language processing to improve legal reasoning. Thus, if you are interested in any aspects of that, please visit our project website.[1] I should also say that there are some people who are in the education department looking at what reforms there should be for the content of the education and training for future lawyers. Something like the present conversation series would certainly be listed as a prime example of what we should be doing.

## TASK-BY-TASK ANALYSIS IS IMPORTANT FOR UNDERSTANDING THE IMPACT OF AI

**Sako:** With that, let me go straight to understanding the impact of AI on lawyers' work. I am going to focus on the notion of an AI-enabled legal service delivery pipeline, which is basically a series of steps that you need to take if you would like to produce and deliver legal services which are enabled by AI. Firstly, I do not think I need to dwell too much on defining what AI is. AI obviously automates tasks ordinarily requiring human intelligence and the use cases in legal services are quite vast and varied, ranging from things like contract analytics to due diligence in M&A to litigation support and legal research. There are different branches of AI, in particular rule-based top-down thinking around expert systems on the one hand, and a more bottom-up, data-based approach focusing on machine learning. The current phase of interest in AI is very much driven by machine learning with lots of computing power and data, enabling the widening and deepening of the application of AI in various domains, including legal services.

AI technology has two effects on what people do and it is important here not to think about jobs, but tasks. A job can be broken down into separable tasks and it is those tasks which are subjected to an AI impact. First, AI substitutes or replaces humans in some tasks, and I will elaborate on what those are in a minute. Second, AI augments humans' work in other tasks. So, it is quite tempting to have a notion of the end of lawyers, which is the title of a book by Richard Susskind[2] where there is this evocative quotation about the fading away of the prominence of certain professions like blacksmiths, tallow chandlers and mercers. Richard's prediction is that lawyers might be going the same way, to fade in prominence. But I think it is

1 'Unlocking the Potential of Artificial Intelligence for English Law' (*Faculty of Law, University of Oxford*) <www.law.ox.ac.uk/unlocking-potential-artificial-intelligence-english-law>, accessed 1 November 2023.

2 Richard Susskind, *The End of Lawyers? Rethinking the Nature of Legal Services* (Oxford University Press, 2008). See also Richard Susskind and Daniel Susskind, *How Technology Will Transform the Work of Human Experts* (Oxford University Press, Updated Edition, 2022).

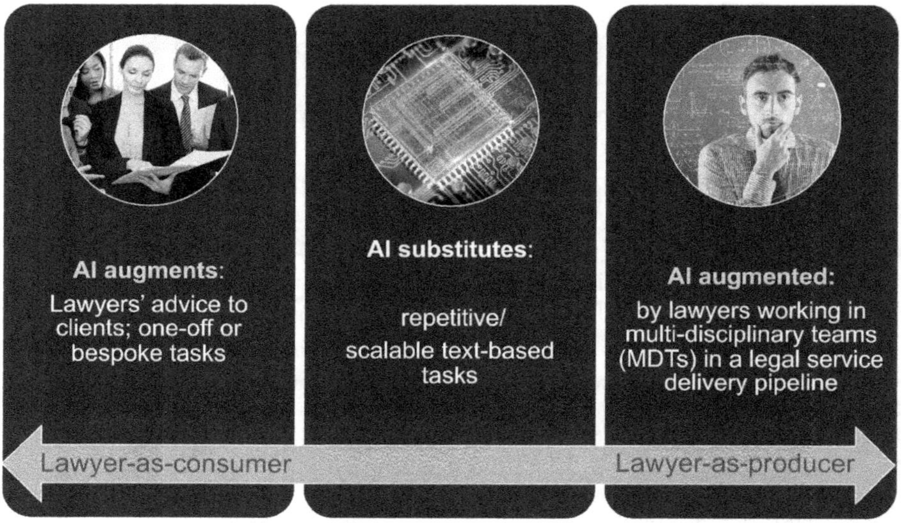


FIGURE 7.1 Three effects of AI on lawyers' work

important to remember that substitution is only part of the story, that AI obviously replaces some tasks that lawyers are doing, but augmentation is equally important. Here, AI augments lawyers' work so that lawyers become better lawyers because they can use the output generated by AI. In that sense, lawyers are consumers of AI. But it is also important to think of lawyers as producers of AI so that AI tools are augmented by lawyers.

Let me say a bit more about the distinction between these two aspects of augmentation by showing you Figure 7.1. In the middle, of course, AI substitutes certain tasks that lawyers are doing. These are the repetitive, scalable, text-based tasks. Here, you may have an image of litigious America in New York where young junior associates are canned into hotel rooms where there are piles and piles of paper that they have to go through to identify relevant text in a particular litigation case, for example. Equally important, to the left of this figure, is AI augmenting what lawyers do. As consumers of AI, lawyers can become better advisors to clients, particularly on one-off or bespoke tasks, and if it is about a bet-the-house litigation case or an important M&A matter, then this is what lawyers are really hired for. This task of advice is bespoke or customised to each client. The quality of that advice is advanced or enhanced due to the application of AI. The right of this figure, though, shows that some lawyers might become much more familiar with what AI is and could actually become producers of AI, in the sense of lawyers working within a multi-disciplinary team. I am going to use this word quite a lot. Multi-disciplinary teams (MDTs) are teams where lawyers work with other professionals like data scientists and project managers. As a team, they become an input into what I call a delivery pipeline.

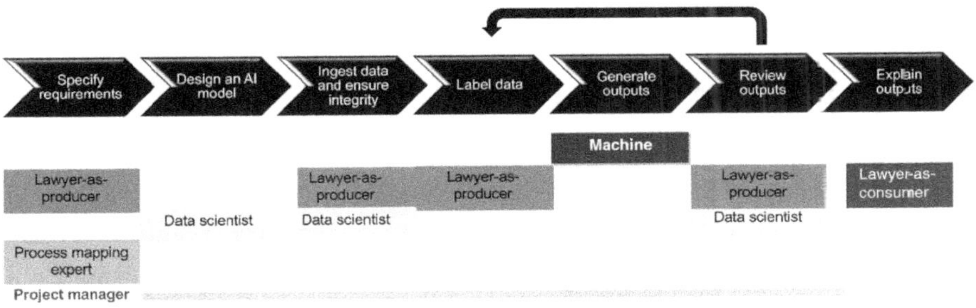


FIGURE 7.2 AI-enabled legal service delivery pipeline

## LEGAL SERVICES AS ASSEMBLY LINES

**Sako:** The delivery pipeline can be thought of as an assembly line. I used to research the car industry. If you visit a car factory there is an assembly line where different components are assembled into a final car. In the past, maybe at the beginning of the twentieth century, a craftsman might have made an entire car on their own. That is where legal work or some of the lawyers' work is, even today. If you introduce an assembly line into what lawyers do, then you can think of it along the following different steps shown in Figure 7.2, while having machine learning like AI in mind.

First, we must specify the requirements. Let us imagine that this is a project which is to improve prediction about which contract clauses are more likely to cause disputes. For this, we need lawyers' input into defining the requirements of the project and then we need some input from process mapping experts and project managers to be able to define the process steps and the project management scoping. Second, we need to define and design an AI model for this project, and the data scientists' input here is essential. Third, we turn to choosing and ingesting data and making sure that there is integrity and security as regards such data. This again involves collaboration between lawyers as producers and data scientists. And then, of course, we need to label the data. Labelling used to be done by junior associates and paralegals, but now this is the work of a lawyer as a producer. Then, the only bit that is totally substituted and automated is the task of generating the output, which is going to be done by the machine. Once it reaches this point, we need some human input again to review the output. There is a bit of a recursive process here if you want to increase the prediction rate by improving the algorithm and thinking about adjusting the labels used. Ultimately, the prediction is used by lawyers as consumers to advise the clients.

In most of the steps, we have a collaborative setting of lawyers working as part of a team. We think of lawyers working with data scientists, process-mapping experts and project managers, as lawyers working as part of a MDT. This is the legal services delivery pipeline, which I hope is a notion that is not too strange to lawyers if you think about other industries like the car industry. I am not saying that this way of thinking would apply to every practice area or every kind of legal work that can be done. But I think that it can be applied to many more situations than a typical lawyer might think today.

## SURVEY OF LAWYERS WORKING IN MDTS

**Sako:** Where can we find these kinds of MDTs? This can be explained using a survey that we conducted about a year ago, in collaboration with the Law Society of England and Wales. The survey asks individual solicitors about their use of LawTech, including, but not limited to, AI, and the kind of training that they have received to be able to use the technology. We distributed the survey online between November 2019 and January 2020, and we obtained 353 responses from qualified lawyers in England and Wales. We asked the respondents about where they worked. About two-thirds, 67 per cent, worked for law firms of various sizes, and 28 per cent worked in-house, inside business corporations. We also wanted to target alternative providers and LawTech solution providers, but the number of responses was not high enough from those categories. Hence, I am just going to compare the responses from those who worked for law firms and those who worked for in-house departments.

Lawyers who work in law firms are less likely to be working in MDTs than in-house lawyers. At the same time, AI deployment is associated with lawyers working in MDTs. Let me show you a few charts to back up that statement. Firstly, one of the questions that we asked in the survey was, 'Which types of specialist experts do you work with on a day-to-day basis?' Notably, as the question specifies, the parameter was everyday work and not just from time to time. We asked the solicitors to select all that apply. You can see that the top two, paralegals and other lawyers, would be lawyers just working with lawyers. But we also put down four separate other categories – legal project managers, process mapping experts, data analysts or data scientists and IT and legal innovation experts. These are emerging new job titles, some of which are used in this way, but there are lots of different labels being applied to what, in effect, are similar roles. Some of you might have heard of legal engineers or legal product architects. All these are new job titles emerging in the field. Those lawyers who only ticked the first two, i.e. those working only with paralegals or other lawyers, were considered not to be working in MDTs. Those who ticked any one of the other four were classified to be working in MDTs. Thus, it is quite a generous definition of MDTs because if you ticked any one of the legal project managers, process mapping experts, data analysts or IT/legal innovation experts, then you were considered to be working with a non-lawyer, if you like, and therefore part of an MDT.

## CORRELATION BETWEEN MDT EXPERIENCE AND AI USE

**Sako:** With this classification, we tried to understand the incidence of working in MDTs for those working in in-house legal departments and those working in law firms. You can see from Figure 7.3 that 48.5 per cent of those who said that they worked in-house, were working in MDTs, whereas the fraction is 35.6 per cent for those working in law firms. Whilst the incidences are reasonably high in law firms, they are higher in in-house legal departments. I will address the possible reasons behind these figures a little later.

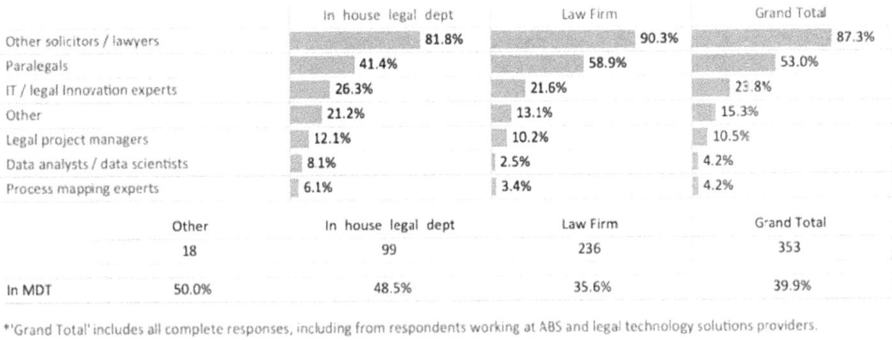


FIGURE 7.3 Opportunities to work in MDTs, by organisation

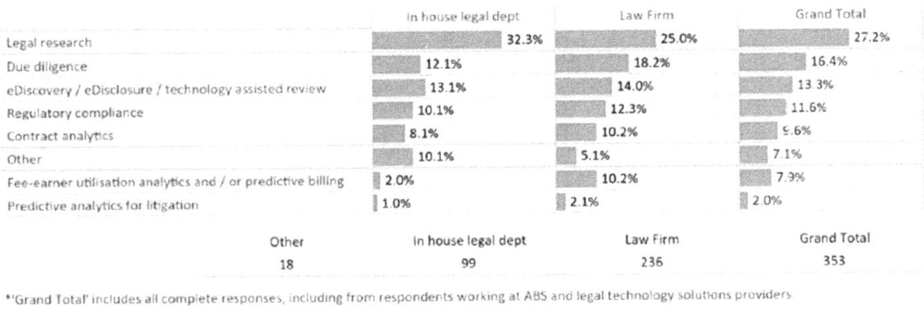


FIGURE 7.4 Usage of AI-assisted legal technology, by organisation

We also asked about the use of AI. We defined AI to include machine learning, expert systems and similar approaches. In Figure 7.4, you can see that apart from legal research, the rate of AI deployment is relatively modest. Similar results are also observed in other surveys which are conducted by other organisations, not just in the United Kingdom, but elsewhere, for example, by the American Bar Association as well.

Figure 7.5 looks at the use of AI by those working in MDTs as compared to the use of AI for the whole population. Whilst this is complex, please look at these two charts to compare and contrast the differences between these two groups. In the case of legal research, 33.8 per cent of lawyers who work in MDTs said that they were using AI, whereas for the whole sample, including lawyers working in MDTs and those who are not working in MDTs, only 27.2 per cent were using AI, which is lower than the former. A starker contrast is evident in due diligence where 40.5 per cent of lawyers in MDTs were using AI, whereas only 18.2 per cent of all lawyers were using AI. Thus, being part of an MDT is more common in-house than in law firms, and being in an MDT is correlated with the use of AI. Now, we cannot say a huge amount about causation here, but this correlation gives you some hint as to the kind of workplaces that are likely to accommodate the use of MDTs and that, in fact, appear to be facilitating the adoption of AI.

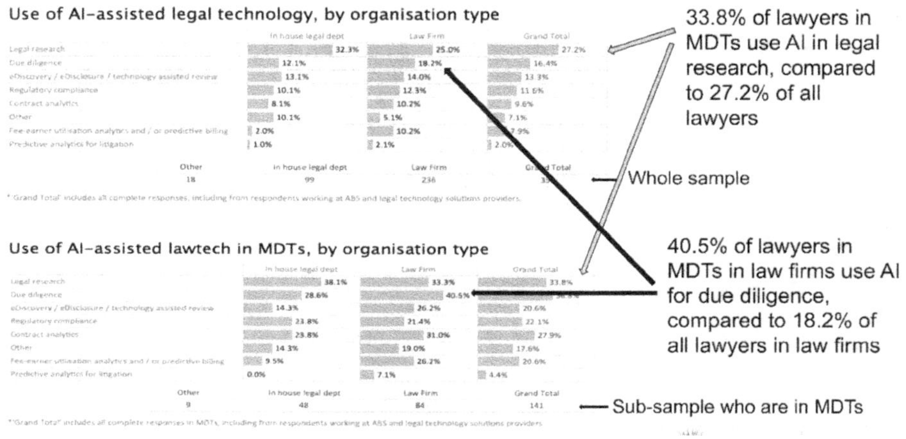


FIGURE 7.5 Usage of AI-assisted legal technology in MDTs, by organisation

Before I go to the next issue, I wish to remind you that we demonstrated the importance of MDTs for the AI-enabled legal service delivery pipeline. I am going to just pause here and see if there are any questions or any comments from you.

**Steffek:** Thank you very much, Mari. I find the differentiation that you made between tasks and jobs very, very helpful for the discussion. It is very helpful for your scientific research, but it is also helpful for discussions about the future of the profession. In my experience, these discussions are often overloaded or made difficult by the over-emphasis on job replacement. To give an example, I introduced to the students a competition that students in Cambridge had organised three years ago where they organised a competition between an AI and lawyers in London. The task was to predict the outcome of certain ombudsman procedures. A conference was organised to discuss the results. Very soon the conference was about job replacement. Also, the way the media reported on the event was dominated by the job-replacement issue and lawyers reacted very sensitively to the topic.

At the same time, I find your assembly line concept very helpful because it shows the other professions involved. It also, at the same time, shows that there are jobs created for other professions. While it shows that there is a replacement of lawyers in the output generation process, there are other people coming into the job market. If you look at it from a societal perspective, then it is not just about lawyers. Lawyers think that lawyers are terribly important, but there are also people who are not legal experts but are still key for access to justice.

## POSSIBILITY OF AI JUDGES

**Steffek:** I would also like to raise a question that concerns legal decision-making. Your research focused on a group that perhaps one could call the advisors, external advisors and in-house advisors. With decision-makers, I mean people such as judges, ombudsmen and arbitrators. A part of the discussion is whether AI may be replacing these decision-makers, the neutrals, perhaps we could call them. I just wonder whether you have a first take on what might be different about them. Compared with the advisors who are often on the side of one of the parties of a dispute, and who even have an incentive to gain competitive advantages over the other party using AI to have better information, the decision-makers are usually neutral and stand between the parties. If you do not mind, could you turn your thoughts to these people?

**Sako:** Thank you so much, Felix. That is helpful because, being based in a business school, the kind of analysis that we are doing is for a segment of the legal market only, the segment which has corporations as clients. Thus, the analysis that I have presented is most appropriate for corporate legal services. Beyond it, John Armour at the law school and I are now extending our attention to what Bill Henderson some time ago called 'people law',[3] where the clients are individual households and small- and medium-sized enterprises – i.e. clients who do not have the same knowledge about law as corporate clients with their in-house legal department.[4] I think that humans are going to continue to be in the loop for corporate legal services because, ultimately, the human lawyer, the trusted advisor is probably always going to be there as an intermediary interpreting the machine learning output. As regards people law there is at least a demand for a chatbot or a robot that can give you some advice on a reasonably simple but nevertheless important query on conveyancing, will writing or whatnot. However, the technology for this might not be there yet. Data aggregation is a real challenge. Humans may be out of the loop eventually. The area that I know the least about is the area that you just talked about concerning the judiciary, where there is a discussion about robot judges. I think eventually some of the simpler dispute resolution could be subjected to AI. Thus, I think the pipeline that I have presented could be extended ultimately to the end point where a lawyer as the consumer could also be replaced by automation or semi-automation.

## ROLE OF AI IN LITIGATION FINANCE

**Steffek:** 'People law' nicely links us to tomorrow's session where we look at the use of technology in law and how it can improve access to justice. The issue of access to law or access to justice for consumers and people who do not have access to prime

3 William D Henderson, *Legal Market Landscape Report: Commissioned by the State Bar of California* (July 2018). <https://board.calbar.ca.gov/docs/agendaItem/Public/agendaitem1000022382.pdf>, accessed 1 November 2023.

4 John Armour and Mari Sako, 'Legal Tech: Levelling the Playing Field in Legal Services?' in David Engstrom (ed), *Legal Tech and the Future of Civil Justice* (Cambridge University Press 2023) ch 2; available at <https://ssrn.com/abstract=3831481>, accessed 1 November 2023; Mari Sako and Richard Parham, *Technology and Innovation in Legal Services: Final Report for the Solicitors Regulation Authority* (July 2021), <www.sra.org.uk/globalassets/documents/sra/research/full-report-technology-and-innovation-in-legal-services.pdf?version=4a1bfe>, accessed 1 November 2023.

legal services needs to be seen against the background that it is either not rational for them to spend that much money on access or that they just do not have the money.

Mari, I wondered while listening to you about the use of AI in law by non-lawyers. In your research, you looked at in-house lawyers and external law advisors. I started wondering whether sometimes non-lawyers are quite good at recognising where they can replace lawyers by using AI. Thus, it is not the lawyers themselves who augment their work using AI, but non-lawyers seeing that they can get even better results than paying a lawyer triple figures per hour. For instance, people engaging in litigation finance may use AI to predict the value of claims. That essentially means knowing whether or not the claim will be successful in court, how long it takes and what the costs are to bring this claim to court. Litigation finance is an area where we see that AI is used. However, these are not lawyers using AI, but finance experts who think that AI may produce better results for the cost. Before using AI, they asked a lawyer to give them an estimate of the possible outcome. Now they may use AI to predict the outcome of such claims themselves. We have seen, in the United Kingdom and the United States, that new areas of litigation finance are being accessed via AI. For small claims, it is not very attractive to take recourse to traditional litigation finance mechanisms as the cost of using lawyers to estimate the outcome is relatively too high. Using AI, however, which is scalable, now provides access to new areas of litigation finance, in particular those concerning smaller claims. Hence, to sum it up, what is your take on non-lawyers using AI in law and how would that fit with your research?

**Sako:** That is a great segue into the next section. The focus really is on what consumers or clients value, and rarely do clients have a legal problem. They have a problem, an issue which could be solved by applying legal analysis. In all areas of law, what AI is most likely to do is redefine the market of legal services. The one-stop-shop solution that some of the clients, whether corporate or individual, are looking for, say, a tax issue in corporate matters or an immigration issue concerning individuals, has a legal aspect, but it also has a non-legal aspect. What AI is able to do is help develop a solution that is packaged, integrating legal and non-legal aspects. This will provide a quicker comprehensive solution to the ultimate client. Whether this is led by a lawyer or somebody who is called a lawyer, as opposed to somebody who is not called a lawyer, is uncertain now.

## CONCEPT OF BUSINESS MODELS

**Sako:** The next part of my presentation is about business models. It is important to note that business models are a particular concept that we use in business schools. We can think of business models in different ways. We have law firms, the likes of Clifford Chance and Linklaters, and legal departments of global corporations like Barclays or BT. That used to be the main thick pipeline of legal services. But we now have new players, law companies like Elevate and UnitedLex, and investors, incubators and data vendors like Thomson Reuters and LexisNexis, which most of you have heard of.

| Business models | What customers value | How value is created | How value is captured |
|---|---|---|---|
| Legal advisory | Bespoke legal advice | Input-based (billable hour) | Trust, reputation, leverage |
| Legal operations | Process efficiency and project management | Output-based (fixed fee) | Process & project management capabilities |
| Legal technology | Technology solutions | Subscription, licensing | Intellectual property (copyright or patent) and platforms |
| Consulting | Consulting advice | Input-based (charged by the hour) | Consulting expertise grounded in legal operations and/or legal technology |

FIGURE 7.6 Four business models in legal services

I am now going to talk about business models using Figure 7.6 as illustration. Business model is a term that has been used in many ways by many different people, but it is basically a way of thinking about how a firm pursues its activities to create and capture value.[5] We start with the customer value proposition, or what customers value. As a provider, you think about how to create value and how to capture value. In our work, which is already published, we identified four different business models, one of which is the traditional legal advisory. What customers value here is bespoke legal advice. Value is created typically through input-based billable hours. Value is captured because lawyers are trusted advisors with a reputation that they can leverage. An organisational complement to this business model is a professional partnership, i.e. a partnership of lawyers only, which is the typical way of organising legal advice in many countries. It is the best mode to deliver this business model because lawyers as peers know each other very well. They can set their ethics and norms, and they can monitor each other well. Consensus decision-making also works well.

Lawyers charge by the hour because legal advice is what economists call a credence good. A credence good is a good or service where consumers cannot verify its quality even after consumption. Think about being a patient and being prescribed a medicine by a doctor. You take it on faith, but it takes some time for the effect to come through. As a patient, you are buying a credence good because you do not have the expertise to understand the medical basis for why a medicine that you have been prescribed works. It may actually work, or it may not. That is the kind of thinking as regards legal advisory.

5 John Armour and Mari Sako, 'AI-Enabled Business Models in Legal Services: From Traditional Law Firms to Next-Generation Law Companies?' (2020) 7(1) Journal of Professions and Organization 27.

If you think about what new business models are being created using AI, then the first type I would like to mention is 'legal operations'. Here, what customers value is process efficiency and project management. Value is created through output-based pricing, the so-called fixed fee. You can predict costs a lot better this way, and you can capture value by having capabilities in process and project management. The organisational complement here is structured so that it incentivises both lawyers and non-lawyers to deploy AI tools efficiently.

A second business model enabled by AI is what we call 'legal technology'. Here, customers value technology-based solutions. Pricing can be through subscription or licensing. Value is captured by the provider typically by way of intellectual property – patents, in some cases copyright – and by offering platform services.

Finally, it is important to consider 'consulting' as a separate value proposition. Clients value advice on what kind of technology to adopt, for example. Funnily enough, here, the value is created again by charging by the hour, just like in legal advisory. Much of the expertise is in the experience of using certain types of technology.

## COMBINING THE BUSINESS MODELS?

**Sako:** There are different ways in which we can combine these business models. Much of the competition that is presently going on concerns different players thinking about how best to combine these different business models.

From the perspective of a law firm, you can have a law firm that remains, if you like, pure play, as in not combining anything, i.e. sticking to legal advisory and externalising everything else. You can access new services by buying rather than making. In that way, law firms can externalise all the complexities that arise from combining business models. This also concerns human capital. But there are certain law firms, which have brought legal operations expertise in-house. A while ago, you may have read about knowledge centres created in places like India, the Philippines or Northern Ireland. Some law firms like Simmons & Simmons have purchased LawTech start-ups like Wavelength Law. So, legal tech can be bought as a service, but acquiring a LawTech company is also a possibility. Other law firms, including Pinsent Masons, have created an in-house consulting wing within the law firm. This is an interesting development.

LawTech companies like UnitedLex, Elevate and Axiom start with expertise in legal operations and consulting and to an extent legal technology. They are not stopping there but are quite ambitious in wanting to get into the legal advisory work as well. A company like Elevate has created its own in-house law firm called ElevateNext. Another company, UnitedLex, has an in-house law firm called Marshall Denning. Without such an in-house law firm they would not have access to premier corporate clients. So, everybody is trying to get into each other's turf, and there is competition in terms of combining different business models.

## WHAT CAREERS DO LEGAL TECH ENTREPRENEURS NEED?

**Sako:** I am now going to discuss the LawTech start-up business model. There is a lot of buzz and a lot of excitement around different types of LawTech start-ups in different areas of law.[6] In our research, we compared LawTech and FinTech start-ups in three locations, London and New York, which are two global financial centres, and the San Francisco Bay area known for its tech start-ups broadly, well beyond FinTech and LawTech.[7] We compiled data concerning the start-ups' social connections by looking at the founders' educational and employment ties – what kind of university they went to in the past, what kind of work they did before they founded the start-ups. We also tried to classify the founders' knowledge according to whether they are coders or whether they are from the financial markets' domain, whether they are lawyers or had a management role beforehand. We ended up with a database of just over 600 founders for just over 300 venture firms. We found that ventures with founders who have denser social ties, i.e. who are located in an ecosystem where there are other people who have gone to the same university or who have worked for the same employer, scale up faster. We also found that founders' knowledge domain matters as well.

Figure 7.7 shows that the founders' social networks are the densest in San Francisco and most sparse in the New York LawTech ecosystem. Moreover, in San Francisco founders with coding skills dominate, which is not surprising. In New York and London founders come from very different knowledge domains, including coding and law, which is an interesting finding.

In Figure 7.8, we analyse how fast start-ups grow, which is the vertical axis, according to what kind of founders are involved – on the horizontal axis. Across FinTech and LawTech, we find that a founding team with coder skills only grows the fastest. I am not going to dwell on the middle bit, but on the extreme right is the founding team with lawyers only. That is the slowest to grow. We conducted some interviews to understand this better. Here are some of the insights in the form of quotations.

A retired managing partner who set up a LawTech company said:

> I was a partner for 20 years. Frankly, I am too impatient and can't be bothered to have to go around seeking external investors and then build our own infrastructure.

He basically says that his retirement venture makes a reasonable amount of money and that scaling up is not his objective. On the other extreme is an ambitious founder with an Oxford PhD in Physics saying,

> Our vision is to help companies unlock the value of their data. So, our play is a data play as opposed to a legal workflow play. Our platform is industry-agnostic.

6 For one of the many diagrams and infographics on this matter, see <www.legalcomplex.com/wp-content/uploads/2019/02/tnw-deloitte.jpg>, accessed 1 November 2023.

7 Mari Sako and others, 'Scaling Up Firms in Entrepreneurial Ecosystems: Fintech and Lawtech Ecosystems Compared' (15 January 2020), <https://papers.ssrn.com/sol3/papers.cfm?abstract_id=3520533>, accessed 1 November 2023.

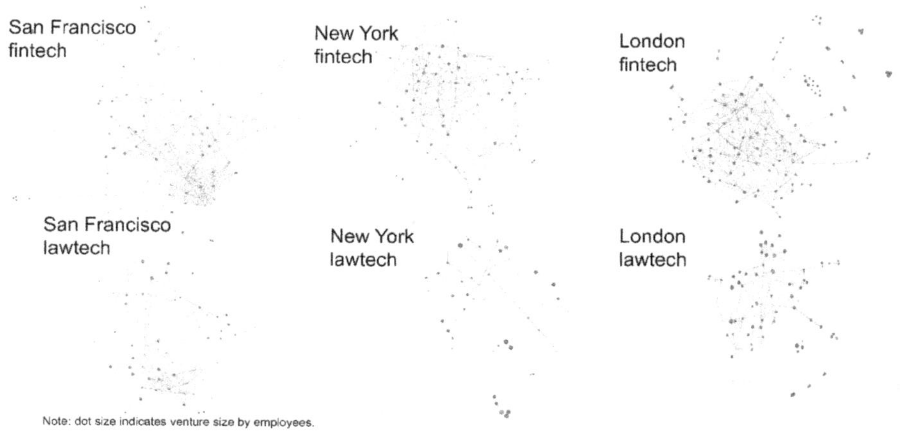


FIGURE 7.7 Founders' social networks

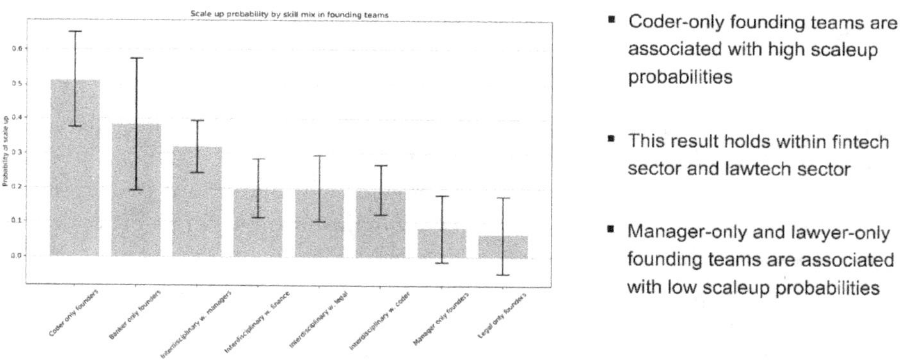


FIGURE 7.8 Speed of scaling up

Industry-agnostic means that his target market is not just legal, but also finance and well beyond. Anything that uses data is his target market. This shows the extreme ends of different ambitions, different corporate aims that have been predicated in part on the background, the knowledge domains and the experiences of the founders. I find that quite interesting.

To sum up, from a LawTech provider perspective, you have business models where you, obviously, start with the legal technology, but can then take different approaches, including selling to law firms or data providers or partnering with law firms. The likes of Thomson Reuters and LexisNexis are in the business of buying these LawTech start-ups. There is a certain amount of consolidation going on. What is interesting about the LawTech start-up scene is that some of the companies are not treating legal services as a defined well-scoped market. The ambition is to go well beyond, to address other markets.

**Sako:** Are there any questions at this point?

**Student A:** Thank you for the presentation. You mentioned that law firms have the choice of internalising or externalising complexities arising from combining business models. Could you explain these complexities in more detail, please?

**Sako:** Sure. What I meant by complexity concerns not only the organisational management complexity but also managing the careers of professionals with different expertise. Law firms are typically partnerships of lawyers only. The career route leads from junior associate to senior associate to partner. Partner is a status involving being an equity owner of the law firm. In many countries, except, however, England and Wales, you can be an equity owner of a law firm only if you are a lawyer. In that context, if you try and combine a business model beyond legal advisory to also include legal operations or legal technology business models, then you need to hire and incentivise data scientists and other specialists who are not lawyers. This is difficult. The complexity arises from the need to recruit and retain different talents who are not lawyers and, as a consequence, do not enjoy the opportunity to get promoted to the top management team.

There are other complexities, but one of the main complexities concerns managing human capital when you have a variety of different professionals and talents. If a law firm does not adopt a different business model and just buys legal technology services rather than having a legal technology operation in-house, then it can rely on somebody else to hire and incentivise those people.

**Student B:** Thank you, Professor, for your informative presentation thus far. I really found your research comparing founders of LawTech start-ups interesting. I was wondering whether you have any further ideas as to why legal-only founders experience slower scale-ups.

**Sako:** Thank you. Our research shows slower scale-up for ventures that had lawyer founders compared with ventures with other types of founders. Some might think of lawyers as being more cautious and not very prone to taking risks, but the reason that has come to light through our research rather concerns the target market. Lawyer founder ventures tend to target the legal market only. That is a vast market because there are not that many start-ups, and there are different types of start-ups. One start-up may be focused on contract analytics, another one on legal research and another one offers on-demand lawyering. The latter means creating a marketplace allowing the hiring of lawyers on a project-by-project basis. Nevertheless, it is a legal market only. This market constrains their ambition to scale compared with a start-up that has, as a starting point, a piece of technology or tool that can be applied to all kinds of markets, including legal, but also finance and marketing and so on. Such companies partner with big corporations like SalesForce for marketing or they partner with DocuSign for all kinds of document signing, not just legal documents.

**Sumida:** Thank you. Would you like to continue with your presentation?

## WHAT YOU NEED TO SURVIVE AS A LAWYER

**Sako:** Sure. I would like to think about the future of lawyers, all of you in the audience, the law students and the practising lawyers. Let's think about the future of law firms. I will avoid black-and-white futuristic projections, terms like 'the end of lawyers' or 'the end of law firms', partly because I am an academic, but partly also because I think there are really important nuances concerning what will stay and what will disappear.

The classical advisory roles of giving valued advice to clients will stay. It will be enhanced in quality but will decrease in quantity. The number of lawyers who are going to be specialised in this role will not be high because some of these services will be substituted by machines. New roles in MDTs, augmenting legal services through technology, will increase in importance. This requires new training and career paths. Importantly, some of these people may not be called lawyers anymore in the future. The MDTs involved may be facilitated in different ways. One can have lawyers and non-lawyers working together in a team seamlessly because they speak the same language, they understand each other. Or lawyers themselves acquire technical skills. This is the notion of the lawyer-coder.

Turning back to the survey, we asked respondents to agree or disagree with the statement, 'I prefer to work with lawyer-coders (lawyers with coding skills) than with non-lawyer technologists (who specialize in coding) to get my work done.' You can see in Figure 7.9 that in the first bar, which represents respondents from in-house legal departments, 11 per cent agreed with that. It is a very low number. In the middle bar, 27 per cent of the respondents from law firms agreed. This is not the majority, but more people working in law firms agreed with this statement.

**Sako:** This gives us some indication of the career path that is available to people who are working in law firms. One of the questions asked earlier concerned the complexity of law firms. The corresponding situation is illustrated by the following quotation: 'We have obviously been a very good firm, with a good brand associated, in terms of access to young talent. In the software space, they normally do not want to join a law firm, they want to go and work for a cool software company.' If you have a choice of working for Amazon or Google or working for a top law firm, however top that would be, if you are a data scientist, I think the choice is rather clear.

## WHAT LAW COMPANIES HAVE THAT LAW FIRMS DO NOT

**Sako:** Here is another statement that we have collected: 'We have all kinds of people who have been practising lawyers, people who have been general counsel who understand the executive communication, we also have people experienced in business process outsourcing, people in IT or HR, people who are process specialist blackbelts. We have change management. We have financial analysts.' Law firms like this one will be able to accommodate a variety of different talents. I think that is the real stark contrast. Thus, if you think about what is necessary in an MDT from a

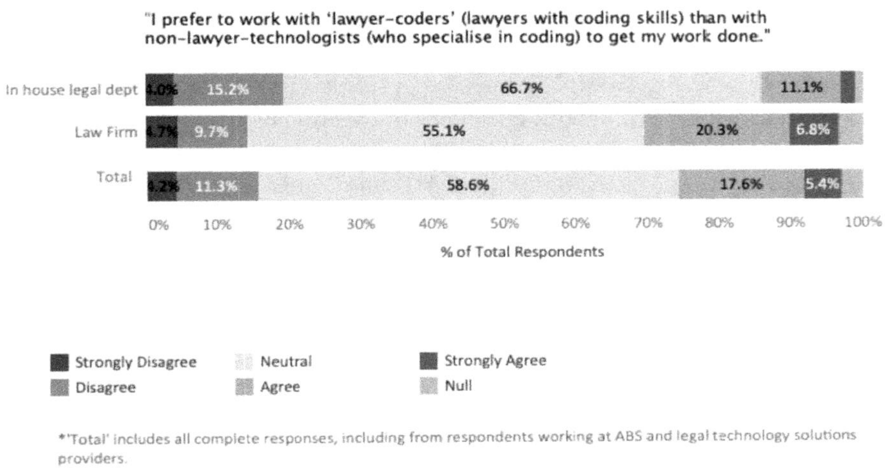


FIGURE 7.9 Lawyers in law firms prefer lawyers with programming skills over technicians

law firm perspective, it is not just about lawyers becoming coders. It is really about mindset and a common language. As one law firm member said, 'I don't think that lawyers should code or need to code. I think that what they need to do is to think about the interpersonal skills, be curious and be willing to adapt. This is really less about a technical perspective and more about how they interact, how they work and how they are continually changing.' I think that is a novel way of thinking about how effective you can be in an MDT.

What would determine the pathways to multi-disciplinarity? It depends on two things. One is to do with what the professional control would look like. What would lie within and what would lie outside of the jurisdictional boundaries of a licensed lawyer. In the United States, you have the notion of authorised practice of law and the opposite of that is the unauthorised practice of law. What is required is a re-definition and revisiting of such definitions. The second factor, which determines the pathways to multi-disciplinarity, is law firm governance. Let me spend a few minutes each on these points.

## THREE CAREER PATHS FOR FUTURE LAWYERS

**Sako:** On the first point, I project that there are three possible futures in twenty–thirty years from now. One is what happens in law firms now. The main body of human capital is licensed lawyers. They are assisted by specialists who are in data science or who are process and project experts. These two categories are support staff and are never going to be a part of the law firm's core hierarchy. A second scenario is what I call incorporation. Here, all licensed lawyers, some of whom become lawyer-coders and some of whom become lawyer-managers, stay within the legal profession. The third is what I call the professional fragmentation scenario. Here, licensed lawyers will work with other specialists and these other specialists are professionals in their own, different rights, be it in legal operations or in legal engineering.

Let's think about these three scenarios, as shown in Figure 7.10, and consider the possible career paths for lawyers. On the left is business as usual, licensed lawyers. I expect that the associate-to-partner progression will remain the main career path. Data scientists and managers are rewarded financially if they are to be attracted to work for law firms. They will probably have to think about a career path which is more self-managed. They will probably be coming into and out of law firms and other kinds of workplaces as well.

In the middle, we have the rise of lawyer-coders. There are some signs that lawyers' technical skills are being accredited, for example by the Law Society of Scotland, which has a certificate for legal engineers. That is an interesting development, but the question here is whether, if you move to specialise in legal engineering, you can also still become a law firm partner.

Finally, in the professional fragmentation scenario, licensed lawyers' work will be fragmented. Some of them will go into legal engineering and others into legal operations. Legal operations experts have their own professional association called CLOC. Some of the entry points for becoming a legal operations expert or legal engineer may not be through getting a licence to be a lawyer. There will be multiple entry points for people who work in legal services.

For the law firms, the implications are quite interesting. I do not think that time is running out for law firms. Some law firms will survive. As you probably know, in the United States, the ABA Model Rules of Professional Conduct 5.4 basically mandates law firms to be owned by lawyers only. Fee sharing is forbidden, except in regulatory sandbox experiments which are going on in the states of Arizona, Utah and California. The United Kingdom is a little bit ahead in permitting what they call

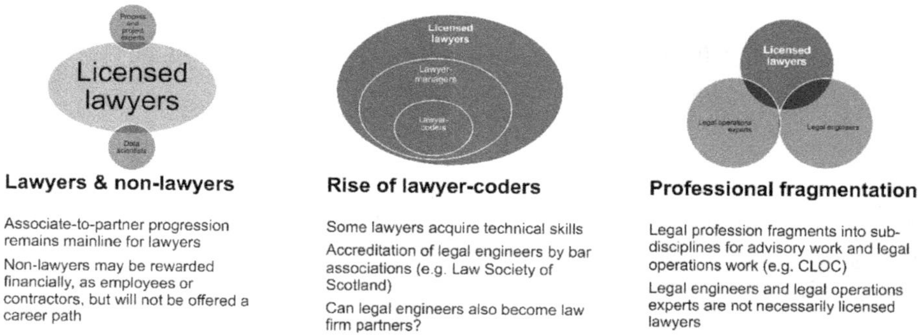


FIGURE 7.10 Possible legal career paths

'alternative business structures'. They enable lawyers to co-own and co-manage law firms with non-lawyers.

### WHY LAWYERS AND NON-LAWYERS CANNOT WORK TOGETHER

**Sako:** Much of the policy concern focuses on relaxing rules so that law firms can get access to outside finance for innovation, including investing in legal technology. But in our interviews, nobody has really expressed concern about lack of finance, outside or inside, for legal tech adoption. In contrast, the key concern appears to be the recruitment and retention of non-lawyer human capital. So, we wish to re-direct people's attention to the career path issue that I have already talked about. The issue is that, if you are a lawyer, you can get to the top, but if you are not a lawyer, you cannot get to the top, and that obviously is damaging to incentives.

There is a puzzle as regards the United Kingdom, which has created the opportunity for an alternative business structure (ABS) where lawyers and non-lawyers can co-own and co-manage law firms. Ten years after the Legal Services Act has enabled this structure, large law firms remain mono-professional partnerships. If you talk to the likes of Clifford Chance, Linklaters and Freshfields, they are not considering using the ABS. The question arises as to why that is the case. We think that they fear that the ABS would risk diluting the reputation and value of the core intangible assets, which are the lawyers themselves.

As a result, what is most likely to happen is that the law firms, some of which are going to just be pure play with the advisory business model only, will remain partnerships. They will be consumers of AI-enabled legal services. There will be other law firms that want to produce AI-enabled legal services by having an in-house technology division. I predict that they will use the ABS model.

Let me conclude by reminding you of the importance of thinking about the impact of AI in terms of the delivery pipeline. We are talking about the end of some things that lawyers do, but definitely not the end of lawyers. AI automates tasks, not jobs. We can think of lawyers as consumers of AI, but also as producers of AI working in MDTs. There is a variety of AI-enabled business models in legal services that many players, whether it is a law firm, a law company or a legal tech provider, are experimenting with, including by combining them in different ways. This has fundamental implications for the future careers of lawyers and also of law firms. I would project that law firms are here to stay as niche players and that with the possibility of three different kinds of scenarios in the future, it is up to not just the regulators and the government, but also the legal professionals themselves to influence which direction they want to take. Thank you very much. I really look forward to some questions and comments.

**Steffek:** Thank you very much, Mari. It was a fantastic talk. We are very grateful that Masakazu Iwakura is willing to provide comments. In his comments, he will consider the situation in Japan. Thank you very much again, Mari. We will come back to you later in the discussion.

### JAPANESE BUSINESS LAW: 30 YEARS BEHIND THE UNITED STATES AND THE UNITED KINGDOM

**Sumida:** Today's commentator is Professor Masakazu Iwakura, a Senior Partner at TMI Associates. Professor Mari Sako has discussed the situation in the United Kingdom and the United States. I thought that Professor Iwakura would be the perfect person to discuss the implications for Japan, drawing from the presentation of Professor Sako. Professor Iwakura, without further ado, the floor is yours.

**Iwakura:** Thank you, Professor Sumida, for your kind introduction. As Professor Sumida mentioned, I am now working as a partner in a law firm, and I have been practising law for the last thirty-four years. Including my time at Harvard University and Hitotsubashi University, I have been teaching in higher education for over thirty years. I was very impressed by the wonderful presentation by Professor Sako. The topic of my talk is the Japanese situation by way of comparative analysis of the materials presented by Professor Sako. I must first let you know that I am not an expert in LawTech. Rather, I am a professional business lawyer. I am involved more in bespoke cases in the areas of intellectual property and M&A. Hence, I am not quite versed in state-of-the-art legal technology. It has been quite an educational opportunity for me today. Going forward, I will be using the knowledge I acquired today.

It is often said that the Japanese legal sector is behind that of the United Kingdom and the United States by 20–30 years. In the areas of LawTech and legal AI, Japan is lagging behind substantially. We are rather primitive in these sectors. But those countries, including Japan, which are lagging behind, are in a position to cherry-pick, making it possible to leap-frog. Thus, we can cherry-pick all the knowledge and achievements that have been made in other markets. Japanese law firms, lawyers and academics can be good students of the innovation we have been exposed to today.

### THE BIG FIVE JOINTLY FOUNDED LAWTECH VENTURES

**Iwakura:** I agree with Professor Sako's key assertions. The propagation of AI in the Japanese legal industry is lagging behind that of the United Kingdom, the United States and China. The speed at which the Japanese legal industry is adopting AI is much slower. That is a unique challenge Japan is facing. In Japan, there are many law firms. We might not have the Big Four or Big Eight firms in the world in the accounting industry, but we have the Big Five law firms – big by Japanese standards. The definition of a big law firm in Japan includes those with more than 400 lawyers. The Big Five firms are all located in Tokyo.

However, the majority of Japanese law firms are very small in scale. Most are one-attorney or two-attorney offices. There is a huge difference in the way of doing business and in terms of aspirations between the Big Five and the smaller law firms. I have belonged to two of the Big Five law firms in the past. Within the Big Five, AI is being adopted at a much slower rate than that seen in the United Kingdom or the United States. All the Big Five firms are engaged in cross-border and international cases. That requires them to be more familiar with AI, especially because they must communicate with their counterparts in the United Kingdom and the United States on a daily basis.

In cross-border cases, the Big Five are, for example, engaged in e-discovery. E-discovery is a process that did not exist in Japan. What I have in mind is not the deployment of AI for e-discovery in Japan, but the use of e-discovery in international M&A or arbitration cases. To support such a case, big Japanese firms must be able to manage the e-discovery process. Legal research, due diligence review and contract drafting also use AI, though the level of reliance is much lighter. Some of the Big Five are now working with LawTech providers. The approach they are taking is to jointly launch LawTech companies.

At TMI, which I now belong to, a company named TMI Privacy and Security Consulting has been launched, separate from the law firm. TMI Privacy and Security Consulting specialises in specific areas of privacy and security. It is aspiring to expand the scope of business to include wider areas of LawTech. Nagashima, Ohno and Tsunematsu have launched MNTSQ, another LawTech firm. I believe that this is a joint venture. So, it is interesting to see that some of the Big Five law firms have jointly launched these specialised LawTech firms.

As mentioned already, small- and medium-sized law firms, even though I really regret and am rather embarrassed to say this, have not engaged at all with AI. This is the result of a survey conducted in 2019.[8] Ninety-eight per cent of the law firms in Japan have ten or less lawyers. One- or two-lawyer firms constitute around 80 per cent of the entire law firm market. Hence, the demography of the law firms is very different compared with the British or the American industries. With technical advances, the proportion may change, and small- and medium-sized law firms may become more interested in the use of AI because AI can possibly augment their skills and capabilities. But as we speak today, the LawTech ecosystem is much less developed in Japan. There is little engagement by small- and medium-sized law firms. The attorneys in the Big Five and junior and upcoming aspirational lawyers may have an interest in creating law firms that have a stronger emphasis on LawTech. They are yet to assert their unique value.

## HAS THE INTRODUCTION OF AI IN THE JUDICIARY MADE PROGRESS?

**Iwakura:** This is a very sensitive issue, and I must be bold to say this to you, but the Japanese Supreme Court is focusing on the wider use of IT. Introduction and

[8] Japan Federation of Bar Associations (ed), *White Paper on Attorneys* (2019) 72, <www.nichibenren.or.jp/library/en/about/data/WhitePaper2019.pdf>, accessed 1 November 2023.

application of IT are being encouraged at the Supreme Court level in Japan. This is also supported by the government of Japan. We are seeing rapid development with regard to the wider use of IT. However, the area of IT usage is focused more on civil procedure practices, not on criminal cases. It, frankly, is not really AI. Instead, the focus is on very basic IT services. Hence, within the Japanese legal sector, AI has very little practical relevance.

What about the legal community in Japan? I am not quite sure if Professor Sumida is of the same opinion, but only a limited number of scholars are versed in AI. Correlations or the relations between AI and the law, or the implications and repercussions that the same may have, have been drawing much attention, however, the level of knowledge is still limited. The younger generation tends to be more interested than the older ones. Younger lawyers are aspiring, and I am hoping that Japanese scholars, too, will become more interested in this area. Scholars of older generations are not quite sure even as to how to use these technologies or how these technologies can impact their areas of research.

## EMERGENCE OF NEW PLAYERS

**Iwakura:** Now, I will turn to new players. While the number of new players is still limited in Japan, there are some LawTech providers starting new businesses. I do not have any personal affiliation with these companies, but I can say that there are new players in the Japanese market of legal technology. Some of them are affiliated with the Big Five law firms. In-house counsel and corporate services are the areas that these players are trying to serve.

A key point raised in Professor Sako's presentation is the emergence of MDTs. As Professor Sako mentioned, compared to in-house lawyers, lawyers at law firms are less eager to engage with LawTech. Within big firms, it is the data scientists that the lawyers work with. TMI and Nagashima Ohno have a joint business alliance with LawTech providers. In that sense, lawyers have opportunities to work with non-lawyers, but especially in small- and medium-sized law firms, MDTs are virtually non-existent.

As far as in-house counsels are concerned, the number of lawyers was earlier limited in Japan, and, as a result, the number of in-house lawyers was also limited. After legal reform, the number of lawyers has increased dramatically in recent years. I became a lawyer about 40 years ago. In that specific year, 450 applicants passed the bar exam. Now, around 1,500 applicants pass the bar each year. That also means that the number of in-house lawyers is increasing. Business firms aspire to have an in-house lawyer and we now have professional associations of in-house lawyers. But looking at the entire pool of lawyers, most of them are not in-house. Since legal issues arise within businesses, LawTech is being sought after by business entities. I think that this is a unique factor in Japan. The Big Five and other larger law firms may consider developing MDTs, but other than those major players, MDTs may be created mainly in non-legal businesses in Japan.

## WHY JAPAN IS BECOMING GALAPAGOS

**Iwakura:** How exactly does the situation in Japan differ from that in the United States, the United Kingdom and China? Be it technology, the economy or even culture, there is something unique about Japan. I am not really a person who worships the uniqueness of the Japanese situation, but I still believe that there are unique factors present in Japan. Legal jargon and legal terms are specific. I have a US bar licence and I also have taught law at Harvard. Against that background, I can say that the Japanese legal language is very different from the English legal language. American court decisions, while they can get philosophical at times, are very articulate and clear in terms of the reasons. In Japan, on the other hand, precedents are not as clear as the judges themselves would like them to be. Precedent is used in a much more multi-faceted way by lawyers in general, and people working in legal roles in companies in particular. One of the reasons for this may be the ambiguity of the Japanese language. This is not to say that ambiguity is generally a bad thing. However, because the Japanese language has such a special character and is not a language used by many people around the world, as is the case with English and Chinese, it may be lagging behind in some of the basics that are useful for the development of legal AI.

Another thing that I mentioned earlier is that the Supreme Court is making progress with IT. But in fact, it is also lagging behind considerably. As reported in the news, Japan has a stamp culture, which is not necessarily the case in other countries. When signing a contract or creating an official document, you have to stamp it. This is considered to be very inefficient, especially since remote working was recommended during the pandemic. This is also a factor that demonstrates how Japan is lagging behind.

## WHEN WILL THE JAPANESE LEGAL PROFESSION CHANGE?

**Iwakura:** Be it law firms or lawyers or legal society, how will they be impacted by legal AI? In my opinion, AI should be used, not only by consuming it but also by producing new LawTech services. I believe that we have such movements in the Japanese legal industry, even though we are still in a nascent phase. We are lagging behind, but we can still learn from and cherry-pick American and British experiences.

Since Japanese lawyers mostly work in small-sized law firms, they have yet to face the immediate consequences of legal AI. Aspiring younger lawyers who wish to work for Google, Apple, Facebook or Amazon (GAFA) may possibly start using AI, thereby changing the landscape of the legal industry. In terms of the management of law firms, I believe that law firms will survive. There is a solid client base for such law firms as well.

Talking about court litigation, not arbitration, courts and judges may feel a sense of resistance against using AI in decision-making. Arbitrators may want to use it for arbitration, but there is little thought of using this technology for court litigation, even though that is the direction we may be heading towards. In terms of litigation, lawyers are paid when the cases are won. So, there is a reward for successful litigation. Lawyers may use AI for the preparation of litigation. Younger scholars or up-and-coming new players are curious about new technologies and start using them. They may start finding new business or research opportunities as well.

Shogi is a Japanese chess game and there is a very young professional Shogi player in Japan whose name is Sõta Fujii. He is still a teenager, and it seems to me that he uses AI technology. He has come up with new skills and he has won two of the seven big major titles of Shogi, defeating big names. So, as is the case with Fujii-san, the Shogi player, it is the younger generation that will bring the change. Looking at the successes of young people, maybe we should be learning from them. I hope that this is the general trend in Japan.

**Sumida:** Thank you very much. Professor Sako, would you like to respond?

## DATA AVAILABILITY IS KEY FOR LEGAL AI

**Sako:** Thank you so much for the thoughtful and insightful comments on Japan, about which I only have a very narrow and blinkered perspective. Having studied a little about in-house legal departments in Japan, I found it interesting that the majority of people are not qualified lawyers. As you say, there are perhaps advantages to being able to incorporate MDTs in a smoother way. In terms of where Japan can be ahead of the game, there is a lot of talk about digital transformation of legal departments including other corporate functions such as marketing and finance. Maybe Japan could be ahead of the game in digitally transforming some of the major Japanese business corporations in that way; and lawyers can play a part there, too.

You also had some questions concerning the situation in the United Kingdom as opposed to that in the United States. It is not an area that I know a lot about, but my understanding is that London is a centre for litigation funding. So, there is equity and other financial capital appetite for the use of AI in predicting court cases. I think that is a major driver. As regards the courts, Richard Susskind has contributed a lot to the application of AI to arbitration and litigation. Much of the use of AI, I think, is in commercial areas, in international arbitration and in minor commercial dispute resolution. Much of the difference between the United States and the United Kingdom is in the availability of data for both academics and others to analyse. Felix may know more about that than I do, but I think there is a huge gap in terms of being able to access court-based data in the United States and China, compared to the United Kingdom where it is much more closed. It is not about digitisation. I think it is more about the will to disclose the data.

## WHAT YOUNG LAWYERS CAN DO TO MAKE A DIFFERENCE?

**Student C:** Young keen and upcoming lawyers in the future may start using AI, as you were saying, but in a former class by Mr Ludwig Bull, we heard that in Japan, data is not really made public, so it is very difficult to use AI. He talked about the scarcity of public data in Japan. So, in this situation, for young lawyers in Japan to act, we need change. What do you think?

**Iwakura:** In Japan, compared to the United States, overwhelmingly, important data is not made public. In the past, court cases were not disclosed. The courts decided whether to make decisions public or not. But now, the Supreme Court is trying to make decisions publicly available on an anonymous basis, if there are no problems regarding privacy. So, there is an improvement, but there is a lot of legal data that is not disclosed in Japan. In my area of specialisation, M&A, in the United States, there is a certain standard under which M&A transaction contracts are all disclosed for listed companies. In the case of Japan, the rules of the Tokyo Stock Exchange do not stipulate for these contracts to be disclosed. I believe that they should all be disclosed like in the United States. I have been saying this for a long time, but for a variety of reasons, these contracts are not disclosed in Japan.

**Student D:** I have a question about AI development. Could the government, or a public institution, provide datasets regarding the law to facilitate the development of legal AI? I would be interested in Professor Sako's opinion on this.

**Sako:** If I understood your question correctly, it concerns the limited availability of legal data, which we have not addressed fully in this session. I do not think that it is just a Japanese problem. This limitation is everywhere in the legal market. We need to distinguish between technical constraints and non-technical constraints on the ability to make data publicly available and/or open-sourced. I think that we will get there, but we need collective action to do this. On the technological side, advances in technology might ease the privacy fear of individuals sharing their personal data. But then, even if technology is solving that aspect, from a business perspective, there is commercial sensitivity around sharing certain types of data, including on M&A. If the data is at the core of the competitive advantage of a particular company, they are not going to be willing to share. So, we need that to be put aside.

Much of the difficulty in aggregating data has to do with the lack of standardisation and the lack of templates for structuring data in such a way that it can be aggregated. In the United Kingdom, there is an initiative, called Engine B, in which the Big Four audit and accounting firms are getting together to try and create a standard for sharing their client data. Similar collective action of the Big Five in Japan or the Magic Circle firms in the United Kingdom as regards aggregating data following a certain standard would make a big difference. But none of those initiatives is happening in the legal field, at least not yet, as far as I know.

**Sumida:** Thank you to our two wonderful guests. This has been a very interesting session.

## CONCLUDING CONVERSATION

**Steffek:** Mari Sako's presentation analysed the use of LawTech applications from the perspective of an economist and a management researcher. I found her presentation fascinating in many respects as she shed new light on the discussion.

**Sumida:** As an organiser, I was so excited to invite Professor Sako to give a lecture at our university. Her suggestions for the Japanese commentators and her ideas on how to organise the session in order to make the dialogue with the students more enjoyable were also very much appreciated. It was a real treat to have the essence of the most advanced research in such a condensed and easy-to-understand format.

**Steffek:** From my perspective, the first point of Professor Sako's presentation is to enlighten the debate on the impact of AI on the legal profession. She makes it clear that lawyers will be either consumers or producers of AI applications, and that where AI applications are used, they may lead to augmentation of lawyers' services, or they may lead to substitution of such services. For the latter, she observed that they are more likely to be concerned with repetitive and scalable 'tasks'. Professor Sako's analysis went beyond the simple question of whether AI can replace human lawyers and showed that lawyers need to ask more differentiated questions about where they can become consumers of technology and where they can produce AI services.

**Sumida:** What surprised me was the way she applied the automobile assembly pipeline to the provision of legal services. By the way, she used the concept of 'task' to analyse the process of providing legal services by breaking down the process into very detailed 'tasks'. I remember that the categorisation of work into repetitive, interactive, cognitive and manual labour, introduced in the Labour Economics study on the impact of information and communication technology on labour, also focused on 'tasks'.[9] However, that study focused on 'tasks' when analysing 'occupation'. The different granularity of the discussion is a point that should not be overlooked.

**Steffek:** That is right. Professor Sako suggests that we look at the individual 'tasks' required to deliver legal services and ask how these will be affected by the use of AI. As a result, she points out that while the generation of outputs, in particular, will be strongly affected, new tasks will also be created, in particular those that require the cooperation with non-lawyers such as data scientists and project managers, who will contribute to legal services with greater relevance in the future. This focus on tasks is useful in order to better understand the impact of AI on the legal profession. From this perspective, we have found that the question of whether AI will replace human lawyers overlooks the potential for AI to create new jobs.

9 David H Autor, Frank Levy and Richard J Murnane, 'The Skill Content of Recent Technological Change: An Empirical Exploration' (2003) 118(4) The Quarterly Journal of Economics 1279. A well-known study in this context is: Daiji Kawaguchi, 'Will People Lose Their Jobs to Machines?' in Mihoko Sumida and Shunsuke Kudoh (eds), *Society Living with Robots – How Does the Law Deal with AI?* (Koubundou 2018) 73 [in Japanese].

It was also very interesting to analyse the business models as regards how firms operate and capture value. For example, law firms traditionally charge on an hourly basis, whereas LawTech start-ups often charge on a subscription fee basis. Also, law firms are traditionally organised as partnerships, whereas LawTech start-ups are organised as capital-based companies. The question for the future will be whether these two types of firms will partner or merge their businesses.

**Sumida:** In explaining why legal advice, the traditional business model of lawyers, is charged on an hourly basis, I was struck by the point that it is a 'credence good' and, like a doctor's prescription, it is uncertain whether it has really worked! I think this highlights the difficulty of preserving this value as new business models emerge and compete with each other.

**Steffek:** After listening to Professor Sako's presentation, I wondered which group of professionals would be best placed to understand the value that AI applications could bring to the legal services market. Is it lawyers themselves, or is it non-lawyers such as litigation finance specialists? At the same time, it was also an interesting observation that people rarely have 'legal problems'. People do have 'problems', and they may use the law to help solve them.

**Sumida:** That was a very memorable phrase for me. It is this perspective that underpins the idea of redefining the market. I think it is also connected to the issue of how to package legal and non-legal solutions in a one-stop solution, which is a topic in the following session.

**Steffek:** Further questions I pondered were whether local lawmakers can effectively shield local legal services markets from international competition as regards LawTech applications. Are there areas where such protectionism is not possible? Just to avoid a possible misunderstanding, I am not proposing that advanced jurisdictions should shield their markets against international competition. I rather wonder whether this is possible at all and, if not, what this means for professionals in jurisdictions where lawmakers are not open to the use of technology in legal services. This links to Mari Sako's analysis of professional laws where she finds that some jurisdictions allow joint business structures of lawyers and computing experts, whereas other jurisdictions exclude outsiders from holding equity in legal services firms.

**Sumida:** Is there a technology side to this question, such as foreign AI applications and language issues? In his comment, Masakazu Iwakura pointed out the Japanese language barrier. In our joint research project, we are discussing how high and how thick the Japanese language barrier is.

**Steffek:** Masakazu Iwakura compared Mari Sako's insights with the situation in Japan and pointed out notable developments, such as the fact that major Japanese law firms are setting up subsidiaries to deal with LawTech, which was very interesting. I also thought that it was important to point out that, in considering the future of LawTech in Japan, it is critically important that there are many smaller law firms in Japan compared to the United Kingdom and the United States. How these law firms relate to and adopt LawTech will be a topic to watch. He also confirmed the earlier speaker's assessment that, although LawTech is slow to take off in Japan, we can expect to see an expansion of AI-powered legal services.

**Sumida:** Masakazu Iwakura pointed out that MDT lawyers in Japan have already started in the big law firms, but apart from that, they are going in-house. I think this is true in terms of legal careers, but if we look at it more broadly, we can point to database companies as employers of MDT in Japan. It seems to me that the most pressing need is to solve the need for datasets, for example by shifting to open data for court decisions. Of course, it is not only Japanese database companies, but also foreign database companies that are expanding their business in Japan, which may be relevant to the issue raised by you.

## QUESTIONS FOR FURTHER THOUGHT

- Should the government interfere with the use of LawTech, or should it be left to commerce and the 'invisible hand' of the market?
- Will non-lawyers be the future drivers of AI applications in law in case lawyers are not moving into this field fast enough?
- What environment is needed for law firms to engage with AI?
- Is an explanation of the slow use of AI perhaps the fact that the services offered are not attractive enough?
- When you start your own legal business in the future, how do you evaluate the incentives for colleagues who are not qualified lawyers?
- Can legal markets insulate themselves such that even if AI is used in other jurisdictions, it will not matter in the insulated market?
- What role will lawmakers play in the future development of the legal profession and its relationship with technology?

# Conversation 8

## Will Digitalisation Help the Five Billion People without Meaningful Access to Justice?

ABSTRACT

This conversation brings together national and international policymakers to discuss the impact of digitalisation on access to justice. The background of the discussion is provided by the United Nation's Global Goal 16 to 'provide access to justice for all'. The policymakers contributing to this conversation represent the ministries of justice of Germany and Japan, the Organisation for Economic Co-operation and Development (OECD), the International Institute for the Unification of Private Law (UNIDROIT) and the Pathfinders for Peaceful, Just and Inclusive Societies. The discussants explore the potential of technology to provide meaningful access to law and justice. They do so within the context of their organisation's policy initiatives such as digitalising courts and other justice institutions. Referring to reform experiences, they pay attention to facilitators and barriers of technological change. The policymakers also consider the risks of technology for access to justice and emphasise the need to keep digital vulnerability in mind.

| | |
|---|---|
| *Speakers* | Philip Scholz, Takashi Kikkawa, Tatyana Teplova, Maaike de Langen, Ignacio Tirado and Anna Veneziano |
| *Moderators* | Felix Steffek and Mihoko Sumida |
| *Concluding Conversation* | Felix Steffek and Mihoko Sumida |
| *Questions for Further Thought* | Felix Steffek |

## IMPROVING ACCESS TO JUSTICE THROUGH DIGITALISATION

**Sumida:** Today, we are hosting an international workshop on innovating access to justice. First, our fascinating guests will give their presentations followed by comments and questions.

**Steffek:** Professor Sumida and I have assembled what we thought was our dream team for today. This last session concludes our conversation series. It is a great pleasure inviting first Dr Philip Scholz to take the floor. Dr Scholz will start this workshop as one of two speakers who represent national governments. The framework of this workshop is that we have two speakers representing national governments, followed by four speakers representing international organisations.

Dr Scholz is Head of Division and the leader of the project group on 'Legal Tech and Access to Justice' in the German Ministry of Justice. In this position, he oversees various activities in the Ministry relevant to today's workshop. In 2020, for example, he and his team organised a major event as part of Germany's EU Council presidency on 'Access to Justice in the Digital Age – Perspectives and Challenges'. He currently initiates and leads digitalisation projects for the German justice system. One of the projects is the development and piloting of an online civil court procedure. Today, he will speak on 'Digitalisation and Access to Justice – a European Perspective'. Dr Scholz, it is a great pleasure to have you on this panel and we are very much looking forward to your presentation.

**Scholz:** Thank you very much. I am very happy to be with you today. I am very pleased to give you a brief overview of digitalisation and access to justice as it is discussed in the European Union.

Germany held the presidency of the Council of the EU in the second half of 2020. The presidency of the Council rotates among the EU Member States every six months. During this period, the presidency chairs meetings at every level in the Council, helping to ensure the continuity of the EU's work in the Council. Perhaps most importantly, the presidency has the opportunity to set thematic priorities. The German Ministry of Justice put the digitalisation of justice systems at the top of its agenda.

An important result of addressing this issue was that the Member States were able to jointly agree on so-called Council Conclusions.[1] These formulated guidelines for the future digital development of our justice systems. The conclusions encourage Member States to make increased use of digital tools throughout judicial proceedings and call on the European Commission to develop a comprehensive EU strategy for the digitalisation of justice. In December 2020, the European

[1] Council Conclusions 'Access to Justice – Seizing the Opportunities of Digitalisation' 2020/C 342 I/01, OJ C 342I, 14 October 2020 <https://eur-lex.europa.eu/legal-content/EN/TXT/?uri=CELEX:52020XG1014(01)>, accessed 1 November 2023.

Commission presented a Commission Statement, a so-called Communication, in which concrete legislative and administrative actions for digitalisation were outlined.[2]

It would be easy to understand these two acts as mere reactions to the COVID-19 crisis and the calls for more digitalisation. But I think this view does not capture the motivation. The digitalisation of the justice systems is and needs to be regarded as an aspect of access to justice, which is a fundamental right and a core element of the rule of law.[3]

This brings me to my next point, the fundamental rights perspective of the issue. The Charter of Fundamental Rights of the European Union states that every person has the right to an effective remedy before an independent and impartial court to have any violation of their rights and freedoms considered in a fair and public hearing. In order to improve the acceptance of justice systems and to strengthen confidence in the rule of law, the right to effective legal protection must also be fully asserted under the conditions created by digital transformation. That means, on the one hand, that the digital development of the justice sector must be constantly guided by and aligned with the fundamental principles of judicial systems, namely the independence and impartiality of the courts, the guarantee of effective legal protection.

On the other hand, and that is the more important aspect for me, digital technologies can be used in judicial systems to advance adherence to rule of law standards, as well as the exercise of and respect for fundamental rights. Even further, to fully ensure the effective protection of fundamental rights, the enhancement of digitalisation in the justice sector might be a necessity and not merely a luxury. The possibilities presented by digitalisation can simplify access to the judicial system for citizens on a very practical level. Some court proceedings can be conducted entirely online and thus provide access to justice for people who otherwise might not have turned to a physical court, for example, people living in rural areas, where the nearest court is far away. The use of videoconferencing in judicial hearings significantly reduces the need for burdensome and cost-intensive travel and may facilitate and shorten proceedings.

2 Communication from the Commission, 'Digitalisation of Justice in the European Union: A Toolbox of Opportunities' COM/2020/710 final <https://eur-lex.europa.eu/legal-content/EN/ALL/?uri=COM:2020:710:FIN>, accessed 1 November 2023. As a follow-up to the Communication, the Commission adopted on 1 December 2021 two proposals – a proposal for a regulation laying down rules on digital communication in judicial cooperation procedures in civil, commercial and criminal matters and a proposal for a directive aligning the existing rules on communication with the rules of the proposed regulation, see <https://commission.europa.eu/publications/digitalisation-cross-border-judicial-cooperation_en>, accessed 1 November 2023.

3 'Rule of law' refers to the idea established in the modern state of following laws enacted by parliament, as opposed to the 'rule of force', in which a powerful person or despot uses their power to arbitrarily administer the law.

## DIGITALISATION OF JUSTICE IN EU MEMBER STATES

**Scholz:** Let us take a closer look at the digitalisation or level of digitalisation of justice systems in the EU. Digital technology is constantly evolving. New approaches and solutions for managing, securing and exchanging information appear all the time. These developments also shape the digitalisation of justice systems. Measures such as the conducting of digital court proceedings, electronic communication between parties, courts and authorities, the electronic transmission of documents and the use of audio and video hearings and conferences have already become important elements of efficient judicial administration in numerous EU Member States. Progress varies greatly from one Member State to another, and I have to admit that Germany is by no means at the forefront of development here. There is still a lot to do, but we are on the right track. The German Federal Government Digital Strategy describes specific projects with concrete, measurable goals to advance digitalisation in Germany.[4] It also includes measures to further digitalise the judiciary.

A dynamic evolution of digital technologies in the judicial and legal sectors of the EU can be observed, in which plans to develop and use new technologies, including AI systems for justice, are increasingly formulated. It can hardly be denied that the further digitalisation of judicial systems has enormous potential to facilitate and improve citizens' access to justice. Digital tools can help to better structure proceedings and to automate and accelerate the handling of standardised and uniform tasks, thereby increasing the effectiveness and efficiency of court proceedings. In this way, digital tools can provide an enormous amount of support to the courts, leaving them with more time to devote to their core business: engaging in judicial deliberation and legal analysis, which no technology can fully replace.

Furthermore, it is important to emphasise the opportunities offered by digitalisation in enabling citizens and legal practitioners to have comprehensive access at all times to legal information, such as legislation and anonymised court decisions, as well as information on the progress of their own cases. But it is also clear that employing digital technologies and means of electronic communication should not undermine the right to a fair hearing, in particular the right to equality of arms and the right to adversarial proceedings, but also the right to a public hearing, including in certain cases the right to an oral hearing in the physical presence of the affected party.

## THE USEFULNESS OF DIGITALISATION AS REVEALED BY COVID-19

**Scholz:** The COVID-19 crisis has exposed challenges and risks as regards the effective functioning of justice systems in exceptional circumstances. It has highlighted the need to strengthen the resilience of justice systems across the EU. It has also triggered a significant shift towards the uptake of digital technologies in our societies. Digitalisation was identified as a tool to address some of the resulting

4 See <https://digitalstrategie-deutschland.de/>, accessed 1 November 2023.

issues, particularly to avoid similar hardships in the future and to clear the backlog caused by the crisis. In the end, the COVID-19 crisis has confirmed that further digitalisation of justice and the enhanced use of new technologies are key factors in ensuring the efficiency and resilience of justice systems. The EU Member States and the EU itself should increase their efforts to promote and further expand digitalisation in this sector, always of course, with a view to ensuring equal access to and availability of digital services for everybody.

It is very important to us, and that is why I would like to emphasise this here in particular, that we follow a citizen-centric approach in the digitalisation of justice. The digital reorientation of court proceedings should focus on expanding access to justice in the service of citizens. If we assume that citizens are the 'users' of the legal systems, this approach could play a key role in the development of new digital solutions in the justice systems. Successful process design should focus on people and their needs rather than on specific institutionalised procedures.

In line with this people-centred design approach, it could be necessary to retain traditional non-digital processes alongside the new digital forms to provide citizens who cannot yet fully participate in technological developments with effective legal protection and access to justice. At the same time, there is a need to provide citizens with comprehensive information in simple and accessible language on how to use digital services and how to assert their rights in this way.

## DIGITAL VULNERABILITY

**Scholz:** Finally, I would like to mention one important point regarding persons who are particularly vulnerable. The digitalisation process must take full account of the needs of the disadvantaged groups. Digital technologies are becoming increasingly user-friendly and accessible to a large majority, regardless of age or level of education, and accessible for persons with disabilities. At the same time, all citizens should benefit from the additional digital possibilities and should enjoy equal opportunities regarding digital access to justice and to fair proceedings. Digital participation must be unconditionally guaranteed to all societal groups without any discrimination. The needs of vulnerable persons, including children and vulnerable adults such as elderly people and persons with disabilities, should be taken into account in particular. The use of digital technologies in justice systems should not diminish procedural safeguards for those who do not have access to such technologies.

Let me come to a short conclusion. The digitalisation of justice systems gives us the chance to further improve access to justice – if we manage to develop and deploy technology in line with the rule of law and put the citizen's needs at the centre of technological development. Thank you very much for your attention.

## WHY THE DIGITALISATION OF JUSTICE IS LAGGING BEHIND

**Sumida:** You gave an excellent presentation, but may I ask you one question? You just said that Germany is not necessarily the frontrunner in the EU in the digitalisation of the justice systems. On the other hand, Germany is known as a technologically advanced country. Can you tell us about Germany and the reasons behind this?

**Scholz:** Thank you for this legitimate question. One reason for the relatively slow development in Germany could be that the judiciary in Germany is mostly the responsibility of the 'Länder'. The Federal Republic of Germany, as a federal state, consists of sixteen partly sovereign federated states. That means, that we are organised on a decentralised basis. That makes certain things more difficult because different Länder have partly developed different IT systems. For example, we have different e-file systems in the judiciary, which do not make it easy to exchange information.

Another reason could be that digitalisation has often been understood as a one-to-one transformation of analogue processes into digital processes. This does not go far enough. The associated potential is not fully exploited. Instead, the previous design of the processes should be reviewed, and processes should be rethought and set up anew.

Nevertheless, things are moving forward here as well. We have several research projects in the area of artificial intelligence (AI) in the justice sector, for example, on the identification of hate crimes on social media, machine translation services for legal documents, anonymisation of court decisions and analysing, structuring and preparing information on the subject matter of cases. In Germany, it is already possible to use videoconferencing technology for hearings in civil and commercial cases. It is also possible to initiate proceedings and file claims in a digital way. Nonetheless, we could do more, and we could be better. At the moment, we are working to create a legal framework to allow court proceedings that can be conducted entirely online, i.e. generally without oral hearings. Citizens are also to be given easier access to justice through the use of digital structuring tools, e.g. web application forms.

**Sumida:** Thank you very much, Dr Scholz.

## DIGITALISING THE JAPANESE JUSTICE SYSTEM

**Sumida:** I would now like to welcome Mr Takashi Kikkawa from the Ministry of Justice of Japan. The Ministry of Justice in Japan handles a wide range of tasks, including drafting the country's civil and criminal laws, immigration and residency management and management of correctional facilities such as prisons. He is responsible for the development and management of the information system, which is the subject of today's discussion. Mr Kikkawa was appointed Prosecutor in 1995 and was in charge of investigations and trials of various criminal cases at the Public Prosecutor's Office in the Tokyo District. He has also served in the Ministry of Justice as Counsellor in charge of legislation such as the amendment of the Code of Criminal Procedure and acted as Director of the Judicial Law Division and Director of the General Affairs Division of the Criminal Affairs Bureau.

**Kikkawa:** Thank you for inviting me here today. In relation to 'Innovating Access to Justice', I would like to focus on the Ministry of Justice's efforts to digitalise the justice system. In the previous sessions, many of you have pointed out the slow adoption of AI, IT and other technologies in Japanese society. I believe that this is precisely the case, and the justice sector is a prime example of this. The justice sector is currently in the process of digitalisation and has not yet reached the stage of sufficient digitalisation, much less digital transformation.

It is often pointed out that the slow introduction of AI, IT and other technologies in Japan is due to the maturity of its society. In other words, it is said that this is because many people are satisfied with the current status of Japanese society and have little motivation to make major changes to the existing systems. I believe, however, that there are further reasons for the delay in the justice sector.

First, I believe that the legal response to AI, IT and other technologies can be divided into two approaches: the substantive law approach and the procedural law approach. The substantive law approach refers to issues such as what effect the law will have on or how it will regulate AI, IT and other technologies. For example, when automated driving of vehicles on public roads becomes possible, who will be responsible for accidents and under what regulations and rules will that be allowed In other words, the question is how the law will tackle issues involving AI, IT and other technologies.

On the other hand, the procedural law approach concerns how AI, IT and other technologies can be used in judicial proceedings, including litigation hearings. In other words, the question is how to integrate AI, IT and other technologies into judicial proceedings.

The two approaches differ in the speed of evolution. Substantive law must keep pace with changes in society. As Japanese society adopts technologies such as AI and IT, it is forced to respond and create substantive laws. The development of rules and regulations for virtual currencies is one such example.

Procedural law, on the other hand, is essentially autonomous. Even if digitalisation and the use of IT advances within a society, there is no reason that the same would be pursued in the judicial field. At least there is no time pressure to achieve that. Moreover, the judicial system is the very foundation of society. In Japan, a certain level of trust is maintained by the public in the judicial system, including the decisions of the courts. Therefore, there has been a tendency to emphasise the negative aspects that could arise from the digitalisation of and use of IT in judicial procedures. This may be the fundamental reason why digitalisation and the use of IT have not advanced quickly in the justice sector.

## THE PUSH FOR THE DIGITALISATION OF JUSTICE

**Kikkawa:** Procedural laws, including the Code of Civil Procedure and the Code of Criminal Procedure, have been amended after controversial discussions in response to changes that have occurred in society. However, the obstacles hindering digitalisation and the use of IT seem to have been particularly difficult to overcome. From a student's point of view, you may feel that it would be a good idea to introduce something convenient as soon as possible, but when trying to create a new system, we must at the same time identify the negative aspects and think about how to deal with them. Also, considerable momentum is needed to make major changes to a system that has been maintained for a long time.

As Dr Scholz pointed out earlier, the justice system must be easily accessible to people. In Japan, the degree of access to justice is at a good level due to the development of one-stop consultation services such as the Japan Legal Support Centre ('Hou-terasu' in Japanese) and the contributions of lawyers and other representatives of the justice system. It would be a mistake to reduce access to justice for the digitally vulnerable by proceeding with digitalisation too hastily. In addition, given the vulnerability of technology to interference by third parties, there is good reason to maintain a paper-based filing system. Furthermore, as judicial proceedings are procedures in which judges find the facts, face-to-face contact in some respects is superior to online procedures. The negative aspects of digitalisation and the use of IT have attracted widespread attention, which has prevented us from being motivated to take quick steps forward.

In recent years, however, consideration has begun to digitalise civil court proceedings. One of the main driving forces behind this is the need to deal with internationalisation. Japan's civil court procedures are no longer for its citizens alone. If Japan's civil court procedures are regarded internationally as difficult to use, this will affect economic activity. I am aware that such external factors have strongly motivated the government to push for the introduction of IT in civil courts, and the heavy wheels have finally started to move. I seek your understanding for the rather long introduction. I hope this background information is useful for what I am about to say.

## THE CURRENT STATUS OF THE USE OF IT IN CIVIL COURT PROCEEDINGS

**Kikkawa:** The Legislative Council of the Ministry of Justice is currently discussing the introduction of IT in civil court proceedings, with the aim of submitting a bill in 2022. This is the very starting point for the digitalisation of the justice sector in Japan. It has the potential to enable the use of new technologies such as AI in the future and to significantly change the nature of the judiciary. This will be a landmark step in the Japanese justice system. Professor Kazuhiko Yamamoto is leading the discussions in the Legislative Council.

The outline is shown in Figure 8.1. Conceptually, the project aims for the full implementation of IT from the filing of the complaint to the judgment. The main pillars of the concept are, 'e-submission', which enables the online submission of complaints and documents containing the parties' claims, etc. 'e-court', which enables both parties to participate in oral arguments and other proceedings via the internet, and 'e-case management', which enables the parties to access the court's servers via the internet at any time to view and download records electronically. The more concrete institutional designs for these pillars are currently being developed.

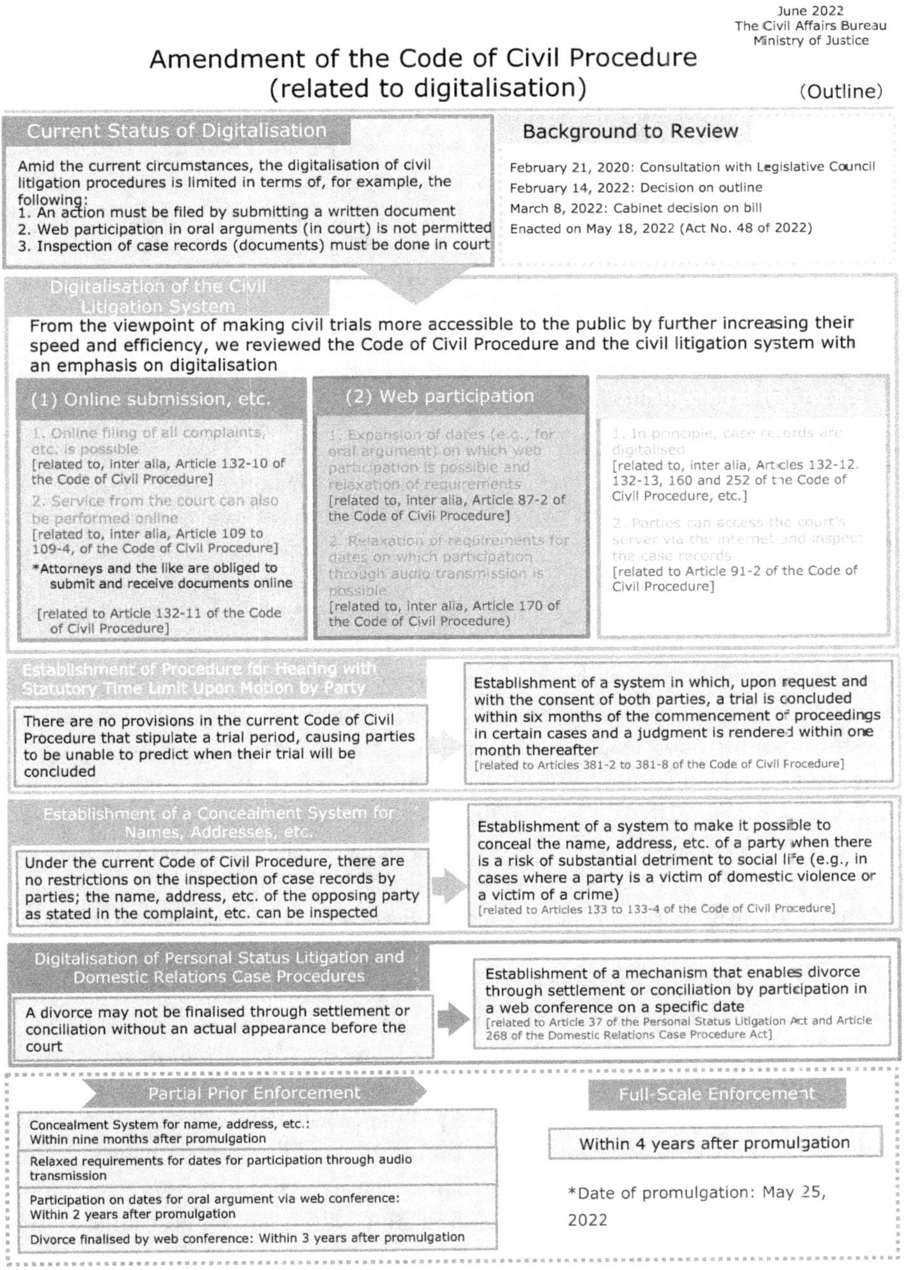


FIGURE 8.1 Digitalisation of civil court procedures in Japan

In this context, a system is being considered whereby judgment documents are digitised and uploaded to the court's data system for downloading by the parties. Access to electronic judgments has been intensively discussed in this conversation series. If the court can digitise and centrally manage judgment documents and turn them into open data, the possibilities for their use will expand dramatically. At present, information on civil judgments and other information is available on court websites, but this is limited to cases, which are important precedents, and cases of high social interest. Currently, a study group of the Japan Federation of Bar Associations is discussing how data should be managed and used, with a view to making civil judgments open data.

## THE CURRENT STATUS OF IT IN ALTERNATIVE DISPUTE RESOLUTION

**Kikkawa:** The use of IT and other technologies is also being considered for Alternative Dispute Resolution (ADR), a procedure whereby civil disputes are resolved by an impartial third party such as a mediator, for example, in claims for damages from a traffic accident. In the case of a claim for damages for a traffic accident, a private dispute resolution organisation sponsors mediation and resolves the dispute by agreement between the parties concerned. This online ADR is called ODR – Online Dispute Resolution. Since ADR is a private-sector activity, it is possible to design procedures that are more flexible than court proceedings. By incorporating IT, it is expected that procedures can be constructed to meet the needs of various users by increasing convenience, speed etc. Currently, possible procedures are being considered, including the establishment of a new dedicated platform common to all ADR-related organisations. Furthermore, if data is accumulated through open data of court proceedings and AI is able to predict the outcome of court proceedings, then it is expected that ADR will benefit.

The IT of civil court proceedings and ADR is currently considered, and beyond that, the IT of domestic affairs and execution proceedings will also be an issue to be addressed. In the future, the digitalisation of the justice sector should lead to a better system as a whole compared with the current one. The result should be that disputes can be resolved more quickly and appropriately in accordance with people's needs and the nature of the dispute. To this end, it is important to think in terms of system design, starting from the legal consultation of the parties to the execution stage.

Figure 8.2 provides an overview of the digitalisation of the justice sector in Japan. The first issue is accessibility. Everyone should have easy access to dispute resolution procedures. A variety of dispute resolution procedures should be available and support should be provided for the digitally vulnerable. The second issue is reliability. Dispute resolution procedures, whether court proceedings or ADR, are based on the trust of the public and users. Procedures must lead to good decisions, ensure adequate security and provide seamless access. The third issue is realisability, i.e. implementation. The content of judgments and other decisions must be implemented smoothly. With these aspects in mind, it is necessary to consider in detail

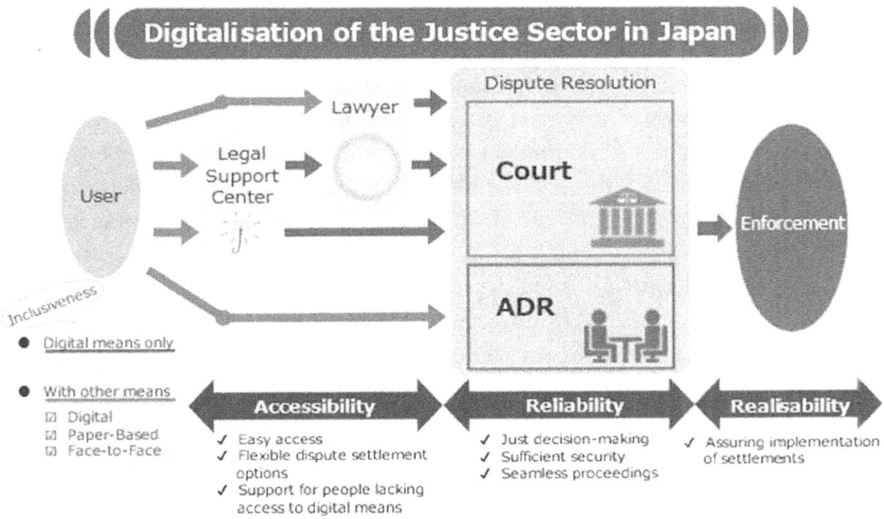


FIGURE 8.2 Digitalisation of the justice sector in Japan

which specific procedures should be digital-only, whether they should be digitalised while allowing a choice of conventional methods to coexist, or whether they should not be digitalised.

## THE CHANGES THAT DIGITALISATION WILL BRING TO THE JUSTICE SYSTEM

Although I have focused on civil matters up to this point, IT considerations will soon begin for criminal proceedings as well. Based on the actual conditions of investigations and trials in criminal cases, a wide range of discussions will take place, including the creation and management of documents using electronic data, the online issuance and receipt of documents when requesting and issuing warrants and trials using an online system. In addition, the Ministry of Justice is also involved in a wide range of other tasks such as correctional services, rehabilitation, immigration control and litigation. We are currently working with experts to examine whether we can make our operations more efficient and appropriate by digitalisation and using AI and other emerging technologies.

AI, IT and other technologies have great potential in the justice sector. If we first promote digitalisation and IT, and if AI and other technologies are further utilised, we will see major changes in the way judicial procedures are carried out. We may even see a new judicial system that is adapted to the digital world. I believe that where we are now is at the very edge of such changes. As society becomes more digitalised, supercomputers and other devices will make various simulations possible, and the day will come when the effects of laws can be predicted to a certain extent in advance. If this happens, the way legislation is made, and the way laws are made may change.

I am very encouraged and grateful that Professor Sumida and other professors are one step ahead in considering the use of AI and other methods, based on the premise of digitalisation, and that various studies and initiatives are underway at law firms and other organisations. I personally believe that speed is very important, but on the other hand, as the judicial system is the foundation of society, we must not allow that people fall through the net of the judicial system or undermine trust in the judicial system due to hasty changes. I think it would be good to have some time in which the digitalisation and digital transformation of the justice sector in Japan can proceed with some delay while referring to the results of studies and practices in other countries. In any case, I sincerely hope that many of you will participate in this major public-private project in the future. Thank you very much.

## LEGAL PROCEDURES, THE INTERNET AND FACE-TO-FACE COMMUNICATION

**Sumida:** Thank you very much. Would anyone like to ask questions or comment?

**Student A:** Thank you very much for your excellent presentation. In your presentation, you mentioned that procedural law is rather autonomous and not strongly connected to societal change, but I think that if the nature of disputes changes with the spreading of the internet, then this will change the nature of procedures.

**Kikkawa:** Thank you for your question. In the past, in response to the differentiation of disputes, there have been changes in the nature of judicial procedures or an increase in the menu of judicial procedures in order to make them suitable for resolving various types of disputes. However, the integration of AI, IT and other technologies into judicial procedures is a somewhat different matter. Even if society's approach to disputes changes as a result of the spreading of the internet, as you have asked, and even if the content of disputes themselves increasingly relates to AI, IT and other technologies, it does not necessarily follow that judicial procedures using AI, IT and other technologies must be introduced in order to resolve such disputes. Whether or not to incorporate AI, IT and other technologies into judicial procedures is an independent decision.

However, as AI, IT and other technologies permeate society, it is inevitable that calls for their inclusion in the judicial sector will grow louder, and that is exactly what is happening now. If digitalisation in the judicial field progresses, and if AI and other technologies are utilised, then there is a possibility that a dispute resolution system will be constructed in a completely different way. It can be faster and more satisfactory for the parties concerned.

**Student B:** Thank you very much for your valuable talk. You mentioned that there may be a need for face-to-face communication at judicial hearings. I understand that in the criminal justice system, it is difficult to see faces or to capture facial expressions in court proceedings when people wear masks.

**Kikkawa:** Thank you for your question. According to media reports, online jury proceedings have been tried in some states in order to overcome the stoppage of jury trials in the United States during the COVID-19 pandemic. Although it is an unavoidable measure, it seems that some cautious arguments have been raised against such efforts. I think it is a common perception in many countries that face-to-face attendance is suitable for civil trial proceedings, which are directed at the determination of facts and decisions based on those facts.

As I mentioned earlier, following the introduction of IT in civil court proceedings, discussions are about to start on the introduction of IT in criminal court proceedings. At that time, the question of which proceedings will be online and which will be face-to-face will be a major debate. Even once the system has been established, I am sure that it will be further improved as technology advances. I hope that the students attending this conversation series will be involved in such discussions in the future.

## JUSTICE PROBLEMS ARE EVERYWHERE

**Steffek:** Now, it is a great pleasure to introduce Dr Tatyana Teplova. Tatyana, you are Head of Division at the OECD for Policy Coherence for the Sustainable Development Goals, which is an urgent call for action adopted by all United Nations Member States in 2015. You are also Senior Counsellor for Gender, Justice and Inclusiveness, which means that you take an inclusive and comprehensive view of access to justice. You are a part of the Public Governance Directorate at the OECD, meaning that you look at what states and lawmakers do in terms of strategies and approaches to justice. Finally, you lead the Justice Department of the OECD, and your team has developed leading guides and reports on access to justice. I can only recommend that everyone look at the website of the Access to Justice team of the OECD.[5] There is a wonderful assembly of guidance and reports. You will speak to us on Access to Justice for All in the Time of COVID-19 and beyond.

**Teplova:** Thank you, Felix. Thank you to you and Professor Sumida for putting together this extremely impressive programme and, of course, for inviting the OECD to join this discussion and to share the highlights of some of our work. As you mentioned, we take a broad approach to access to justice, but I also feel that there are many elements that were already highlighted by the previous speakers from Germany and Japan. Hopefully, my presentation will be complementary to what was already said but perhaps offer a slightly broader approach.

As you can see in Figure 8.3, we at the OECD look at access to justice as part of the policy action on inclusive growth, which is a key strategic priority for the OECD. We are not concerned only with income and equality, but also focused on how inequalities can touch every aspect of people's lives, from employment and likelihood of getting employment, educational outcomes, to where you live and even how long you live.[6] As you mentioned already, Felix, access to justice is a key part of the 2030 agenda and the full spectrum of the targets for sustainable

5 See <www.oecd.org/governance/global-roundtables-access-to-justice/>, accessed 1 November 2023.

6 The following is based on The OECD White Paper on Building a Business Case for Access to Justice, <www.oecd.org/gov/building-a-business-case-for-access-to-justice.pdf>, accessed 1 November 2023.

FIGURE 8.3 Access to justice as an enabler for creating prosperity and sustainable development

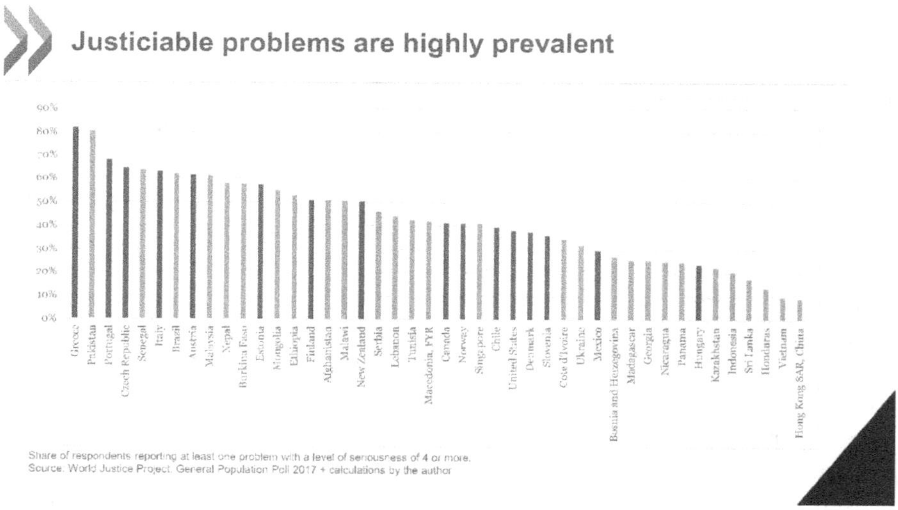


FIGURE 8.4 Justiciable problems are highly prevalent

development goals and, specifically, Target 16 where countries have committed to provide access to justice to all, to leave no one behind and to build effective, accountable and inclusive institutions.

In Figure 8.4, we see that legal problems are not rare, they are not unique. We know that nearly every aspect of people's lives, from health to employment, depends on sound legal frameworks. Any problem or dispute that arises within those

FIGURE 8.5 The most vulnerable to legal problems – Australia Law Legal Needs Survey

sectors, by necessity, can bring into play laws and regulations. What we see in the data, which comes from the World Justice Project, is that legal problems are ubiquitous and that they can flow from everyday life and can be experienced by many on a daily basis. For example, this figure shows that on average, around 50 per cent of the people who were surveyed among 45 countries experienced legal problems in a given two-year period. So, such problems are quite frequent. Actually, the proportion of unresolved legal problems can also go as high as 50 per cent, meaning that these problems did not get resolved either because the legal justice system was inaccessible, or people decided not to take legal action for a variety of reasons. I will touch a bit on those.

Looking at Figure 8.5, we also see that these legal problems tend to cluster together with issues related to employment or debt, housing or health problems. This can trigger a vicious cycle for already vulnerable populations. We know that not all groups have equal experiences in accessing justice, as was already highlighted by the German speaker, Dr Scholz. Indigenous populations, people with disabilities, women, single parents and the elderly face a higher prevalence of legal problems. This is what we see from the data in Figure 8.6. These groups can also experience particular barriers when trying to resolve these problems such as language, distance or lack of digital skills. This is particularly relevant for the discussion today. The greater reliance on technology can improve the efficiency and effectiveness of the justice system, but it can also create a new layer of marginalised populations who lack digital skills. It is important that to be truly accessible, justice systems take into account this dimension.

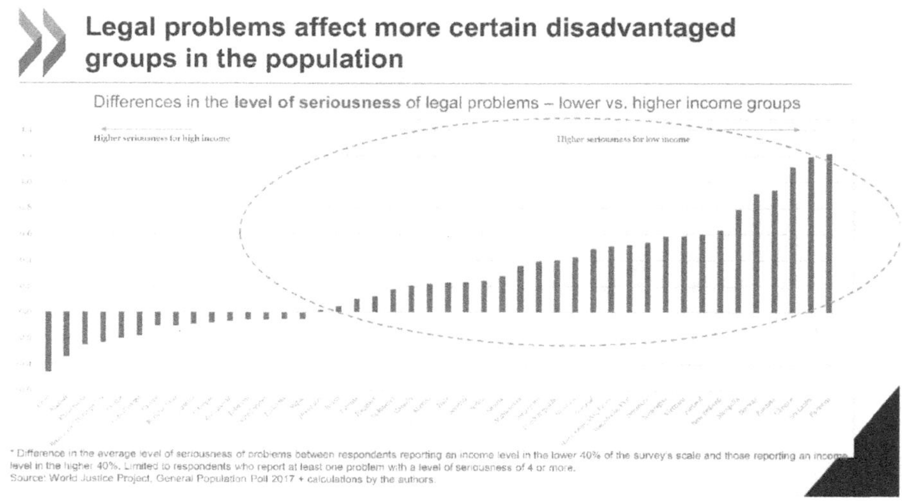


FIGURE 8.6 Legal problems affect certain disadvantaged groups more severely

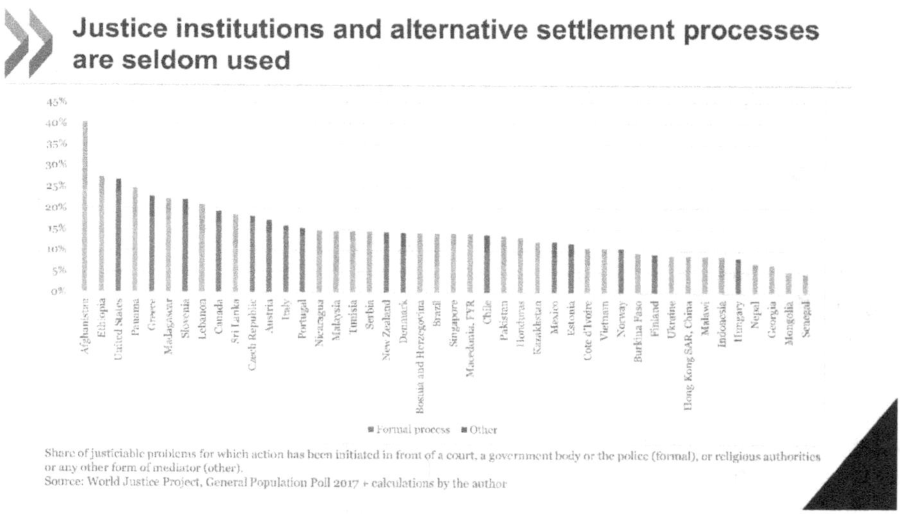


FIGURE 8.7 Share of justiciable problems for which action has been initiated in justice institutions

## BARRIERS OF THE JUSTICE SYSTEM

**Teplova:** Figure 8.7 shows that only a small fraction of people deal with their legal problems through the formal justice system. This reinforces the need to increase access to alternative, but also cost-effective, dispute resolution mechanisms that are tailored to the needs of people and to the nature of the problem that they face.

We know that the cost is actually one of the top reasons why people choose not to do anything about their legal problems. But there are also many other barriers, such as the complexity of the justice system and the complexity of the legal language. In some cases and, actually, more frequently than we anticipated, it is the lack of trust in the justice system that is a barrier to addressing legal problems.

The COVID-19 crisis has had a profound impact on the legal needs of people and of businesses, but also on the justice systems themselves. In multiple discussions in the OECD Access to Justice Roundtables, we have seen that legal needs are increasing as a consequence of the crisis due to rising unemployment, growing business disputes, company insolvencies, increased medical issues, insurance problems, difficult access to healthcare and a rise in domestic violence. This is, unfortunately, a worrying trend in many of the OECD Member countries. We also know that the cost of unmet legal needs, i.e. the cost of not doing anything about them, was already extremely high. It was quite significant even before the crisis, reaching up to 3 per cent of the gross domestic product (GDP) on average across OECD Member countries. If legal needs are increasing as a result of the COVID-19 crisis, then of course, the cost to society is also quite likely to increase.

As we already heard, justice systems have been severely affected during the COVID-19 pandemic. Note the closure of many courts in OECD countries, the suspension of many procedures and the difficulties of providing legal aid during the pandemic. It has also generated significant case backlogs in many countries during the crisis and recovery phases. There is also a brighter side in that we also observed unparalleled innovations in the justice systems, including through digitalisation, which is, again, particularly relevant for today's discussion.

## OPPORTUNITY FOR A DIGITALISATION REVOLUTION

**Teplova:** I would like to highlight some key lessons in terms of the justice systems' responses during the crisis. First, globally but also individually, justice systems should not miss the opportunity. Usually, change is slow due to various constraints, be it the governance arrangements in the justice system, be it the legal culture, be it that it is difficult to develop digital skills. We know from years of discussions on this topic that the adoption of technological innovations can be quite slow across the justice sectors. The crisis has offered an opportunity to accelerate such change. In many, many countries, change is already here. It is happening. The big question is how to capitalise on this opportunity.

It is important to embed, from the outset, an understanding of what works for whom under what circumstances. Technology should not be adopted blindly and it should not disadvantage groups that have already been marginalised. Data and evidence will play a critical role in making the most effective policy in this area, but also in allocating already scarce resources in the best possible way.

We have observed that the responses have been most effective when countries have established cross-functional teams to lead the change and adjust the justice systems to respond to the growing needs. The whole-of-government approach, but also the whole-of-justice chain approach have been most effective – when the task forces included courts, ministries of justice, health ministries, social ministries and ministries of labour or business development. So, horizontality is crucial to best support the needs of the people.

We also saw that clear communication with citizens is particularly crucial. This is specifically relevant for groups which are at risk of even further marginalisation during the crisis. It is important to ensure that they know which legal remedies are available to them and how to access them. On the topic of technology, we saw that it has massive potential to improve accessibility and efficiency of justice. We also learned that special efforts must be made to maximise the benefits of technology while minimising the absorbed risks and challenges. We saw that procedural simplification is possible and there have been many examples across the OECD membership when countries looked at their legal procedures with a view of simplifying them. Of course, such change should aim to maintain quality, ensure the rule of law and a fair trial, but still reduce unnecessary steps in the legal process to ensure that access to justice is improved.

If you take a look at Figure 8.8, you will see key country innovations that we observed during the COVID-19 pandemic, a period of unprecedented change and opportunity. Many of our Member countries have adopted innovative approaches. This included using technology, which has been one of the biggest accelerators of change during the crisis. There is also the growing use of ADR mechanisms, for example, in Chile, or procedural simplification in Portugal. In terms of technology, countries invested in maintaining the continuity of legal services, trials and legal aid through different technical means such as remote trials via videoconferencing or phones. As already mentioned, we need to be mindful of the risks in the use of these

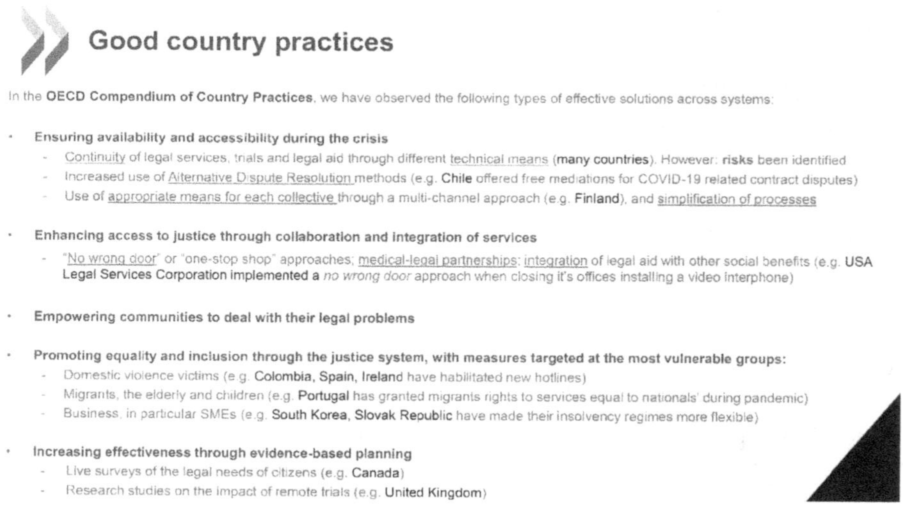


FIGURE 8.8 Good country practices

technologies and multi-channel service delivery remains an important priority. The Finnish government has taken particularly active steps in this regard. Other countries have applied a no-wrong door approach or a one-stop-shop approach to justice services. For instance, in the United States, there is a growing use of medical-legal partnerships as well as integration of legal aid and other social benefits. So, when people are applying for unemployment insurance, legal aid is integrated into the package that was offered as part of this support.

Finally, I would be grateful if you took a quick look at Figure 8.9. The OECD has been developing resources to support countries in their efforts to bring justice closer to the people and to implement their commitments under the 2030 Agenda for Sustainable Development. We are also one of the co-custodians of the new indicator on Access to Justice to Leave No One Behind. I would like to encourage you to take a look at our materials and, of course, I am happy to answer any questions and provide any further information. Thank you so much for your attention.

**Sumida:** Thank you very much for talking so clearly about how access to justice is linked to social issues. I would now like to invite Professor Kozuka to comment.

## CHALLENGES ASSOCIATED WITH COMMERCIAL DISPUTE RESOLUTION SOLUTIONS

**Kozuka:** Thank you very much, Dr Teplova, for your fruitful presentation on the subject. When we think about the digitalisation of justice, we come across the issue of the use of the proprietary commercial system. Strong countries like Germany or Japan may be able to create a digitalised judicial system through government funding but, from the perspective of an international organisation, this is not the

FIGURE 8.9 Justice for growth and inclusion: towards people- and business-centred justice systems

case in all countries. Some countries may need to rely on commercial systems, which may have a proprietary nature that is not disclosed, or it may have biases. How do you think such a commercial system can be controlled and how can it be led in the right way to help people have access to justice?

**Teplova:** Thank you for this question. I am afraid that I do not have a straightforward answer to this question. This is a dilemma that is faced by many of our Member countries. The role of the OECD is to work together with the countries in developing principles that could guide the use of commercial systems for public purposes. This includes principles concerning the reliance on public systems, be it the judiciary or the broader public service delivery for many other areas. So, this is a big question. What is the role of the governments in regulating technological solutions? How do we ensure the appropriateness of the public-private interface? We know that many countries are developing public-private partnerships with clear guidance and clear principles surrounding these partnerships. So, there is no single answer to your question. We do know that, of course, the private sector is offering many innovative solutions and that for governments there is certainly scope to benefit from and to build on those solutions through partnerships. Governments, of course, also have the responsibility to protect the public interest. This is where there must be clear regulations and strict precautions to ensure privacy, data protection and so on. This is something that we are looking forward to developing further together with our Members.

## ACHIEVING SUSTAINABLE DEVELOPMENT GOALS BY 2030

**Steffek:** Thank you very much again, Tatyana, for a very interesting and rich presentation. It is now a great pleasure to introduce Maaike de Langen, who is the Programme Director for Justice for All with the Pathfinders for Peaceful, Just and Inclusive Societies,[7] a programme of New York University's Center on International Cooperation. Maaike has over fifteen years of experience leading national and international programmes and teams in the areas of governance, rule of law and legal empowerment. She has worked in the Netherlands, Mali, Chad and New York. To pick just one of her stations before she came to her current role, as Policy Specialist on Legal Empowerment of the Poor for the UNDP in New York, she was involved in drafting the report of the Commission on Legal Empowerment of the Poor and created UNDP's first global project on legal empowerment of the poor.

**de Langen:** It is a great pleasure speaking to you today about innovating access to justice. Firstly, I will speak about access to justice and about a global movement that is coming together to improve people's access to justice around the world. Secondly,

[7] The Pathfinders is a group of UN Member States, international organisations, civil society and the private sector, that works to accelerate the delivery of the SDG goals for peace, justice and inclusion by 2030.

I will speak about justice in a pandemic and about the impact of the COVID-19 pandemic on justice services and people's justice needs. Thirdly, I will talk about technology and innovation, the theme of this programme, and I will present seven principles for innovation with a people-centred justice perspective.

What is access to justice? I will tell you about the context in which we operate, which is the United Nations Sustainable Development Goals. The United Nations adopted these 17 global goals for the world to achieve by 2030.[8] Goal 16 focuses specifically on issues related to peace, justice and institutions. One of its core components is to provide access to justice for all. In 2015, all the countries of the world together embraced this universal ambition and committed 'to having systems that provide equal access to justice for all by 2030'. This goal was new in the global development agenda and a group of countries came together as Pathfinders to accelerate delivery of these goals. They developed the Roadmap for a Peaceful, Just and Inclusive Society, which sets out strategies and a plan to achieve SDG 16.

## 5.1 BILLION PEOPLE DO NOT HAVE MEANINGFUL ACCESS TO JUSTICE

**de Langen:** Justice had a high priority within the Roadmap because it is one of the three central components in SDG 16. One of the first things the Pathfinder countries did was to establish a Task Force on Justice, to identify strategies and plans for achieving the goal of providing equal access to justice for all. As shown in Figure 8.10, the Task Force was led by ministers from Argentina, the Netherlands and Sierra Leone, together with the Elders. A group of countries and international organisations came together in this process, which led to the publication of the 'Justice for All' report[9] and a series of other reports.

The Task Force asked the following question: 'If we want to provide equal access to justice for all, we must know, first, where we are today. So, we must find data on the global justice gap. What is the gap between the justice people receive and the justice that they need?' And once the data was assembled by the World Justice Project, the Task Force reached a shocking conclusion. It found that, across the world, 5.1 billion people do not have meaningful access to justice. This is the global justice gap. It is composed of 4.5 billion people who are excluded from social, economic and political opportunities that the law provides; 1.5 billion people who

[8] The 2030 Agenda for Sustainable Development, adopted by all United Nations Member States in 2015, provides a shared blueprint for peace and prosperity for people and the planet. At its heart are the 17 Sustainable Development Goals (SDGs), which recognize that ending poverty and other deprivations must go hand-in-hand with strategies that improve health and education, reduce inequality, and spur economic growth – all while tackling climate change and working to preserve our oceans and forests. See <https://sdgs.un.org/goals>.

[9] The full report, in multiple languages, is available at <www.sdg16.plus/resources/justice-for-all-report-of-the-task-force-on-justice>, accessed 1 November 2023.

FIGURE 8.10 Taskforce on Justice: Pathfinders for Peaceful, Fair and Inclusive Society

have a criminal, civil or administrative justice problem that they cannot resolve and 253 million people who live in extreme conditions of injustice without any meaningful legal protections.

So, how can this global justice gap be closed? One crucial step is to bring together evidence of what works to increase people's access to justice. In the Justice for All report, we developed the notion of people-centred justice, putting people at the centre of the justice system and at the centre of what you are trying to achieve. This is the perspective that we take when we speak of access to justice. It is really about people's justice problems and resolving and preventing them.

## 'SHADOW PANDEMIC' TRIGGERED BY COVID-19

**de Langen:** I will now turn to my second point, on access to justice in a pandemic. How has the pandemic impacted people's access to justice and what was the impact on justice actors and the justice sector more broadly? We have produced a series of briefings around that. They are shown in Figure 8.11. The first one focused on the public health emergency.[10] When the pandemic hit in March and April 2020, we saw in country after country that there were measures being taken – lockdowns were imposed, public health emergency measures were put in place and justice actors were on the frontline of this pandemic. Justice actors were helping to enforce lockdowns. There were tensions between justice actors and people who were objecting or protesting against lockdowns and other public health measures. There was a risk of abuse. A lot of questions arose around prisons. Could prisoners

[10] Available at <dx.doi.org/10.2139/ssrn.4755459>, accessed 1 September 2024.

FIGURE 8.11 Reports by Pathfinders on Justice in the pandemic

be kept safe? There were releases of prisoners in some countries. A separate problem was the increase in domestic violence. During lockdowns, it was widely reported from across the world that there were massive increases in domestic violence, to the extent that UN Women even called this a 'shadow pandemic'.

The second dimension of the pandemic that we looked at is the economic crisis.[11] Due to the economic crisis, access to justice and the problems that people face in obtaining justice are changing. We have seen, for example, increases in unemployment, which brings with it justice problems. There is an increased risk of evictions, increases in divorce, increases in domestic violence and so on. At the same time, we saw that justice actors had difficulty operating because of the restrictions. They could not meet with their clients. Courts closed and had to change their procedures. Suddenly, the justice sector, which is not the most innovative and which does not change procedures very often, had to be creative.

Our third pandemic-related briefing[12] assessed the role of justice in mitigating the long-term negative social and political impacts of the pandemic and in helping societies to 'build back better' in its wake. Justice actors are critical intermediaries for the social contract between states and citizens, but if countries are to recover from the pandemic, they will need to work to strengthen societies' resilience against crises, reach out to all population groups, solve the problems that matter most to people and engage people to develop solutions to injustice.

We call what has happened during the pandemic the triple crunch. On the one hand, you see justice problems increasing because of the public health emergency, the economic crisis and the social impacts of the virus. In parallel, justice actors are facing restrictions that limit their ability to respond. They cannot meet in person.

[11] Available at <ssrn.com/abstract=4762622>, accessed 1 September 2024.

[12] Pathfinders, 'Justice for All and the Social Contract in Peril', 2021, available at <ssrn.com/abstract=4802282>, accessed 1 September 2024.

They cannot have regular procedures. So, the operations of paralegals, lawyers and judges are heavily restrained. And thirdly, due to the economic crisis, there is a lack of funding across the board, including in the public sector. As a result, investments in innovations are more difficult to make.

The result of this triple crunch is that we must do more with less and provide more access to justice with fewer resources. What we have seen is that this leads to three things: innovation, creativity and collaboration. Court procedures had to move online, documents suddenly had to be exchanged in digital format, case management systems had to be implemented, hearings were held online, etc. Using technological solutions became a necessity overnight.

The exact technological solutions have been discussed in the rest of this course in more detail than I can give you. What I will focus on is the question of how you can improve people's experience and people's access to justice while using these new technologies. What are the principles of people-centred justice innovation?

## SEVEN PRINCIPLES FOR PEOPLE-CENTRED JUSTICE INNOVATION

I have seven principles that I will discuss. First, putting people at the centre. This is the basic principle of people-centred justice. It means that you must understand people's capabilities. Not everybody is highly educated. Not everybody is very competent in using computers or has access to technology. Another principle of the SDGs is that we want to leave no one behind. We must keep that in the back of our minds with every access to justice solution. Is it easy for all people to understand? Can they access it? Can everybody use it?

The second principle is to focus on the reality of people's lives and experiences. What are the problems they are facing? How can the justice services we provide really address those problems? Focusing on resolving justice problems requires a broad perspective. You must look at clusters of problems, try to address the underlying issues and be conflict-sensitive in the approaches used. A procedure or technical solution can either promote conflict behaviour or de-escalate conflict. It is important to keep this in mind in the design phases.

The third principle is the need to create better justice journeys. What is the journey that people are taking when they resolve their problems? What is their access to justice? How are they empowered to access the justice system? What people-centred justice services are available? Interestingly, that means that digitising the process as it currently exists should not be the goal. As we have seen, 5.1 billion people are excluded from meaningful access to justice. Digitising existing processes, which exclude so many people, will not help. We must use the process of digitalisation, the process of using AI and other advanced technologies, as an opportunity to improve the justice journey and to improve the way the system serves people.

The fourth point I would like to raise is that we need to be open to different actors. Often, there is a focus on the courts. The exact percentages may differ from country to country, but it is true everywhere that, in the vast majority of cases, the courts do not come into play when people are faced with a justice problem. So, if you want to resolve people's justice problems and really provide them with access to justice, you must look at different actors, such as lawyers, paralegals, civil servants, police officers, trade unions and other organisations that help people address these issues. We must focus on collaborations and there are technologies that can support those kinds of collaboration between different actors with the objective to serve people better. Collaborations across sectors are also needed. For example, lawyers can collaborate with social workers or with psychologists depending on the justice problem being addressed.

The fifth principle is that we must create standard solutions. If you digitalise, you must develop a standard process that is more efficient than the traditional way of providing justice services. However, people are not standard and problems are not standard. So even though you design a standard process, you must make sure that there are individual escape routes. What if I must tick a box but none of the boxes apply to me? What if I must perform the next step but I want to go back to the previous step? These are simple examples but they are important to keep in mind when you digitalise processes. Standard solutions need individual escape routes. If you have those standard solutions, there are economies of scale, because many cases are similar and can be resolved much more easily than is typical in our current justice systems.

Point six refers to the importance of collecting data and then using that data to learn and to improve. For technically minded people this is a natural way of working. You try something, then you collect the data and you improve it. That is how the process develops. The justice sector is often less focused on data and on using justice data to really understand what the problems are that people are facing, how they are experiencing the process, what the solutions are that really work, how you can better serve people and how you can make improvements in the justice services they provide.

That brings me to the last principle, preventing justice problems by learning from individual cases. This, too, is about using data to learn and improve. But now it is about the justice problems that people face and the structural issues in the legal system. If you really understand the sum of these individual cases, you can identify the bottlenecks in regulations, in the laws or in their implementation. What are the obstacles that people are facing? Where do things go wrong and do problems emerge? This information can help identify structural solutions and contribute to preventing justice problems from occurring in the first place. This also reduces the justice gap.

I hope this people-centred approach to justice is useful as you think about technological solutions for innovating justice services and improving people's access to justice. The pandemic has forced innovation at a much higher speed in the justice sector than we had previously thought possible. So, there are amazing opportunities, especially if we work together and put people's justice problems at the centre of our efforts. There is a lot of work to do and a lot of improvements that can be made to help close the global justice gap. Thank you.

## UNIDROIT PROMOTING GLOBAL MODERNISATION AND ECONOMIC GROWTH

**Steffek:** Thank you very much, Maaike, for this excellent and thought-provoking presentation. Now, we are blessed to have both the Secretary-General and the Deputy Secretary-General of UNIDROIT as our final speakers. UNIDROIT is the International Institute for the Unification of Private Law based in Rome. Professor Ignacio Tirado was appointed as Secretary-General in summer 2018. Before that and in addition to this, he is a professor at the Universidad Autónoma of Madrid. Previously, he was a senior legal consultant at the World Bank's Legal Vice-Presidency and the Financial Sector Practice for almost nine years, having also consulted for the IMF on insolvency-related matters, as well as for the Asian Development Bank on commercial legal reform. Amongst others, there are many accolades I could mention, but I will only mention two. He is a founding member of the European Banking Institute and a director of the International Insolvency Institute.

Anna Veneziano is the Deputy Secretary-General of UNIDROIT. She is also a professor, in that case, Professor of Comparative Law at the University of Teramo in Italy, and she was affiliated with the University of Amsterdam in the Netherlands as a Professor of European Property Law. She has published widely, for example, on international comparative law, European contract law, secured transactions and international insolvency law. We are very grateful that you are taking the time. We know that you are very busy, and you have many projects going on at UNIDROIT. We are very grateful, Ignacio and Anna that you are here with us today. You will speak on UNIDROIT's initiatives concerning access to justice, with a particular focus on the enforcement of creditor claims. Thank you very much and over to you.

**Tirado:** Thank you very much, Felix. We would like to start out by wholeheartedly thanking the University of Cambridge and Hitotsubashi University in Japan, and especially Professors Steffek and Sumida, who have very kindly invited us. As Professor Steffek mentioned, it is not usual for both the Secretary-General and the Deputy Secretary-General to participate. We do this because of the importance of the project and the importance that the United Kingdom and Japan have for our institution. We very much look forward to continuing this important collaboration moving forward. Fortunately for all of you, most of the important speaking will be done by Professor Veneziano, while I will just give a very quick overview of our institution.

We should not take for granted that you all know what UNIDROIT is. I am, therefore, going to take a minute to talk about it. It is one of a group of organisations

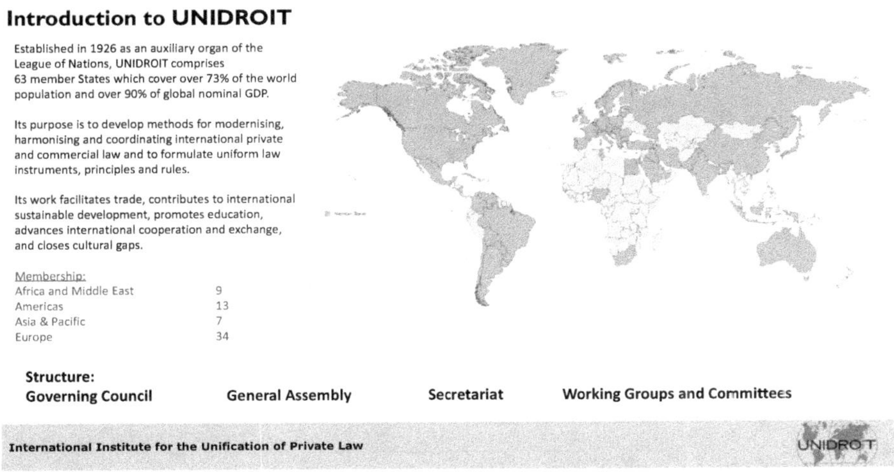


FIGURE 8.12 Introduction to UNIDROIT

known as the three sisters, the three organisations around the world working on transnational law and the unification of private law. The three sisters are the Hague Conference on Private International Law, the United Nations Commission on International Trade Law that is UNCITRAL and UNIDROIT. We are a bit older than UNCITRAL, having been founded in 1926 and thus approaching our first century celebration. UNIDROIT was founded in the context of the League of Nations, which, as all of you will know, was the predecessor of the United Nations. This is important because the *raison d'être* of the League of Nations, which was created after World War I, very much influences the principles of our organisation. Our principles are international collegiality and ensuring the harmonisation of private law as a mechanism for fostering economic growth and peace amongst nations. We currently have 63 constituent countries, which may sound like about one-third of the countries in the world, but in truth represent almost 75 per cent of the world's population and about 90 per cent of the world's nominal GDP. These very relevant countries are shown on the map in Figure 8.12.

Our work is on private law in a broader sense. Most of our work is concentrated on commercial law and the commercial sides of private law, but there are also important exceptions. Figure 8.13 presents a clustered summary of our instruments, both those that are already in force or at least have been approved and those that we are currently working on. All of them pretty much relate to access to justice in one way or another because they are legal instruments, after all. One of the main areas of work concerns international commercial contracts, an area in which I would like to highlight the UNIDROIT Principles of International Commercial Contracts. These Principles are deemed an international best practice or standard in international contracts, not only because they are a very high-level instrument from a technical

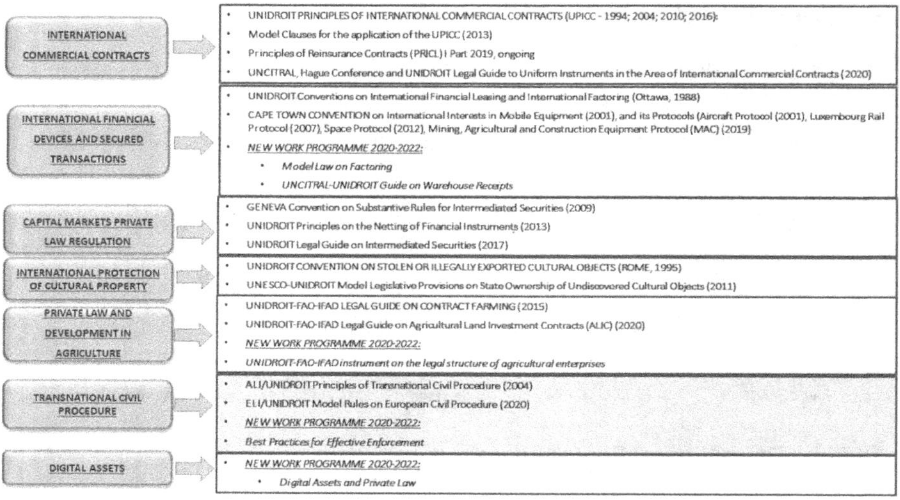


FIGURE 8.13 UNIDROIT instruments

standpoint, but also because they strike an extraordinary balance between common and civil law perspectives of contract law. This makes them extremely useful for arbitration, for model legal reform and for other uses. Countries such as China, Russia, Argentina and France are but a few that have recently amended their civil codes and their contract laws according to the UNIDROIT principles on international commercial contracts.

We also have important projects on secured transactions and access to finance, including one of the most successful commercial law treaties in the world, which is the Cape Town Convention. Most transactions concerning aircraft, such as aircraft engines and helicopters, take place using the Cape Town Convention, prepared by UNIDROIT and for which we are the Depositary. We are currently working on drafting a model law on factoring and another on warehouse receipts, which are key in access to finance, especially in developing nations. This is an area where modernisation and harmonisation of law are most needed to lower transaction costs and, thereby, increase investment growth. We also have an important practice in capital markets, which I will not get into as it has little to do with access to justice.

## CONTRIBUTING TO CIVIL PROCEDURE

**Tirado:** An important, procedural part of our work concerns cultural property. The UNIDROIT Convention on Stolen or Illegally Exported Cultural Objects of 1995 is a milestone of our signature instruments. It has fifty signatory states and it keeps growing. It is an important instrument to ensure that cultural heritage, especially in developing countries, is not unduly taken away. It basically dries out private markets and facilitates the recovery of those assets. So, that is another side of our work which you might find interesting. You might be interested in an area of our work where access to justice is still very much in the making, which is digital assets. We are currently working on digital assets and private law. How litigation and other problems that might arise in the market practice of digital assets are to be addressed nationally and internationally remains to be seen.

We have now reached the final part of my introduction, which concerns national civil procedure. We have done quite a lot on this front. We proudly approved the American Law Institute/UNIDROIT Principles, which are deemed a world standard for procedural principles that facilitate arbitration and transnational litigation.[13] They provide a meeting point between common law and civil law approaches to procedural law, which hopefully makes them useful and relevant. Following suit, we have recently approved the European Law Institute/UNIDROIT Model European Rules of Civil Procedure, which are more detailed, more European, ad-hoc, tailor-made, but pretty much consistent with the general principles approved before.[14] We are hopeful that in the future, we can continue and produce similar types of instruments for Asia, Latin America and Africa. Those three regions are yet to develop common procedural principles.

Our current work is focused on enforcement. While access to justice is important around the world, the place, the moment, the when and where in which access to justice fails the most, is when it comes to implementing decisions, i.e. when it comes to enforcing the rights of the parties. This is not just a problem in developing nations but also in fully developed nations. Legal enforcement is often too late and too costly. Anna Veneziano will speak about all of this in detail.

## WHAT IS REQUIRED TO ENFORCE A CLAIM?

**Veneziano:** Thank you very much, Ignacio, and thank you, of course, Professor Steffek and Professor Sumida, for the invitation. The second part of our presentation will focus on a current UNIDROIT project, which is directly connected to the topic of access to justice. As the Secretary-General mentioned it focuses on the development of best practices for effective enforcement.[15]

This is a project that we have only just begun. We held the first Working Group session in December to discuss the scope of the project and were fortunate enough to involve Professor Steffek in our work. There is, therefore, a caveat to bear in mind

[13] See <www.unidroit.org/instruments/civil-procedure/ali-unidroit-principles/>, accessed 1 November 2023.

[14] See <www.unidroit.org/instruments/civil-procedure/eli-unidroit-rules/>, accessed 1 November 2023.

[15] See <www.unidroit.org/work-in-progress/enforcement-best-practices/>, accessed 1 November 2023.

because the project is so young: we have more questions than answers at this stage. Nevertheless, sometimes posing the right questions is also important.

We decided to focus on this topic for two main reasons. The first reason is, as noted by Ignacio, that enforcement is often neglected when discussing issues of access to justice. With the term enforcement, we mean the actual execution phase, to use a term that is more familiar for civil lawyers, i.e. the procedures and mechanisms to execute creditors' rights when creditors are granted such rights in a judgment or when they are exercising remedies extrajudicially. This is, as mentioned, often neglected, but remains an integral part of access to justice and of the legal framework for a developed credit market, improved access to credit, increased trade and investment and overall economic development and sustained growth. These are all goals that were also mentioned by previous speakers. However, there are growing concerns in many legal systems as to inefficient enforcement mechanisms for creditors, delays, costs, lack of transparency and insufficient satisfaction. This is the backdrop against which the proposal of the World Bank to develop a guidance instrument for policymakers in this area was accepted by our governing bodies.

The second reason why we wanted to focus on this project is the impact and role of technology. In our view, as well as according to the views of the experts, technology will play an essential part in this project, much more so than in previous UNIDROIT instruments on civil procedure. The European Law Institute/UNIDROIT Model European Rules of Civil Procedure mentioned by Ignacio do contain several provisions on the appropriate use of electronic communication between courts and parties and among parties (such as video or audio conferencing, video recording of hearings, use of technology in evidence taking, disclosure, production of electronic data and electronic platforms in collective civil proceedings) and also emphasise settlements, which can be achieved using technology. However, they do not go into detail, which is what we would like to do with this new project.

There are two related issues of more general importance on this matter that I would like to present, and then I would like to go into some more detailed questions that were posed by the experts participating in the group.

## ADVANTAGES AND CHALLENGES OF TECHNOLOGY

**Veneziano:** First, there are considerations as to the double role of technology. While it is a tool to tackle traditional obstacles to effective enforcement, it is also a source of new potential problems. Previous speakers have mentioned, for example, issues pertaining to monitoring, accountability and respect of fundamental rights. The second general issue is the challenge of technological neutrality. Experts advise us of the need to ensure the neutrality of legal instruments with respect to specific types of technology, which ensures that the instruments are future-proof and can be applied globally. This, however, is easier said than done. How does one ensure the development of a technologically neutral instrument in this area? What about the issues of compatibility and interoperability that might also arise?

This leads us to the specific issues raised by experts. One of them concerns the development of new architectures, such as the platforms that can be used in civil procedures for different purposes. They can also be used for enforcement. There are clear benefits, such as limiting delays and the costs of enforcement, as well as enhanced transparency. Depending on the purpose of the technologies employed, they can enhance effective asset liquidations, in the case of e-auctions for instance, and they can create secondary markets. But what about the challenges? This indeed raises further questions: Who is responsible for the management of the platform? What is the role of private actors? Should a monitoring system be introduced? How do we deal with possible concerns as regards the applicable law?

Other issues relate to automation, such as the automatic partial or total performance of agreements, including the enforcement of obligations. How should we deal with the opacity of the decision-making process and the possibility of errors or misuse? Is there a need to introduce mechanisms to protect the debtor's rights? In our opinion there is, but what would be an efficient and fair way to go about it: ex-ante, or ex-post? Finally, questions arise as regards new types of assets, namely digital assets. How shall we adapt existing concepts or procedures, such as the concepts of repossession and control, to this new environment? Alternatively, should we develop a completely different set of legal tools and soft concepts to deal with enforcement in a digital environment? These are all topics that the experts have begun discussing and where they have not identified a very straightforward and clear answer for the time being.

As anticipated, I have presented more questions than answers but our project will try and tackle these problems and come up with suitable solutions and advice. Thank you once again for the invitation to participate in this very interesting workshop. Further information about UNIDROIT can be found on our webpage.[16]

**Sumida:** This is a world that is not very familiar to our audience, but the presentation was an excellent reminder of the breadth of the issues. Thank you very much. Professor Takeshita, may I ask you for some comments?

## THE IMPACT OF TECHNOLOGY ON ENFORCEMENT

**Takeshita:** My name is Keisuke Takeshita and I am based at Hitotsubashi University. Thank you very much for your very interesting presentation. The issue of 'enforcement' is very important from the perspective that law is not a 'picture in a box' but is only meaningful if it is implemented in reality. I represented Japan at the Hague Conference on Private International Law in 2019 when the Convention on

[16] See <www.unidroit.org/>, accessed 1 November 2023.

the Recognition and Enforcement of Foreign Judgments in Civil and Commercial Matters was newly adopted. This Convention only obliges states to guarantee enforcement but does not deal with issues beyond that, namely, how to enforce foreign judgments in concrete terms. This is related to the fact that, traditionally, the issue of actual implementation, such as enforcement, has been left to the sovereignty of the states. Even today, each country has its own system of enforcement, which would make global unification very difficult.

From what you have said, UNIDROIT does not only look at the enforcement of judgments but at an even wider range of enforcement, including the enforcement of security interests and enforcement against digital assets. This breadth makes it a very challenging project. I would like to ask whether you intend to focus on the use of new technologies in enforcement against digital assets, or whether the project will deal with enforcement issues more broadly and generally.

**Veneziano:** Thank you for the question and for mentioning the work by other organisations on the international enforcement of judgments, such as the Hague Conference. Our project is dealing with enforcement in general. Its aim is to introduce best practices that might help enforcement, both when it is done in a judicial situation and when it is done extrajudicially. Therefore, we are considering enforcement regardless of whether you have a decision by a court, and you would like to enforce it, or the creditors wish to enforce extrajudicially, for example, in a situation where they hold a security right. Technology will play an essential role because we think that if you use technology and mechanisms that are based on technology, you can do two things. One is that you may support the development of more efficient enforcement proceedings, as it is already happening in some legal systems. I mentioned some possible uses of technology such as e-auction platforms, for instance. The other aspect that we touched upon is the creation of new assets through technology. There, enforcement must be linked to this technology. So, we look at enforcement in general, but technology will play a very important role.

**Sumida:** Thank you very much. Now, are there any questions from the students?

## THE FEASIBILITY OF AN AI JUDGE

**Student C:** I think it is conceptually possible to create an AI judge and that AI makes legal decisions, even in arbitration. However, I have a question about the feasibility of such concepts. If AI can be used to make legal decisions in a very short time and if the quality of such decisions can be ensured by eliminating bias, then I would consider the use of AI in law to be very positive. However, I would like to ask whether this can really be achieved and, if so, what the challenges are.

**Sumida:** Thank you very much. How about you, Dr Scholz?

**Scholz:** We discussed the question of AI in judicial systems during our negotiations on the Council conclusions. AI systems in the justice sector offer great opportunities. In the future, these systems will be capable of performing increasingly complex tasks, like structuring and preparing information on the subject matter of cases, automatically transcribing records, anonymising court decisions, estimating the chances of success of a lawsuit and so on. The use of AI tools has the potential to improve the functioning of justice systems by assisting judges and judicial staff in their activities, accelerating court proceedings and enhancing the comparability, consistency and, ultimately, the quality of judicial decisions.

On the other hand, we see that the application of AI in the justice sector may also contain the risk of perpetuating and possibly strengthening existing discrimination and of allowing distorted or opaque decision-making. The outcomes of AI systems based on machine learning can in certain cases not be retraced, leading to a black box effect.

Against this background, we think that the use of AI in the justice sector should not interfere with the decision-making power of judges or judicial independence. A court decision, in the end, must always be made by a human being and cannot be delegated to an AI tool. I hope this answers your question, at least partially.

**Sumida:** Thank you very much. Mr Kikkawa, would you like to add something?

**Kikkawa:** I agree with what you have just said. Since technology has advanced so far, it will continue to progress by leaps and bounds and advance to the level of humans. The question will be, which decision-maker users place more trust in: what the machine does or what a human does? If a lot of people place more trust in what the machine does, then that may take priority, but, I think, that at the end of the day, people will place their trust in the decisions of a human. So, I believe that AI should only perform auxiliary tasks.

**Sumida:** Thank you very much. Finally, Felix, could you please provide us with a summary?

**Steffek:** Thank you very much, Mihoko. I have prepared an attempt to summarise today's proceedings. However, in the interest of time, I will not present it. However, it is not only time that brings me to this conclusion. I have two substantive reasons. First, I think our speakers have been so excellent and have presented us with such rich content that it is not necessary for me to attempt to summarise it. The speakers were so fantastic that they stood up for themselves. Second, we will publish the presentations and discussions in a book. So, I can write down my comments and we will have a chance to read them later.

It is a nice outcome that our work, our conference, our thoughts and our discussions will be available in the form of a book. It is also part of access to justice that experts and those studying law do not keep to themselves, but that they engage with the wider society. So, the book that we are planning is one that makes our topic accessible. It will be directed to our audience in a way that makes our thoughts accessible also to non-experts. I am very grateful to Mihoko Sumida, who has proposed this, and I will hand it back to you, Mihoko, to close our conference.

Thank you.

**Sumida:** Thank you. I would like to thank the students for their patience with our very challenging sessions. During this time, Professor Steffek and I, who organised the event, have received feedback from the guests who collaborated with us, saying that they had a very enjoyable experience interacting with the students. I think this is due, above all, to the students who participated in the conversations with great enthusiasm and asked excellent questions. This conversation series started with the topic of 'Legal Innovation', but in fact, the main aim was to encourage and nurture the seeds of innovation. I am very happy to say that, thus far, we have achieved that objective.

Finally, please give a round of applause to our guests, who gave really wonderful presentations. I would like to conclude now. Thank you very much.

## CONCLUDING CONVERSATION

**Sumida:** It really was a great feast of discussion on innovations in access to justice, with a host of magnificent guests! Discussing 'access to justice' from different perspectives was like a kaleidoscope, with commonalities and diversities, inviting us to a new understanding. What does it mean to view access to justice from an SDG's perspective, and how should we think about access to justice after the era of COVID-19? I was very excited to be able to share this cutting-edge understanding.

**Steffek:** I am sure the guests enjoyed themselves and it was a really great finale. So, without further ado, let me give you my own summary of the day.

The first thing that became clear throughout this workshop is that technology can be very powerful in closing the global justice gap and providing equal access to justice for all if we put people at the centre of the justice services we design. Maaike de Langen of the Pathfinders emphasised this. Similarly, the OECD – represented by Tatyana Teplova – estimates that gaps in access to justice can cost up to 3 per cent of the GDP. In addition, the OECD emphasises the importance of access to justice for inclusive growth, well-being and even health. This is in line with national governments such as the German Ministry of Justice – represented by Philip Scholz – placing great importance on the need to employ technology to protect vulnerable groups. Ultimately, all speakers based their statements on a people-centred approach, i.e. on an approach that puts people and their interests at the centre of access to justice.

Generally, and I agree, the lawmakers presenting in this workshop think that technology can be useful in facilitating access to justice. All of them, however, also agree with UNIDROIT – present via the contributions of Ignacio Tirado and Anna Veneziano – cautioning to keep in mind that there remain risks and challenges. This is also the approach taken by Takashi Kikkawa speaking for the Japanese Ministry of Justice. The Japanese Ministry has very actively engaged with the advantages and risks of using technology in the justice sector and is currently preparing draft legislation.

**Sumida:** Nevertheless, I was really surprised by the global gap in access to justice, i.e. that there are 5.1 billion people in the world – two-thirds of the world's population – who do not have meaningful access to justice. If I remember correctly, this number is almost three times the number of people without bank accounts – the 'unbanked'. Given the scale of the problem, I thought that this creates an imperative to utilise technology.

It was meaningful for Japan to have this international workshop at a time when the digitalisation of civil justice is about to start in earnest. We were able to share the big picture and share excellent know-how, awareness of issues and challenges. By the way, Mr Kikkawa's presentation was very advanced in content and full of power. The students seemed to be greatly inspired and asked a lot of questions.

**Steffek:** Yes, I was impressed by Mr Kikkawa's progressive views. I was also very much in favour of the workshop consistently taking a comprehensive approach to 'access to justice' and not just considering the courts. Mr Kikkawa stressed the importance of out-of-court dispute resolution. This is in line with the OECD's and Pathfinders' insight that many problems faced by citizens are ultimately not dealt with by the formal justice system. This is why legal practitioners need to look at the stage before a dispute goes to court.

This comprehensive view was further expanded by UNIDROIT's presentation on the importance of enforcement for access to justice. As regards enforcement, even advanced jurisdictions face challenges. Technology could fundamentally change the way enforcement happens. In particular, technology might have the effect of making public enforcement institutions superfluous in part.

**Sumida:** Traditionally, when people refer to 'access to justice', they tend to think of it as the threshold for using the justice system to find solutions to people's problems. Here, instead, we used the term in a very broad and comprehensive way to cover the entire legal system and how it solves people's problems. We included not only which rights are recognised, but also the enforcement stage of realising those rights. When you start to think of it that way, you realise why Sir Geoffrey Vos said that the justice system provides an economic infrastructure.

On a personal note, it was eye-opening to hear Professor Tirado talk about UNIDROIT's mission in terms of 'access to justice'. My understanding of what it means to study comparative law and what the harmonisation of law means for society and the economy was renewed.

**Steffek:** Both national lawmakers, for example, Takashi Kikkawa, and international organisations, for example, the OECD, stressed the importance of data for the future development of access to justice. This requires involving society, both in terms of sharing data with society but also listening to the concerns society has about data. The societal challenge we are facing is not just a technology challenge, but also a data challenge.

Considering the effect of COVID-19, the OECD and the Pathfinders showed that the pandemic has not only facilitated the use of technology to improve access to justice but that the pandemic has also created new justice problems. The Pathfinders call this the triple crunch of (1) more justice problems, (2) operational constraints and (3) funding constraints. This was picked up in the discussion by a question asking how states that do not have the funds to use technology in the justice sector should proceed.

The workshop ended with speakers and commentators agreeing that a broad perspective was necessary when dealing with access to justice and that this broad perspective was also necessary when considering the implications of technology for access to justice. I very much agree with this perspective as it is the perspective of the people who are, negatively and positively, affected by the law and legal conflicts.

## QUESTIONS FOR FURTHER THOUGHT

- What is the relationship between technology and law? Does law trump technology or vice-versa? Is there a possibility to develop a system in which law and technology cooperate?
- Will private justice solutions become more attractive than public justice solutions, i.e. might start-ups offer more attractive services such that parties do not use state institutions in the future? If this happens, how should legislators react?
- How should governments deal with the challenge that technology will first require costly investment before it achieves cost-saving in the future?
- Should technology try to mirror the current justice system or are there aspects of the current justice system that technology could improve?
- Will technology have the effect that citizens can better understand the law before they take action and will, therefore, have fewer disputes later?

# Epilogue

## *What Is Legal Innovation?*

ABSTRACT

In the epilogue, the editors reflect on the series of conversations. They revisit the definition of 'legal innovation' and what they have learned about it through the discussions. Their perspective on legal innovation is twofold. On the one hand, technology transforms the reality of law and fundamentally changes the way we access and experience law and justice. On the other hand, law evolves, adapts to changes in society, but can also facilitate and implement innovation. They conclude by considering what it takes to initiate legal innovation.

*Speakers* Felix Steffek and Mihoko Sumida

**Sumida:** This conversation series was a really fun and enlightening experience. I very much enjoyed thinking about legal innovation and technology with our guests and students. While our research project 'Legal Systems and Artificial Intelligence' is still in its infancy, it was great to be inspired by the best concepts explained by the best guests we can think of. To have received so much support and to have the opportunity to publish these conversations – well, I am just thrilled! Against this background, I thought that we, the organisers, could present what we have arrived at through this experience – with each other and sharing it with our readers.

### DEFINING LEGAL INNOVATION

**Sumida:** My understanding is that the concept of 'legal innovation' is similar to the 'theory of legal evolution', which captures the 'adaptation' of law to changes and innovations in the environment, including society and the economy. In discussing what legal innovation is, it would be a bit perverse to treat it as if it were a legal rule and define its requirements and effects in order to establish a basis for discussion.

If legal innovation was treated in this way, the discussion would not be able to proceed. On this point, Felix, as you suggested the term 'legal innovation' for this conversation series: what did you mean by 'legal innovation'?

**Steffek:** When I proposed that the topic of this conversation series should be 'legal innovation', I had two things in mind. *First*, technology is transforming the reality of law in the sense that it is fundamentally changing our access to and experience of the law. Therefore, I thought that this course should deal with advances in technology dealing with the law, i.e. LawTech. Artificial intelligence (AI) can be used to gather information about the law, analyse the law, predict the law and communicate the law. Blockchain technology can be used to design smart contracts. Smart contracts will not always rely on public authorities to enforce the performance of contracts. Instead, this can be achieved by algorithms. It is important to understand how technology will affect the administration of law and what will drive such changes.

*Second*, there is also a change on 'the other side': innovation from the side of the law, responding to a new reality. Like technology, law is not static, it evolves. In many cases, such evolution occurs in stages. External shocks can also significantly change the structure of law. How will the use of advanced technology and Big Data affect the law? I thought it would be useful to engage with the forms and causes of the change in law. In this course, I wanted to examine these changes through the lens of technology. This also means recognising the importance of the contribution of lawmakers in creating change in society. By lawmakers, I mean both public ones, such as parliaments and courts, and private ones, such as professional service providers and professional associations. It will be interesting to see how lawmakers in this broader sense react to current technological advances.

Looking at legal innovation from these two perspectives – technology and law – raises the question of priorities. Will technology dominate the law, for example, when contracts become algorithms that do not require a legal system? Or will the law prevail over technology, for example, will parliaments come to ban certain algorithms and regulate others? Or will there be a future cooperation between technology and law, where law adapts to technological progress and technology respects the normative constraints imposed by law? The world we live in today faces many challenges, and I am thrilled that we live in a time where these questions are being asked. So, the modern age we are living in provides us with a wonderful opportunity to think about 'legal innovation'. That is what I was thinking.

It is true that legal innovation has a completely different dimension compared with legal norms. In that sense, I agree with your proposal to introduce the theory of evolution into the way in which we think about law. Professor Simon Deakin has written ground-breaking articles on applying evolutionary principles to law.

## NOW IS THE TIME TO TACKLE STRUCTURAL PROBLEMS

**Sumida:** The challenges we face 'here and now' are large, deep and numerous, with many of them raising fundamental questions. Especially for Japan, which is facing a number of social and economic structural problems, Professor Koda has made the important point to use the post-COVID-19 period as a chance for progress. There is a need for a radical new approach that is not an extension of the old system. Specifically, we must turn to innovation that uses technology to solve social problems. He also spoke of his expectations for legal innovation as a way of thinking about how law should reflect innovation, how legislation should be drafted and interpreted and how legal innovators should be facilitated.

**Steffek:** Similarly, the social problem-solving approach was mentioned by Ludwig Bull, the founder of a LegalTech start-up. Legal innovation should contribute to normative goals, such as improving well-being and achieving justice through law. The two vectors of law and technology that I mentioned earlier can be understood in terms of social and economic change and law. When an innovative technology is invented, such as blockchain-based value transfer, legislators will develop new rules on how to fit it into the existing legal system. Interestingly, social and technological change will often precede and the law will follow. On the other hand, there may be a form of law reform that aims to bring about changes in society first, such as the liberalisation of the law of professional legal services to provide legal service providers with a framework to accommodate technology-based legal services.

## INITIATING LEGAL INNOVATION

**Steffek:** The actors of legal innovation may be public institutions – e.g. parliaments and courts producing statutes and case law – or private ones – e.g. commercial actors and consumers producing company articles of association and contracts. While the former concerns the public order, innovative private ordering is no less important and often precedes public legal innovations. In this sense, legal innovation can be understood more broadly to include not only formal law, e.g. statutes and contracts, but also legal practice, e.g. court procedures and modes of operation of law firms. Again, both public and private actors are involved in legal practice.

**Sumida:** It is an important point to take a broad view of the actors of legal innovation. However, we should not forget Sir Geoffrey Vos, one of the highest judges in England and Wales who is leading the digital transformation of civil justice, and his idea of civil justice as economic infrastructure. I was overwhelmed by the persuasive power of his logic.

**Steffek:** That's very true (laughs). As far as the private actors are concerned, good corporate governance will generate profits by using technology to solve people's problems and improve people's lives. I agree with the direction set by the Ministry of Economy, Trade and Industry (METI) in Japan. My own summary of the 5Ds of corporate governance changes brought about by technology is as follows: (1) Data: more and better data analysis; (2) De-centralisation: less central direction and oversight; (3) Democratisation: a stronger relationship between social welfare and governance; (4) Disruption: fundamental changes in corporate governance and (5) Design: more pre-design of legal relationships and less post-dispute litigation.

**Sumida:** I have studied the METI study group's proposals. Its direction of integrating AI governance into corporate governance was inspired by the insights of our joint research project's UK Principal Investigator, Professor Simon Deakin of the University of Cambridge. Based on many years of research on corporate governance in Japan, he investigated the prospects for a period of radical change brought about by technology and came to the conclusion that Japan's long-standing characteristics can be resilient.

In that sense, there is no need to be quick and assume that the Japanese language – with its ambiguities – is unsuitable for AI. This is supported by the spectacular results of AI research based on Chinese language texts. The point made by AI researcher Dr Yamada that as long as the data environment is in place, AI research can proceed and improve prediction accuracy, is also very encouraging for Japanese readers. I am sure that they will share the sense of longing that the direction of Japan's policy is right and that we are waiting for its realisation as soon as possible.

## INNOVATING ACCESS TO JUSTICE

**Steffek:** In a recent development related to our research project, the OECD has launched the project 'Digital Transformation for Access to Justice: Towards a People-centred Justice System'. The project is led by the Access to Justice Team of the OECD under the guidance of Dr Tatyana Teplova and the Latvian Court Administration. I have the great honour of being the scientific advisor of this project. This project is still in progress and the final report is still in draft form. Against this background, all my comments are preliminary.

The report is based on a questionnaire which was sent to the OECD Member countries. The questionnaire covers four areas in terms of access to justice and technology: strategies and institutions, technology for legal services, technology for dispute resolution services and data-driven access to justice. The responses show that the digital transformation of justice services is driven by the demand for high-quality and differentiated access to justice. This transformation has been facilitated by advances in technology, limited by public resource constraints and accelerated by the COVID-19 pandemic. The flexibility and willingness of citizens in these countries to accept technological changes in justice services during the pandemic were also reported to be excellent. At the same time, care must be taken to avoid the formation of a digitally abandoned citizen base. Overall, the speed and depth of integration of technology into judicial services varies across countries. Some countries are taking a progressive approach, while others are still searching for direction.

**Sumida:** It is a very interesting project. I am looking forward to the publication of the report. By the way, the Japanese team of our research project is tackling a serious social issue in the online-first era: anonymous defamation on the internet.[1]

[1] Our research project 'Legal System and Artificial Intelligence' is carrying out AI development experiments in collaboration with the research project 'Explainable Dispute Resolution Prediction Models for Civil Disputes' (JST Strategic Creative Research Promotion Project ACT-X: JPMJAX20AM), conducted by Hiroaki Yamada, in cooperation with LIC Inc.

Of course, AI is already used to detect hate crimes, but this is mostly based on learning large amounts of data from social networking sites. In contrast, our approach is to develop and test a prediction system for civil dispute resolution, using civil judgments as training data. We aim to see how far we can go in solving the problem of bias, which has become prominent in recent years.

When I started this research, I realised that court proceedings that produce the learning data in the form of judgments are not only a matter for me as a legal scholar, but also a matter for technology experts. As a legal scholar, but also as a 'technology conscious' person, I am curious to see what the courts will do. I am particularly focused on privacy. It has a direct impact on the data environment.

Take the example, where a family court investigation officer published an academic paper on a juvenile protection case that he was in charge of, first in a prominent journal and later in a book. The Japanese Supreme Court, while taking into account the characteristics of the juvenile protection case, denied any violation of privacy in view of the manner of publication and the fact that the purpose of the publication was 'to promote an important public interest'.[2] This decision reversed the decision of the High Court, which had found an invasion of privacy.

When I came across this judgment, I felt that the term 'important public interest' implies the intention to protect the environment in which the collaboration between judges and family court investigation officers, who have a background in psychology and psychiatry, can function effectively. This has supported the quality of judicial decisions in juvenile protection cases. In the context of the new business model for providing legal services, Professor Mari Sako talked about multidisciplinary teams as a keyword for the future of legal professionals. However, it can be said that the 'correctness' of judicial decisions in difficult cases, such as juvenile protection cases, has traditionally been ensured by working in multidisciplinary teams. In addition, providing a one-stop solution by collaborating with other actors in dispute resolution is also important in the context of human-centred judicial innovation.

Having been exposed to the idea of automation of 'execution' using technology, I felt that this also requires the generation of compatible data – an issue that you have pointed out as a new mission for lawyers and data scientists. From the point of view of preparing for such a digital transformation, I think that the recent decision of the Supreme Court of Japan points in the right direction.

Felix, I saw that you have been appointed Director of the Law Tripos at the University of Cambridge, where you will also be working on curriculum development for the Faculty of Law.

**Steffek:** I like your point of view on technology consciousness! A legal innovator is not a bystander to change, but an agent of change. As regards teaching law and technology at Cambridge, I am currently developing a LawTech Workshop for our

[2] Japanese Supreme Court Judgement, 9 October 2020, Supreme Court Reports (civil cases) vol. 74, no. 7, p. 1807.

students.[3] The main idea is that this Workshop should not focus on the law as it regulates the use of technology. Hence, the Workshop will not focus on intellectual property law or data law. Instead, it will concentrate on technology as it is used in legal practice. For example, we will have a demonstration on the screen in a classroom for the students, of what a legal database looks like, how a machine learning algorithm is constructed and how it develops predictions. I hope this will be a worthwhile learning experience for the students as many read and discuss LawTech, but not that many law students have seen the technology in operation. However, it is only after seeing and understanding the relevant technology that one can really discuss its ethical implications.

**Sumida:** Because legal innovators are experimenting, experimenting and experimenting again.

3 Felix Steffek, 'Technology and Law: A Research and Teaching Agenda' (2019) 1155 New Business Law 41 (in Japanese).

# Index


Access to justice, 62, 74, *See* Artificial Intelligence: Access to justice, *See* Online Dispute Resolution, *See* OECD
  Commercial dispute resolution solutions, 217
  COVID-19, 202–3, 215, 220–22
  Digital vulnerability, 203
  Digitalisation, 200, 202–3, 209–10
  Fundamental rights, 201
  Innovation, 238
  People-centred approach, 203, 222–24
  Risks, 228–29
  United Nations Sustainable Development Goals, Goal 16 of, 219–20
AI and jurisprudence, 55–57
AI decision-makers
  Discrimination, 231
  Humans, role of, 178–79, 231
  Opaque decision-making, 231
AI in dispute resolution, use of, 41–42
  AI in court, 48
  Preconditions, jurisdictional differences in, 49–51
AI in law, role of, 43
  Access to justice, 61
  Analysis, 43
  Decision, 44
  Information, 43
  Rationality, 44–45
Application Programming Interfaces (APIs), 148
Artificial Intelligence
  Access to justice, 81–82
  Co-existence, 23, 52, 55, 84, 173–74
  Difficulties unique to law, 23
  Ethics, 48
  Goal-based regulation, 136–37
  Human lawyer, preference for, 36–37, 53–54
  Jurisdictional differences in research and use of, 59–60
  Liability, 53
  Limitations, 68, 82–83
  Outcome prediction precision, 39–41
  Risk bias, 45–46, 62, 135–36
  Social values, 140–41
  Transparency, lack of, 46–47, 51–52, 62

Blockchain, 157, 161–62
Business innovation
  Japanese economy, fall of, 4–5, 9–11
  Transition, need for, 8–9
  Venture ecosystem, 11–15
Business models, 180
  Combination of, 182–83
  Consulting, 182
  Legal operations, 182
  Legal technology, 182
  Value creation, 181

Capital market, 3
Case Crunch Lawyer Challenge, 33–36
Civil Code of Japan
  Natural disaster, legal liability for, 89–90
Coase, Ronald, 132, 139
Companies Act, Article 14 of, 128
Corporate governance, 237
  Artificial Intelligence
    AI principles, placement of, 130–33
    Fusion approach, 137–38
    Misora Habari revival, 130
  Audit, 123–24, 141–42
    Digital transformation, changes due to, 122–23
    Supply chain, 132

Council conclusions, 200
COVID-19
  Challenges, 120–21
  ESG priorities, change in, 124–25
  Regional disparity, 7
  Triple crunch, the, 221
COVIDX, 121
Credence good, 181
Crisis, financial, 120

Data protocols, 168
Datasets
  Accuracy, 68
  Anonymisation, 51
  Availability, 49–50, 54, 80, 194–95
  Civil Law system, 51
  Digitalisation, 51
  Limitations, 82–83
  Organisation, 65–66
Development, approaches to
  Relay race, the, 115
  Rugby, the, 115
Digital innovation, 237
  Big-boned policy, 16
  Capital market, interlinkage with digital market, 3–4
Digital transformation, 16
  Design, 125
  Five Ds, 121–22
  Fundamental changes, need of, 17–19
Digitalisation, lag in
  Germany, 204
  Japan, 204–5
DX, *See* Digital innovation, Digital transformation

Enforcement, change in *See* Blockchain, *See* UNIDROIT
  Accountability, 158
  Court, role of, 159–60
  Digitalisation, 157
  Infrastructure, lack of, 158
  Public-private collaboration, 158–59
Entrepreneurship, 15, 69
Experimentation, role of, 66, 69
  Passion, role of, 66
  Vision, role of, 67, 69–70

Finance, decentralised, 161
Financial Services Agency, *See* FSA
Financial services, change in, 161, 164–65
Financial supervision, *See* FSA
  Banking as a service, 160
  Corporate number, effective use of, 151–52
  Data analysis, automation of, 152
  Data collection, 148, 163–64
  Data, normalisation of, 150–51
  Digitalisation, 148–49
  Efficiency, improvement in, 153–54
  Financial institutions, working together with, 152–53
  Financial Services Agency and Bank of Japan, data sharing between, 149
  Granular data, utilisation of, 149–50
  Securities and Exchange Surveillance Commission, 156–57
  Surveillance, 167
FinTech, 156
FinTech Proof of Concept Hub, 155
FinTech Support Desk, 154
FSA
  Change in, 160, 162–63, 165–66
  Culture, 163
  Digitalisation, 162
Future lawyers
  Programming, 186
  Three career paths, 187–89

Good country practices, 216
Great White Shark, 21
Group decision-making, three ways of, 130

Horizontality, 216

Industry, automotive, 114
  Autonomous driving, 113
  CASE, 113
  Red Flag Act, 114
Industry, technology, 71
Innovation, 86
Investment
  ESG, 11

Japan, adoption of Artificial Intelligence in, 190–94
Japan, AI governance in, 133–34, 138–39
  Social Principles of Human-Centric AI, 129, 134–35
Japan, Big Five firms in, 190
Japan, social challenges, 8
  Population contraction, 5–6
  Regional disparity, 6–7
Justice for All report, 219–20

LawTech start-ups, 183–85
Lawyer, ideal, 89
Legal innovation
  Actors of, 237
  Functional equivalence, 126–29, 143–44

Human resources for (wise leaders), 114–18
Meaning of, 2, 235–36
Measurement, difficulties with, 116
New goods and services, 112
Path to, 118
Role models for, 115–18
Structural problems, 237
Legal NLP, 60
Legal prediction tools, creation of, 37–39
Legal procedures, change in, 205–8, 210–11
Legal service delivery pipeline, 175
Legal system
Human resources, cultivation of, 27–28
Social immune system, 24, 26
Legal transplantation, 128
Litigation finance, 179–80
Litigation strategy
'De facto counsel', role of bereaved families as, 93–97, 106–7
Documents, digitisation of, 107
Lawsuits, difficulties with filing, 109–10
Media, involvement of, 101
Negligence, organisational, 108
Praising people, importance of, 107
Small team, 95

Machine-Learning Operations (ML-Ops)
Human-In-the-Loop (HITL), 85–86
MDTs, *See* Multi-disciplinary teams
Multi-disciplinary teams, 174–75
AI use, correlation with, 177
Lawyers, survey of, 176
Mindset, 187
Non-lawyer human capital, retention of, 189

Negligence, 90
Negligence, organisational, 100, 110
Foreseeability, 99–100, 105–6
Liability, 98–99, 102–3

OECD, 217
Inclusive growth, 211
Justice system, barriers of the, 214–15
Justiciable problems, high prevalence of, 212
Vulnerable populations, 213
Okawa Elementary School Tsunami, 91
Online Dispute Resolution, 30, 208–9

Open innovation
Closed innovation, problems with, 19–21
Culture of, 20–21
Ore Ore Swindles, 21–22

Pathfinders, 219
Platform business model, 17
Professional fragmentation, 188
Public-private collaboration, 18, 169, *See* Enforcement, change in: Public-private collaboration

Rational contradiction, 91
RegTech, 147–48
Regulation, 48
Academia, role of, 77
Economic analysis and human rights, 72–74
Ethics, different from, 77
Financial services, 75–77
Regulatory sandboxes, 20
Risk management, 78–79
Tiered, 77–78
Robotic process automation, *See* Financial supervision: Data analysis, automation of

School Health and Safety Act, 101–5
SECI Model Theory, 80
Shadow pandemic, 221
Shigenobu, Hozumi, 117
Substantive law, change in, 205
SupTech, *See* RegTech
Susskind, Richard, 173

Task Force on Justice, 219
Tasks, 196–97
Three lines of defence, 122

UNIDROIT
Automation, 229
Enforcement, 227–30
Introduction, 224–27
New architectures, development of, 229
Technology, double role of, 228

Volkswagen example
Mistakes, 24–25
Response, difference in, 25–26
Vos, Sir Geoffrey, 29–30

World Justice Project, 213

www.ingramcontent.com/pod-product-compliance
Lightning Source LLC
LaVergne TN
LVHW011812200926
848484LV00005B/1154